What Nazism Did to Psychoanalysis

I0130470

What Nazism Did to Psychoanalysis explores the impact Nazism had on the evolution of psychoanalysis and tackles the enigma of the transformation of individual hate into mass psychosis and of the autocratic creation of a neo-reality.

Addressing the effects of the Holocaust on the psychoanalytic world, this book does not focus on the suffering of the survivors but the analysis of the concrete mechanisms of destruction that affected language and thought, their impact on the practice of psychoanalysis and the defences that psychoanalysts tried to find against the linguistic, legal and symbolic chaos that struck the foundations of reality. Laurence Kahn discusses the struggle against the appropriation, by the Nazi language, of key terms such as demonic nature, drives, ideals and, above all, the *Selbsterhaltungstrieb* (the self-preservation drive), which became, with Hitler, the axis of the living space policy, the "*Lebensraum*".

Covering key topics such as trauma, transgenerational issues, silence and secrecy and the depredation of culture, this is an essential work for psychoanalysts and anyone wishing to understand how strongly the development of psychoanalysis was affected by Nazism.

Laurence Kahn is Training and Supervising Analyst at the French Psychoanalytic Association (APF) and is a former President of the APF (2008–2010). In 2014, she received the Maurice Bouvet Award, and in 2021, she received the IPA award for Extraordinarily Meritorious Service to Psychoanalysis.

Psychoanalytic Ideas and Applications Series
Series Editor: Gabriela Legorreta

For more information about this series, please visit: www.routledge.com.

What Nazism Did to Psychoanalysis

Laurence Kahn

Translated by Andrew Weller

Routledge
Taylor & Francis Group

LONDON AND NEW YORK

Cover image: Richard Ross / Getty Images

First published 2023
by Routledge
4 Park Square, Milton Park, Abingdon, Oxon OX14 4RN

and by Routledge
605 Third Avenue, New York, NY 10158

Routledge is an imprint of the Taylor & Francis Group, an informa business

English translation of the introduction by Dorothée Bonnigal-Katz, Laurence Kahn, and Andrew Weller.

English translation of all other chapters by Andrew Weller.

British Library Cataloguing-in-Publication Data
A catalogue record for this book is available from the British Library

Library of Congress Cataloging-in-Publication Data
Names: Kahn, Laurence, author.
Title: What Nazism did to psychoanalysis / by Laurence Kahn ; translated by Andrew Weller. Other titles: Ce que le nazisme a fait à la psychanalyse. English
Description: Abingdon, Oxon ; New York, NY : Routledge, 2023. | Series: IPA psychoanalytic ideas and applications | Includes bibliographical references and index.
Identifiers: LCCN 2022007353 (print) | LCCN 2022007354 (ebook) | ISBN 9781032294551 (hardback) | ISBN 9781032294537 (paperback) | ISBN 9781003301660 (ebook)
Subjects: LCSH: Psychoanalysis—Political aspects. | National socialism—Psychological aspects. | Holocaust, Jewish (1939–1945)—Psychological aspects. | Psychoanalysis—History—20th century.
Classification: LCC BF175 .K28613 2023 (print) | LCC BF175 (ebook) | DDC 616.89/17—dc23/eng/20220609
LC record available at https://lccn.loc.gov/2022007353
LC ebook record available at https://lccn.loc.gov/2022007354

ISBN: 978-1-032-29455-1 (hbk)
ISBN: 978-1-032-29453-7 (pbk)
ISBN: 978-1-003-30166-0 (ebk)

DOI: 10.4324/9781003301660

Typeset in Palatino
by Apex CoVantage, LLC

In Memory of My Grandfather.

To My Mother, Andrée May.

Contents

Series Editor's foreword

The Publications Committee of the International Psychoanalytic Association continues, with the present volume, the series "Psychoanalytic Ideas and Applications".

The aim of this series is to focus on the scientific production of significant authors whose works are outstanding contributions to the development of the psychoanalytic field and to set out relevant ideas and themes generated during the history of psychoanalysis that deserve to be known and discussed by present-day psychoanalysts.

The relationship between psychoanalytic ideas and their applications needs to be put forward from the perspective of theory, clinical practice and research in order to maintain their validity for contemporary psychoanalysis.

The Publications Committee's objective is to share these ideas with the psychoanalytic community and with professionals in other related disciplines to expand their knowledge and generate a productive interchange between the text and the reader. The IPA Publications Committee is pleased to publish the translated English version of Laurence Kahn's book *What Nazism Did to Psychoanalysis,* which was first published in French with the title *Ce que le nazisme a fait à la psychanalyse* in 2018 by Presses Universitaires de France.

This book is a rigorous and remarkable undertaking that conveys, in a strikingly convincing and at times disquieting manner, the impact of Nazism on psychoanalysis and on our culture more generally. Only someone who is seriously concerned about preserving the essence of Freud's tenets of psychoanalytic theory and practice and as passionate and erudite as Laurence Kahn could have explored this topic in such a rich and in-depth manner. As a philosopher, a polyglot philologist and a psychoanalyst, her book goes beyond the discipline of psychoanalysis to cover topics related to history, linguistics and philosophy. She presents, in an extensive and in-depth manner, documentation that helps one understand the establishment of Nazi culture in Hitler's Germany and its repercussions in psychoanalysis in Europe and the transformations that occurred in North America. Kahn describes how Nazism put an end to a psychoanalytic culture that existed before the Shoah and founded a new culture that impacted psychoanalytic theory and practice.

Using her wealth of knowledge of the history of language, Kahn denounces the corruption of language in Nazi culture. Words such as *Führer*, whose German meaning is "the leader", were distorted by Hitler to mean the absolute authority in Germany's Third Reich. Freud used this same term in *Moses and Monotheism* to refer to the great leader who forbids murder and provides the sediment of civilization. Kahn argues that in Nazi culture this term was deformed; it became associated with the absolute authority of Hitler, who legitimized murder, destroyed the foundations of civilization, and established a culture of death and effectively undermined the founding principles of civilization. In its entirety, it was characterized by a regression to prehistoric barbarism, a time before *Totem and Taboo*.

Another example of the corruption of language was the misuse of some tenets of psychoanalytic theoretical concepts by Nazi culture, in particular, the theory of drives. Nazi ideology corrupted the notion of self-preservative drives and used them to justify the need to bring the German people together and unite them based on the idealization of, and the need to "preserve" their Aryan identity, which in turn justified for them the murder not only of Jewish people but of anyone who did not possess their racial identity.

A major contribution of this book is Laurence Kahn's thorough examination of the repercussions of the Shoah and Nazism on psychoanalytic theory and practice. The author traces the origins of ego psychology and argues convincingly that its emphasis on a rational perspective and on reinforcing adaptive functions was a response to counteract the destructiveness of the drives witnessed by psychoanalysts in Europe. Heinz Hartmann, who immigrated from Austria to the USA, was one of the most important contributors to ego psychology. He elaborated a theory of psychic life where the precedence of the ego, with its capacity to judge reality and its relative autonomy from the drives, would allow the individual to resist the overwhelming forces stemming from the "mass psychoses" which psychoanalysts witnessed during the war in Europe. This theory may be thought of as Hartmann's attempt to oppose the ego's libidinal autonomy with the madness of Nazi ideology that took hold of the individual consciousness and existence outside of the Nazi's mass culture, which did not tolerate individual free will. Following this line of thought, ego psychology and the importance given to the notion of empathy could be seen as possible consequences of the fight against Nazi culture. This perspective not only deeply altered the tenets of psychoanalytic concepts, such as the unconscious and the drive theory, but also changed the aims of psychoanalytic treatment. Throughout her book, the author elucidates one of the major impacts of what Nazism did to psychoanalysis, that is, the gradual suppression of the concept of the death drive (Thanatos) and associated concepts such as masochism and sadism. According to the author, this suppression of the importance of destructiveness led to prioritizing the notion of empathy as the central standpoint in the treatment of victims. This minimized the presence in every human being, including victims, of the existence of guilt, unconscious fantasies, amnesia, deformation and repression, forces that remain active in the psychic life of survivors. Following this line of thought, the author examines in detail the American literature on trauma and highlights the way in which this theory has been dramatically altered from the original concept of trauma in Freud's theory. The latter emphasized individual response to trauma depending on the subject's unique psychic reality, taking into consideration the notion of "nachträglichkeit" ("après coup") a freudian concept central to the psychoanalytic understanding of trauma. In this manner, the author identifies a progressive transformation of psychoanalytic theory.

Skilfully organized in 12 chapters, the book covers a myriad of perspectives, such as the collapse of the autonomy of laws, the attempt of Nazi culture to "purify psychoanalysis", the corruption of the German language and the surge of ego psychology as a response to the experience of mass psychosis during Nazism, to name a few.

This book is a remarkable contribution to the study of the impact of Nazism on psychoanalysis, both theoretically and clinically. Its availability to the English readership is a significant contribution to the creation of bridges between different psychoanalytic cultures. One should be thankful to Dr. Kahn for her rigorous research, her insights and her creative contribution. I believe this volume should become an historical reference in psychoanalytic theory.

Gabriela Legorreta
Series Editor
Chair, IPA Publications Committee

Introduction

Old words, new meanings[1]

"It is superfluous to comment on the general international situation. Perhaps we are only repeating the ridiculous act of rescuing a birdcage while the house is burning down" (letter from Freud to Jones dated 26 April 1932 in Paskauskas, 1993, p. 693). In 1933, "isolated and stranded", Freud wrote, "I will for once not write about the bleak misery of these times which at present stifles all more meaningful activity for me" (letter to Jones dated 23 August 1933, ibid., p. 726). Yet, as certain as he might have been that Hitler's movement would also spread to Austria, he nevertheless retained the vague hope that national socialism would be bound through the alliance with the other rightist parties. Granted, "the transition toward a rightist dictatorship . . . means the suppression of social democracy" (letter to Jones dated 7 April 1933, ibid, p. 716). However, the Austrian Jews would perhaps be better protected because of the clearly expressed rights of minorities in Austria's 1920 peace treaty.

We know what happened. A witness until his death of the formidable transferral of the psychoanalytic world's centre of gravity from the East to the West, Freud emigrated to London in June 1938. As he underlined, when the British Society was founded in 1919, he could not have foreseen that he would find refuge in its midst a quarter of a century later: "It is still quite remarkable how unsuspectingly we human beings approach the future" (letter from Freud to Jones dated 7 March 1939, ibid., 769).

Was it conceivable that psychoanalysis could remain unscathed by the disaster begotten by Nazism? One of the first consequences undoubtedly consisted of the displacement of its living sites and, with it, a profound modification of the intellectual horizons within which its theory and practice had come into existence. In areas where logical empiricism and analytic philosophy led to a severe critique of metaphysics in the wake of the Vienna Circle and Wittgenstein, analysts who had recently emigrated to the United States had to face onslaughts against the theoretical grounds of metapsychology. Regarded as an "occult force", the notion of drive was bound to be discredited by those for whom the only criteria guaranteeing the validation of discoveries consisted in observation-based verification and strict demonstrative logic. Enjoined to justify the causal "illusions"

DOI: 10.4324/9781003301660-1

fostered by its pseudo-scientificity, psychoanalysis therefore appeared to be the emanation of metaphysical thinking, the pure product of philosophical errors belonging to an obsolete era of thought. The openly anti-metaphysical aim pursued by the Freudian project mattered very little, even though, on this very specific point, it was aligned with Kant's critical position. It was of no consequence, therefore, that for Freud reality was unknowable and that theoretical reason should renounce all direct knowledge of first things. Kant was treated as an essentialist and Freud as a Platonist.

However, the effects of the exile of numerous analysts to the United States are but one aspect of the blow to psychoanalysis inflicted by Nazism. Like the whole Western world, psychoanalysis was affected by the implacable disruption of the linguistic foundation on which it rested. This seismic shock was perceived by many writers, sometimes immediately – Klemperer, Cassirer, Adorno, Kertész, Celan, Orwell, Beckett, and others. The mystification of meaning, the fascination exerted by an irrationality concealed within the eloquence of pseudo rationality, an outrageous rhetoric of dichotomy with a systematic use of simplified oppositions, were all so operative simply because the Nazi language took root in very close proximity to the very language of culture. To Thomas Mann, who, in 1936, celebrating Freud, asked, "Has the world ever been changed by anything save by thought and its magic vehicle the Word?" (1936, p. 110), history somehow replied that the magic of the word would turn the world into ruins.

Klemperer, a philologist, immediately pointed out this change in the function of language. "All language freely practiced fulfils all human needs", he argued; "it serves reason as well as emotion, it is communication and conversation, soliloquy and prayer, plea, command and invocation" (2013, p. 23). Yet besides "the forcing into line" of its speakers ordered to conform to this unique model, the language of the Third Reich was so poor because it was only used for invocation. And invocation is magic. This is also underlined by Cassirer (1946): not only were new words coined, but old words were used in a new sense; they underwent a change of meaning that "depends upon the fact that each word that was formerly used for descriptive, logical or semantic sense are now used as magic words" (p. 283), not for the symbolization of thought but for the edification of an invulnerable myth, "impervious to rational arguments".

When one ponders what Nazism did to psychoanalysis, it is therefore the corrupt use of words that must first be considered. For example, how does the extensive use of the term *Trieb* by Hitler and Alfred Rosenberg clash with the Freudian "drive"? Or what are the consequences for the drive of self-preservation [*Selbsterhaltungstrieb*], when the latter becomes the axis of a foreign policy of living space in the form of the survival instinct? And what about the use of *Ausrottung*? In Freud's text, this word highlights the fact that the "extirpation" of infantile wishful impulses is by no means the ideal aim of psychic development (1910, p. 53); or that education in no way leads to "eradicating" evil because the drives in themselves are neither good nor bad, they are simply prohibited, or not, by the human community (1915, p. 281). In Nazi discourse, this word, *Ausrottung*, very concretely means Extermination – that is, the final solution. As Olivier Jouanjan (2009) stresses, Nazi law has one goal – the triumph of "concrete thinking" – and a watchword: *logos* is always *polemos*. According to Schmitt, the words of political law "are unintelligible if we ignore who these words were concretely supposed to harm, combat, and deny" (ibid., p. 71). This was the case for the drive, self-preservation, as well as the ideals of purification and racial "hygiene". How could psychoanalytic language not have been affected by such a corruption?

Originally published in 1947 in East Germany, where its author continued to reside after the war, Klemperer's *The Language of the Third Reich* gradually fell into oblivion. This linguistic picture, which was painted *in vivo* by a Jewish philologist who had been banned from teaching, was finally published in West Germany in 1966 under the new title chosen for a new edition: *Die unbewältigte Sprache* – "The Unmastered Language" (Klemperer, 1966). The choice was intentional and was based on Klemperer's statement: "Whatever it is that people are determined to hide, be it only from others, or from themselves, even things they carry around unconsciously – language reveals all" (2013, p. 11). However, this new title also resonated with a question that haunted German thought at that time, the question of "the struggle to overcome the past" [*Vergangenheitsbewältigung*]. This was a question raised by Adorno in 1959. The philosopher suspected that, in the very formulation of this "struggle to overcome", there was a catchword aimed at smoothing out the façade of a heritage that was allegedly superseded but was in truth topical and operative. Sugar-coated phrases, the prevalence constantly given to a "realistic" present, the fact that, at the time of the defeat, there had also been a lack of "the panic" that, according to Freud's (1921) theory in *Group Psychology and the Analysis of the Ego*, "sets in whenever collective identifications break apart" (p. 96) – all this indicated the extent to which, in his view, the collective narcissism of Germans, damaged by the collapse of Nazism, was but awaiting its reconstitution – if only under the cover of the "economic boom" promoted by such "industrious" people (ibid.). Therefore, it is on the basis of a "psycho-socially unmastered past", on a "*unbewältigte Vergangenheit*", that the adaptation to reality, the obstinate resistance to psychoanalysis, the categorical rejection of the critical reflection it proposes, sought, in his opinion, to draw a line under it all.

To Klemperer, this unmastered past dwells at the very heart of the language, for the method that consistently ordered Nazi stylistics consisted of invalidating the definitions of words by disordering their meaning. It was not only true of *Aktion, Sturm, Einsatz, Figuren, Schmattes* or *Anschluss* (*Aktion* being used to describe the operations of massacre; *Sturm*, the storm becoming the assault; *Figuren*, puppets, and *Schmattes*, rags, the names imposed by the Nazis to refer to the exhumed bodies when all traces of the Extermination were erased; *Anschluss*, a connection in physics, now referring to annexation). It was also true for *Ich*, *Moral* and *Tod* – ego, morality and death – in other words, for the most fixed aspects of humanity. The aim of the transformation of the German language into a vast "Barnum" – a combination of romanticism, business and advertising, the most powerful and secret agent of propaganda – was the elimination of thought: inebriating it in order to stupefy it – "Language which writes and thinks for you", "a poison which you drink unconsciously [*Unbewusst*] and which has its effect" (Klemperer, 2013, p. 63; translation modified). This verbal alchemy that was brewing backstage and was springing up in the Nazi harangues thus wrapped the *organisch* and *Organisation* [organic and organization] in "benign" respectability, "the most commonplace expression to describe an activity which had itself become commonplace" (ibid., p. 106) – however overpowering the smell of blood might be. In this "seizure of the individual ego by the collective discourse, History with a capital H performs fervent and life size practical work on the destiny of words", Nathalie Zaltzman (2006, p. 86) writes.

Sternberger et al. (1957) had the same project – studying Nazism's corruption of language – when, between 1945 and 1948, they published a series of articles in the monthly journal *Die Wandlung* [The Change], which would become *Aus dem Wörterbuch des Unmenschen* [Dictionary of Inhumanity].[2] For the same reason that language is the spirit itself, in the authors' view, there is "no difference between the barbarity of language and the barbarity of spirit". "Each word changes the world", and this change remains registered in the use of language. Yet, while the alteration of words alters humanity itself, the quasi-supernatural secret of language is that it ultimately betrays its speaker. In the eyes of the authors, this applies first and foremost to the impregnation of German words by Nazi usage, well beyond the fall of the Reich.

The damage undoubtedly goes deeper. The very struggle against alteration can in fact bring about changes that, in turn, will impregnate language in the long term and distort the notions that it carries. The analysts of the time naturally strove to combat the hijacking of the terminology of psychoanalysis during those dark times. But were they not betrayed by the transformation of the analytic theorizations they were then led to introduce? Did not the new paths they opened up in their struggle contribute profoundly to changing analytic theory and shutting down its practice?

The question arose for me when I discovered a proliferation of texts written between 1928 and 1938 by German and Austrian analysts, including Freud, as they were directly faced with the rise and then the triumph of Nazism. The topic of these texts is the relation between psychoanalysis and a "worldview" (*Weltanschauung*). Reading about persecutions and the Göring Institute, about the theft of language and the "purification of psychoanalysis"' about *Mein Kampf* and the "dictatorship of reason", about scientific arguments and ethical questions, I began to see the emergence of the very first foundations of ego psychology. It is well known that Lacan (1991) levelled scathing criticism against the "triumvirate" or "troika" – Hartmann, Loewenstein and Kris – against their systematic attempt to re-join classical psychology, against their conception of a desexualized – if not "delibidinized" – libido and a "de-aggressivized" aggressiveness. He criticized, in short, the "reform" of the subject that they pursued through a reliance on "objective" data (pp. 24–25; 164). Lacan (2019) inveighs against a version of psychoanalysis that gives prevalence to structuring elements based on ego organization – an ego adapted to its efficient mobility within constituted reality – and goes as far as to assert that the reality promoted by their technique resembles "the world of American lawyers" (pp. 364 and 482).

French psychoanalysis is aware of its debt to Lacan, and my aim here is not to run to the rescue of ego psychology. But it does not prevent us from considering that, at its very beginning, it was a theory that sought to confront the disruption of thought and the distortion of reality, exactly when "nature" and its "biology" had forced their way into the political and ethical spheres. It is a hard endeavour if we take into account the fact that, in the wake of naturalness, the scientific *Weltanschauung* para-doxically became the argument in defence of the value of the new order and the "liberation of living forces". It was in this context, where the fate of words themselves was in the balance, that Hartmann put forward the notion of "the ego's adaptation to reality". He then sought to develop a theory of psychic life in which the precedence of the ego, its capacities to judge reality and its relative libidinal autonomy would permit the extrica-tion of consciousness from "mass psychosis". What was at stake for Hart-mann in the struggle against the autocratic creation of a neo-reality as manufactured by Nazi discourse was an overarching ethic, buttressed by a superego able to repudiate mass identificatory subjugation and hold the objective links of causality firmly. But, as we know, Freudian theory was distinctly affected, if only in the form of ego inflation.

Inversely or correlatively – there in fact lies one of the questions – when from 1960 onwards, American psychiatrists and psychoanalysts instigated major research among Holocaust survivors and published the results, they were visibly seeking to rethink the possible re-founding of a private sphere, after the onslaught of what they consistently referred to as an "extreme traumatic experience". In doing so, they contributed to the rise of the notion of "massive trauma", associated with a simplification of the concept of splitting, thereby fuelling the model of a psychic func-tioning mainly ruled by survival. The will to remember and testify, based on listening to first- and second-generation Holocaust victims, held thera-peutic action as its first aim. Strangely enough, the conclusions turned out to be quite uniform. The ineffable void and the psychic death resulting from the event, the idea of "black holes" reverberating in the form of unfathomable silence, gradually outlined the preferential tool designed to help, cure and communicate, namely, empathy. At the same time, every withdrawal, every absence, every deficiency in the psychic fabric became signs of discontinuity in the individual, if not of the individual's annihilation. This ultimately referred psychic work and the theory underpinning it to a rather rudimentary scaffolding (see the detailed analysis by Apfelbaum (2007): the first reason was that trauma did not seemingly have to be defined because the historical event as such elicited its characterization; the second reason was that diachronic linearity, distortion, screen memories and substitutive formations appeared to have disappeared from the survivors' psychic life; the last reason was that the unrepresentable seemingly became the paradigm of a "lived experience that cannot be lived", an irreversible, non-metaphorizable, cumulative and transmissible experience whose sequelae consisted in internal fragmentation and the disintegration of representations, as epitomized by the "*Muselmann*".[3]

These models are very far removed from the one proposed by Freud, if only because the very notion of massiveness spares us from having to take into account the individual drive-related vicissitudes and their psychic economies. Yet, with his introduction to *Psychoanalysis and the War Neuroses* (Abraham et al., 1921), *Group Psychology and the Analysis of the Ego* (1921) and *Civilisation and its Discontents* (1930) Freud bequeathed to us tools to envision the relations between the amplitude of social phenomena and the struggle of each individual with his internal enemy. Very few analysts in these investigations made use of the role of identifications, which can drive us to heroism and murder alike and serve destruction as well as civilization.

In their defence, one must underline that, regardless of how they related to Freud's theory, they were the first to open up this path. During the 1960s, Europeans, or the French at least, were all very busy with the return to Freud. It suffices to observe the quasi-absence of any mention of the Holocaust in Castoriadis's work.[4] As for Lacan, he hardly dwelled on it. In his lecture of 24 June 1964 (Lacan, 1977, pp. 274–276), the sacrificial metaphor presided over his mention of the extermination of the Jews: "There is something profoundly masked in the critique of the history that we have experienced. This, re-enacting the most monstrous and supposedly superseded forms of the Holocaust, is the drama of Nazism" (ibid., pp. 274–275). Once we posit that "no meaning given to history, based on Hegeliano-Marxist premises, is capable of accounting for this resurgence – which only goes to show that the offering to obscure gods of an object of sacrifice is something to which few subjects can resist succumbing, as if under some monstrous spell", we still have "ignorance, indifference, an averting of the eyes" to "explain beneath what veil this mystery still remains hidden" (ibid., p. 275). But where is this mystery located if we consider that the specific characteristic of the Holocaust in ancient Greece was to be a Chthonian sacrifice? Is it in the function of the infernal gods? Is it in the choice of the victim? Or is it in the identity of the sacrificer? In 1971 and 1976, Lacan returned to it when, tackling the three Freudian forms of identification, he underlined the scope of *Group Psychology and the Analysis of the Ego* with regard to the Nazi phenomenon. In 1971, he mentioned the "little moustache" and its function as a unary trait: "It is indeed in the measure that something in every discourse that appeals to the Thou provokes a camouflaged, secret identification, which is simply to this enigmatic object that may seem to be nothing, the tiny little surplus enjoyment of Hitler, that went no further perhaps than his moustache. This was enough to crystallize people who . . . had nothing mystical about them!" (Lacan, 1971–1972, pp. 43–44). In 1976, the little moustache persisted: "A person may be indifferent and a unary trait be chosen as the basis for an identification. It is not indifferent because this is how Freud believes he can account for the identification with the Führer's little moustache which, everyone knows, played a big role".[5]

Lacan's 1958 comment on "the figure of the Führer and the collective phenomena" signals the fact that he saw this "object reduced to its stupidest reality", operating "for a certain number of subjects as a common denominator" likely to "bring about an identification of the ideal ego to the very moronic power of misadventure that the ideal ego turns out to be at its core" (2006, p. 567). However, it also indicates how he overlooked the relationship that tightly links Hartmann's attempt to oppose the ego's libidinal autonomy to the madness of Nazi ideality that seized individual consciousness. He ignored it, if only to mock it,

> since, in a comical reversal of what Freud wanted to contribute by way of a remedy to civilization's discontents, the very community to which he bequeathed this remedial task has proclaimed the synthesis of a strong ego as a watchword, at the heart of a technique in which the practitioner believes that he obtains results by incarnating this ideal himself.
>
> (ibid.)

Which community is at stake? Is it the analytic community? The Jewish community? In truth, it does not really matter: how does the charge against the capture of the Ideal by the Führer relate to its possible return in the form of the analyst offering himself as ideal?

It does not really matter, because the main issue lies in the consequence. I see it specifically in the fact that, after the very first publications on antisemitism and propaganda (such as the work of Kris, Loewenstein, Nathan Ackerman and Marie Jahoda, along with Ernst Simmel and Paul Federn), the movement that gradually combined empathy, intersubjectivity, co-narrativity and relativism began with the second wave of psychoanalytic research on the Holocaust. The treatment of the latter no longer involved questioning the mechanisms of anti-Jewish persecution or the enigma of the transition from individual to mass hatred. It focused on the event and its inconceivable nature. Yet, as Ruth Klüger (1994) writes, the terms "unspeakable" and "unrepresentable" are both "*kitsch*", a "sentimental flight before reality" (p. 55). This is why she rejects videotaped testimonies that give rise to "the greyish broth of a pseudo-scientific commentary imbued with sentimentality" courting the unconscious (ibid., p. 60). Indeed, what does it mean to exacerbate emotional participation when envisioning the concentration camp negation of humanity? As Olivier Jouanjan (2013) suggests, virtuous or pathetic indignation before barbarism is not enough. The Nazi killing machine had methodical, rigorous and powerful tools at its disposal. There was a logic to the irrational and a coherence to the monstrous. The task of the historian – of the law historian, in this case – must therefore consist of taking Nazi law seriously. This means, Jouanjan adds, seeking, as the psychoanalyst does, to step into the turmoil of the other, even of the most dangerous psychopath, while sustaining a theoretical gaze – a decontaminating gaze – as survival equipment.

But the fact is that the psychoanalytic reflection on the Nazi fury mainly focused on the pathology of the victims. The unspoken things, the incurable insecurity, the shame and the hidden, silence and secrets; there was sometimes the question of reactualization under the blow of another loss; and almost always the idea that the pathology of the survivors is distinct from any other in that it bears witness to the impossibility of historicizing the past. The fact that the psychoanalytic treatment of the Holocaust took the unspeakable trauma as its main route of entry is perhaps a consequence in itself.

Nathalie Zaltzman's (2007) reflection certainly suggests another path which places the role of "collective identifying constructs" at the heart of the work of culture. She starts with the neo-formation of the horde, which is not the return of some primal prehistory but the creation of a new type of group, organized on the basis of a "totem without taboo" (p. 21). She then questions the process at work in the regression of civilization. This regression necessarily operates at the level of ego agencies, since it involves both individual and collective narcissistic libido. Yet, according to her, the primacy granted by Freud to drive-related renunciation in his reflection on the cultural process leaves this identificatory axis in the dark to the advantage of libido taming. However, as the agency of psychic lucidity, the task of the work of culture should not be subjected to any allegedly pacifying or supposedly consensual idealization of the community. It should not be subjected to any wish for a so-called harmonious reappropriation of the subject declared "civilized" at last. The ability, without any hope of "reparation", to "transform the collapse of the representation of the species – a self-inflicted collapse – into a thinkable event that can be thought of by the species itself" (ibid., p. 24) is the condition for an enrichment of the consciousness conquered by men over whatever exceeds them. Failing that, Nathalie Zaltzman adds, we are doomed to send the criminal dimension of the human condition back into limbo.

However, how can we possibly tackle the implosion of analytic language under the effect of criminal discourse? When a new order adopts "the transvaluation of all values" as the slogan for the regeneration of its community and its law, this of course resonates with Nietzsche in the way he was celebrated by the Third Reich.[6] But, for the analyst, is there not also the echo of "the transvaluation of all psychical values" (Freud, 1900, p. 330) in the midst of the changes in emphasis which the dream or the symptom carries out? To Freud, this transvaluation is the operator of disguise, whose instigator is a mobile quantity that can cathect some representational segments indifferently, overlooking their qualitative value. This disorganizes not only the referential systems between words and things, but also the rational links between "real" facts and psychic productions. Dispensing with the "factor of reality" (ibid., p. 329) is therefore the stance required of the analyst who seeks to locate the unconscious lines of force; this implies, in turn, a kind of "indifference" appropriate for examining the subjection to emotional or sensory presence of manifest productions.

Yet, we must admit, indifference – in reference to the German term *Indifferenz*, which is translated into French as "neutrality" – has become almost inadmissible today. At a time when affective authenticity participates in the wish to "humanize" the analytic relationship, the dream experience or the emotional experience of the transference should mobilize our full attention as much as the affective reshuffling that they invoke. Empathy thus won its first spurs by listening to the survivors. But what sort of humanization are we talking about here? The unmediated legibility of affects spares the mischief of suspicion, and one thing is certain: when related to the disaster of trauma, indifference quickly takes on the tone of the slaughterer's coldness. Therefore, apprehending the close relationship between narcissism and the deleterious impact of the superego without sacrificing to the identity *vibrato* or giving up before what has been declared unimaginable has seemingly become a complicated task.

In this context, we will also have to consider whether the rejection of Freudian energetics – the principal mover of the psychic apparatus – and the renunciation of drive theory with the procession of theoretical and practical consequences that we know, are in part consequences of the following: the contamination of drive-related energetics as theorized by Freud by Nazi biologism and its use of "the liberation of living forces' drawn from the nocturnal and demonic depths of nature. Required under the argument of scientificity, this abandonment might in fact reveal extreme distrust towards a notion recruited in the service of obscure and catastrophic drives.

"*Unimaginable*: a word that doesn't divide, doesn't restrict", Robert Antelme (1992) wrote. "The most convenient word. When you walk around with this word as your shield, this word for emptiness, your step becomes better assured, more resolute, your conscience pulls itself together" (pp. 289–290).

Notes

1 Translated by Dorothée Bonnigal-Katz, Laurence Kahn, and Andrew Weller.
2 According to its founders, Jaspers and Sternberger, this "humanist" monthly based its reflection on the Kantian notion of "criticism" and on Humboldt's linguistic positions: thought is closely linked to the singular properties of each language. It appeared from November 1945 until 1949, and included among its contributors Hannah Arendt, T.S. Eliot, and Viktor von Weizsäcker.
3 "The word 'Muselmann'", Primo Levi (1979 [1958]) writes, "I do not know why, was used by the old ones of the camp to describe, the weak, the inept, those doomed to selection." And: "They, the *Muselmänner*, the damned, form the backbone of the camp, an anonymous mass, continually renewed and always identical, of non-men who march and labour in silence, the divine spark dead within them. . . . One hesitates to call them living: one hesitates to call their death death, in the face of which they have no fear, as they are too tired to understand" (p. 96).
4 Daniel Blanchard, a member of the *Socialisme ou Barbarie* group, said during a conference on "Castoriadis and the imaginary" (Cerisy, 6–10 June 2003): "There is above all one fact, that Castoriadis, that all of us at *Socialisme ou Barbarie*, have ignored – and we were not the only ones – a set of facts so abrupt and so deleterious that they still seem unassimilable today by the conscience of the time – I mean obviously, the fact of concentration camps, the holocaust, the genocides. . . . I say *ignored*, in the English sense of the word, because to look it in the face would have challenged what there was still a functional requirement in the rationality in the name of which we were criticizing modern society and would have undermined the optimism which supported us." (Blanchard, "The Idea of Revolution and Castoriadis", online on the Dissidences website: http://dissidences.hypotheses.org/5591).
5 J. Lacan, On a discourse that might not be a semblance, lesson of 20 January 1971, and L'insu que savoir de une-bévue s'aile à mourre, lesson of 16 November 1976 [references taken from the transcription of the International Lacanian Association]; see also Stern (2007, p. 243).
6 See the article in the *Völkische Beobachter* on 15 October 1934: Nietzsche is praised there as a "hero of willpower", "the founder of a new ethics" who, thanks to transvaluation of all values, caused an initial breach in the wall of obsolete "world views". The phrase was used as the subtitle of the volume of close to 2,400 aphorisms published by the Nietzsche Society in 1940.

References

Apfelbaum, L. (2007). Limites du modèle traumatique. *Libres cahiers pour la psychanalyse*, 16:21–30.
Cassirer, E. (1946). *The Myth of the State*. New Haven: Yale UP.
Freud, S. (1900). *The Interpretation of Dreams*. S.E. 4–5. London: Hogarth.
Freud, S. (1910). *Five Lectures on Psychoanalysis*. S.E. 11. London: Hogarth, pp. 1–56.

Freud, S. (1915). *Thoughts for the Times on War and Death. S.E.* 14. London: Hogarth, pp. 273–300.

Freud, S. (1921). *Group Psychology and the Analysis of the Ego. S.E.* 18. London: Hogarth, pp. 65–144.

Freud, S. (1930). *Civilization and Its Discontents. S.E.* 21. London: Hogarth, pp. 57–146.

Jouanjan, O. (2009). 'Pensée de l'ordre concret' et ordre du discours 'juridique' nazi: sur Carl Schmitt. In: *Carl Schmitt ou le mythe du politique*, Y.-C. Zarka (ed.). Paris: Presses Universitaires de France, pp. 71–119.

Jouanjan, O. (2013). Prendre le discours juridique nazi au sérieux? *Revue interdisciplinaire d'études juridiques*, 70: 1–23.

Klemperer, V. (1966). *Die unbewältigte Sprache. Aus dem Notizbuch eines Philologen-LTI.* Darmstadt: Joseph Melzer Verlag.

Klemperer, V. (2013 [1957]). *The Language of the Third Reich. LTI – Lingua Tertii Imperii: A Philologist's Notebook*, trans. M. Brady. London: Bloomsbury.

Klüger, R.(2006). Missbrauch der Erinnerung: KZ-Kitsch. In: *Gelesene Wirklichkeit: Fakten und Fiktionen in der Literatur*. Göttingen: Wallstein Verlag, pp. 52–67.

Lacan, J. (1958). Remarks on Daniel Lagache's presentation. In: *Ecrits*, trans. B. Fink. New York: Norton, 2007, pp. 543–574.

Lacan, J. (1971–1972). *The Seminar of Jacques Lacan XVIII (1971–1972): On a Discourse that Might not be a Semblance*, trans. C. Gallagher. Unpublished Translation.

Lacan, J. (1977/1973). *The Four Fundamental Concepts of Psycho-Analysis*, trans. A. Sheridan. London: Hogarth.

Lacan, J. (1991 [1975]). *The Seminar of Jacques Lacan, Book I: Freud's Papers on Technique (1953–1954)*, trans. J. Forrester. New York: Norton.

Lacan, J. (2006/1958). Remarks on Daniel Lagache's presentation. In: *Ecrits*, trans. B. Fink. New York: Norton, 2007, pp. 543–574.

Lacan, J. (2019 [2013]). *Desire and Its Interpretation: The Seminar of Jacques Lacan, Book VI (1958–1959)*, trans. B. Fink. Cambridge: Polity Press.

Levi, P. (1979 [1958]). *If This Is a Man*, trans. S. Woolf. London: Penguin Books.

Mann, T. (1936). Freud and the future. *International Journal of Psychoanalysis*, 37: 106–115.

Paskauskas, R.A. (ed.). (1993). *The Complete Correspondence of Sigmund Freud and Ernest Jones, 1908–1939*. Cambridge, MA: Harvard University Press.

Stern, A.-L. (2007). *Le Savoir-deporté*. Paris: Le Seuil.

Storz,G. Sternberger, D., Süskind, W.E. (1957). *Aus dem Wörterbuch des Unmenschen*. Hamburg: Claasen Verlag.

Zaltzman, N. (2006). L'impact des mots. *L'Esprit du temps/Topique*, 96(3): 85–91.

Zaltzman, N. (2007). *L'Esprit du mal*. Paris: Editions de l'Olivier.

1   The law beyond the law

Let us admit that psychoanalysis was faced with difficulty in conceiving the Extermination. And, further, let us admit that the analytic operation that consists in "referring to the past" the current reality embodied in the transference did not initially find any other possible territory than the translation offered by "life histories" and their narratives. There was no doubt, however, that a remnant was there, which was related neither to the treatment provided nor to the virtues of mutuality. Referring subjectivities to the objectivity of facts or restoring lived experiences through narrative seem more like resurgences of what at that time had fractured the world of analysts. There is a hint of this break in the fact that, for a long time, there was rarely any reference to one of the points of departure of *Group Psychology and the Analysis of the Ego* (Freud, 1921) and *Civilization and its Discontents* (Freud, 1930). Yet, if collective psychology is the oldest human psychology (Freud, 1921, p. 69, 123), during Nazism, we witnessed in detail the defeat of the subtle mixture between singularity and sociality. Such a dispossession of minds therefore forced us to think again about "mutilated life".

But how should the perimeter of this mutilation be delineated? John Kafka (2000), following Elisabeth Domansky, recalls what happened during the speech delivered by Philip Jenninger on the fiftieth anniversary of the "Kristallnacht".[1] Jenninger, then president of the West German Parliament, dared to break the taboo by speaking of the criminals rather than the victims. Many parliamentarians left the room and were unable in the days that followed to explain their reactions. Was this for the reason that Kafka gives? "From a psychoanalytic point of view", he wrote, "one could say that focusing on the victims is a defence against elements of identification with the criminals". In this sense, he adds, commemoration may contribute to the "organized amnesia" (ibid., p. 90). A remnant, therefore, was there, which concerned the anthropology of the collective bankruptcy, and it was claiming its due.

Strangely, for a long time, it was left to philosophers, poets and men of letters to deal with this remnant. Think of Adorno (2005), who takes up Freud's idea that "that civilization itself produces and increasingly

DOI: 10.4324/9781003301660-2

reinforces anti-civilization" (p. 191) – "especially in connection with Auschwitz" (p. 192). Who would suspect that guilt can easily be exchanged in a communicational system devoted to the duties of memory? If the task of sociology is "to comprehend the incomprehensible, the advance of human beings into the inhuman" (Adorno, 1965, p. 147), it cannot, in his view, do without Freudian sociology, because it alone has the merit of taking into account the bankruptcy of the compensations provided by culture in return for the instinctual drive renunciations imposed on individuals. Thus, the philosopher rejects the "resuscitated culture", which plays its part by pretending to ignore that it was this very culture that gave birth to genocide.

And think of Kertész, who takes a different approach, but with great obstinacy, to the "long, dark shadow" cast by the smoke of the Holocaust over Europe, whose "flames have etched an indelible mark in the sky" (1998a, p. 59). This shadow spreads over the whole of the civilization in which it took place. Our civilization must now live with the burden of and consequences of what happened, which is not the burden of pathetic suffering, nor that of a new chapter of Jewish martyrdom logically succeeding previous trials and ordeals. In a strong voice – and not as a "surviving witness", a character who, in his eyes, participates in the stylization of Auschwitz – Kertész never ceases to affirm that the "Nazi counter-culture" whose culmination was the infernal laboratory of Auschwitz, contains the general potentialities of humanity, and therefore of our own too. What "we experience as irrational, incomprehensible, or rather what we declare as being so, resides in our internal world" (Kertész, 1995, pp. 119–120). Therein lies the burden in this "recent invention" through which "it turned out that murder is a liveable and possible way of life, and is therefore *institutionalizable*" (p. 127, Kertész's emphasis).[2]

However, the earthquake that made "Auschwitz" neither the name of a camp nor even the name of a genocidal event, but rather the paradigm of a new state of the human condition, first and foremost affected the law. This is where Kertész sees the dimension of universality introduced by the Shoah.[3] The National Socialist movement, its "negative heroes" and their destructive power entered the circle of civilization thanks to the "breach of contract", a real engine of power (p. 57). This mode of action cannot therefore be treated as a crime. It was a real operation whose purpose was to place "the law beyond the law" (pp. 47–48). That is why, according to him, our task is to consider "the Holocaust as culture" (ibid.). But culture must still tolerate being fertilized by that which shattered it, conceding nothing to pathos, conceding nothing to the heroization of the experience. Contrary to "kitsch as crude as a Spielberg dinosaur" (p. 133 and p. 154), we should refuse to adapt, for instance, to the rituals of commemoration and to the forgetting that it nourishes. "I would remind you", writes Kertész (2008), "that in my last little essay, I tried to show that one could no longer speak of Auschwitz in the language of the period before Auschwitz.

Before Auschwitz, it really was incomprehensible, during and after Auschwitz, it became *natural*" (p. 64). "Natural", given that the order now accepted may have been ordered by nature.

Many commentators have credited this "*natürlich*" and the phrases "undeniably", "that goes without saying" and "obviously" to the narrative method. In *Fatelessness* (Kertész, 2004/1975), the teenager has no idea of what is going to happen and, step by step, he organizes the "candid" logic of events. But this "*natürlich*" says much more than that. "Anti-Semitism as a matter of ancestry", writes Klemperer (2013), "is ineradicably tenacious; thanks to its claim to being scientific it is not an anachronism, but rather entirely appropriate to modern ways of thinking" (pp. 137–138). Thus, from Goethean *Natur* to "nature" according to the Nazis, the biologization of discourse has hatched "a frightfully simplistic form of mysticism, one which everyone can understand easily and unconsciously" (p. 120). Thus Kertész's "*natürlich*" resonates like the disconcerted echo of what Nazi policy entrusted to "naturalness": the naturalness of the race, the animal naturalness of the parasite (the Jew), the natural impulse towards racial unity,[4] nothing less than the impulse for life based on the state and culture – I will come back to this.

Yet, faced with the question raised by Kertész – how does a crime take on "the proportions of a turning point in the history of mentalities, of an open wound"? (1998b, p. 46) – it was as if psychoanalysts, by rehabilitating the trauma with a precedence justified by the material reality of the facts, had nourished the hope of freeing themselves from the impact of the Shoah on the disorientation inflicted on their own field and on the weakening of their communal "We". For example, the breach of contract that placed the law beyond the law involved revisiting the series of psychic compensations that Freud had placed at the centre of the fragile equilibrium of civilization. Compensations at the individual level when renunciation of the cathexes of infantile objects is required, when the instinctual drive sacrifice made by the ego to the superego ceases to rely on the reward of additional parental love, when the ego, which serves several masters, tries, in order to satisfy the impaired psychic "interests", to invent the path of desexualized diversions towards other aims. These individual compensations are in fact tied to the satisfactions offered by the social group: it is this group that guarantees at the collective level the psychic transactions that are supposed to compensate for the harm of the impaired interest. But this has a condition, namely that the community remains unaware of the fact that it is compensating the individual for a restriction that it itself imposes and which is its foundation. Illusion and compensation are therefore responsible for the coexistence, owing to the same misunderstanding, of both the interests of the group and the interests of the individual, which are in fact perfectly antagonistic. And yet they both support each other by referring to the same judicial foundation of consciousness: the commandments enunciated by the law exert a constraint which derives its efficacy from the inner tribunal that is the superego.

Now the breach of contract that placed the law beyond the law not only provided individuals with the immense narcissistic gain obtained by belonging to a fundamentally homogenous group, but – and this was an open wound in the Freudian understanding of the development of culture – it was based on a "renewed" theory of law that challenged the abstract conceptualization, necessary for legal order – which, according to Hans Kelsen,[5] must be based on rigorous neutrality in the relationship between the law and its object. This neutrality is at the very foundation of the norm that tends towards universalization by rising above individual cases and subjective value judgments. The first condition of equality before the law is that it must refer to an impersonal rule capable of treating an indefinite plurality of cases in the same way, which implies that it must be free from any political expectations, *a fortiori* when these are backed up by "natural" references.

Contrary to such an "abstraction" of legal categories, the overthrow of all values implemented by Nazi law began by erasing the dualism between being and having to be, between the order of life and the order of the norm. To do this, it broke up the separation between the subject of knowledge and the object of knowledge, whereas the legal discipline must in principle systematize its object – which can only be done by means of concepts that make it possible not to carry over into the object non-legal contents of a political or moral character. On the contrary, Nazi law made itself the spokesperson of an "intimate" normality, founded on "good morals" of the "normal type" (the good family father), carried out "in good faith". The guiding principle of Nazi law thus became that of "concrete orders" which, through the discriminatory power of the statutes – for example, that of "non-indigenous alien" – legitimized the "objectivity" of the natural foundations of order. With the equation of "the spirit of the law" with "popular common sense", equality before the law consisted of an equality circumscribed by the sense of belonging to the "German type". Nazi law was no more than the "order of community life" – the "principles of National Socialism" being immediately and exclusively decisive in the application and implementation of general legal clauses, according to Carl Schmitt.

In fact, in the eyes of its theorists, Carl Schmitt in the first instance, Nazi law was first and foremost part of a logic of incarnation. This meant that it did not depend on a separation between the rulers and the ruled; that it owed nothing to the principle of the representation of the people; and that the *Führer*, the bearer of the popular will, was not an authorized proxy. It created the common will as an objective fact – pure immanence. "Nazism thinks 'substantially', without 'fiction', without 'representation'", writes Jouanjan (2006), "and the community is always already, as if fused in its *identity*, substantially united, and united around its leader of whom it is no more than the following, the trusting troop" (p. 149).[6] It is the end of pacts, the end of contracts: "The common life of spouses within marriage, members of the family members within the family, members of the clan within the clan, members of a corporation members within the corporation, state officials, clerics of a church, comrades in a work camp, soldiers of an army, none of this can be dissolved either by the functionalism of laws defined in advance nor by contractual rules" (Schmitt, cited by Jouanjan (2002) in Colliot-Thélène & Kervégan, 2002, pp. 196–197).

What puts the law beyond the law is therefore nature converted into the law of the identity of nature, *natürlich* – an unprecedented version of the cultural universality which Kertész nonetheless relies on when he firmly refers to Freud: "We can see how the horror of the Holocaust takes on the proportions of a universal experience and, if I were not afraid of being misunderstood, I would say, of a culture – as does Freud who links the origin of monotheism, the highest moral culture, to the original parricide" (Kertész, 2009, p. 58).[7]

Notes

1 The reader will find great interest in the (1992) article by E. Domansky, "'Kristall- nacht' the Holocaust and German Unity: The Meaning of November 9 as an Anniversary in Germany", *History and Memory*, vol. 4 (1), pp. 60–94.
2 Imre Kertész's work as a whole is translated in French by N. Zaremba-Huzsvai and C. Zaremba.
3 Although the word Shoah is much less familiar than the term Holocaust for des- ignating the extermination of European Jews, I nevertheless alternate between the two terms, Holocaust referring, in my view incorrectly, to the chtonian sac- rifice in Ancient Greece. How was this great slaughter sacrificial?
4 A. Hitler (1936), *Mein Kampf*, complete edition, Zentralverlag der NSDAP, Munich, in particular vol. II, chap. 1: Weltanschauung und Partei [Concept of the world and the party], pp. 411–424, and chap. 2: Der Staat [The State]; see also vol. I, chap. 11: Volk und Rasse [People and race], pp. 311–362 [viewed online (1936 edition): https://archive.org/details/Mein-Kampf]; see also A. Rosenberg (1986) *Le Mythe du XXe siècle*, Paris, Avallon, pp. 595–648 [viewed online on archive.org].
5 On Hans Kelsen – a great Austrian jurist, a major representative of the positivist movement of the philosophy of law, the author of *Pure Theory of Law* (Kelsen, 1967), a bête noire of Nazi jurists and a reader of Freud – see Rodières-Rein (2017, pp. 81–98) as well as Jouanjan (2009, pp. 71–119).
6 "What does a perfect group of followers do? It doesn't think, and it doesn't even feel any more – it follows" (Klemperer, 2013, *LTI*, p. 252).
7 Kertész was the translator into Hungarian of *Totem and Taboo*, of *Moses and Monotheism*, and of "The Moses of Michelangelo".

References

Adorno, T.W. (1965). Society, trans. F. Jameson. In: *Salmagundi* 10–11 (Skidmore College) (Fall 1969-Winter 1979), pp. 144–153.
Adorno, T.W. (2005). Education after Auschwitz. In: *Critical Models, Interventions and Catchwords*. New York: Columbia University Press, pp. 191–204.

Domansky, E. (1992). 'Kristallnacht' the Holocaust and German Unity: The meaning of November 9 as an anniversary in Germany. *History and Memory,* 4(1): 60–94.

Freud, S. (1921). *Group Psychology and the Analysis of the Ego. S.E.* 18. London: Hogarth, pp. 65–144.

Freud, S. (1930). *Civilization and Its Discontents. S.E.* 21. London: Hogarth, pp. 57–146.

Hitler, A. (1936). *Mein Kampf* (complete edition). Munich: Zentralverlag der NSDAP.

Jouanjan, O. (2006). Justifier l'injustifiable. Astérion [Online Review], 4/2006, (https://asterion.revues.org/643#tocto1n4).

Jouanjan, O. (2009). 'Pensée de l'ordre concret' et ordre du discours 'juridique' nazi sur Carl Schmitt. In: *Carl Schmitt ou le mythe du politique,* Y.-C. Zarka (ed.). Paris: Presses Universitaires de France, pp. 71–119.

Kafka, J.S. (2000). L'individu traumatisé dans la société traumatisée : traitement, mémoire et monuments commémoratifs. *Revue française de psychanalyse,* 64(1): 81–96.

Kelsen, H. (1967 [1934]). *Pure Theory of Law.* Berkeley: University of California.

Kertész, I. (1995). *Ce malheureux 20ème siècle.* In: Kertész (2009), pp. 113–136.

Kertész, I. (2008). *Sauvegarde. Journal 2001–2003.* Arles: Actes Sud.

Kertész, I. (2009). *L'Holocaust Comme Culture.* Arles: Actes Sud.

Klemperer, V. (2013 [1957]). *The Language of the Third Reich. LTI – Lingua Tertii Imperii: A Philologist's Notebook,* trans. M. Brady. London: Bloomsbury.

Rodières-Rein, C. (2017). Kelsen et Freud. In: *Naissances inconscientes du droit.* Paris: Gallimard.

Rosenberg, A. (1986). *Le Mythe du XXème siècle.* Paris: Avallon.

2 The man Moses or brother Hitler

Moses and Monotheism was finished. Protected, thanks to emigration, from external impediments, the book could now come out of hiding. It was still awaiting its translation into English, which was a matter of the greatest urgency because, with the "relapse of the German people into almost pre-historic barbarism", with the assertion of a new order which presented itself "without being attached to any progressive ideas" (Freud, 1939, pp. 54–56), culture was faced with the collapse of the figures of guilt. As Hannah Arendt (1994) would write, "Hitler-Germany demonstrated that an ideology which almost consciously reversed the command 'Thou shalt not kill' need meet no overwhelming resistance from a conscience trained in the Western tradition. On the contrary, Nazi ideology was often able to reverse the functioning of this conscience" (p. 383).

This was what Freud saw head-on when, fifteen years after *Group Psychology and the Analysis of the Ego* (1921), he looked again at the question of the leader in an entirely different way. With *Moses and Monotheism* (1939), of course, he reaffirmed his conviction, established since *Totem and Taboo* (1912–1913), that religious phenomena must be understood according to the model of neurotic symptoms. But this time he put the hypothesis to the test of monotheism by thinking again about the conditions of the education of a people over a long period of time, where the treatment of transgression leads not to some sort of theogony, not to some sort of fra-ternal pact, but rather to ethical legislation. Returning to the question of the historical truth of the tragedy of the primal father, he reengaged with a theory of trauma, nourished by the "posthumous effects" of mnemic registration and its subsequent returns.

It is nonetheless striking that, throughout *Moses and Monotheism*, the "great man" is called *Führer*. Admittedly the word is commonplace in German and was used in the very first German translations of Rousseau's *Social Contract* (1762) to designate the "leader" of peoples. And this is how it found its way into *Group Psychology* . . ., although it is absent in *Totem and Taboo*. Nevertheless, by 1938, the designation *Führer* had become bur-dened with a load that cannot be underestimated. Thomas Mann (1944), moreover, tackled this violently and ironically in *The Tables of the Law*,[1] a

DOI: 10.4324/9781003301660-3

short story showing Moses in the guise of a *Führer* who, from the exodus from Egypt to Kadesh, "shaped" the uneducated horde that had gathered around him in order to make a law-abiding people out of them. *Volksbildung* [education of a people] was no doubt a fanciful notion from the point of view of tradition, but powerfully oriented from the ethical point of view against the policies of the Nazi *Führer*. Did not Hitler want to sculpt the immediate facts of life like raw material, in the same sense that marble is the sculptor's raw material? (see Michaud, 1996).

In this language of culture transformed into the language of assassins, *Führer* is one of the petrified words, just like *Sonderbehandlung* ("special treatment") or *Endlösung* – an ordinary word meaning the complete resolution of a difficulty and which was ordinarily consonant with *Erlösung*, redemption). Everyday words, which subsequently required a glossary to decode their National Socialist meaning (see, for instance, Schmitz-Berning, 1998), words that were now "poisoned" as Klemperer and Adorno say. This was how the value of the word *Führer* was slewed once and for all in Schönberg's eyes, between 1928, the date of the first outlines of *Moses and Aaron*, and 1932, the date when the composition of the opera ceased. "*Wo ist der Führer?*" asked the people abandoned in the desert by Moses at the end of the first act. Having become a refugee in the United States, Schönberg broke off his work, not for a lack of inspiration but because in the meantime he had put himself at the service of international solidarity, building programmes designed to help the seven million Jews at risk in Europe to get out and to provide for their needs (Merlin, 1999).

Words and a culture, then, which turned on their own hinges: this was the theme Thomas Mann was still dealing with in 1938 in another short text that caused a scandal, "A brother" (Mann, 1942). This cultural brother, a sadist steeped in resentment and a mediocre orator to boot, nonetheless had a hysterical propensity and ability to deafen the German people with promises, and also to rouse their feelings by proclaiming his insulted grandeur. And yet, there is no denying it, this individual who suddenly managed to "make the people's suffering a vehicle for his own greatness" (p. 157) inspired fascination. Is there not a form of genius in this, as humiliating as this fraternal kinship is, as shameless as primitivism as a "Weltanschauung" ['outlook on the world'] (p. 158) is? "How a man like this must hate psychoanalysis!" (Mann, 1974), p. 850). Mann continues. "I have a private suspicion that the élan with which he marched on Vienna had a secret spring: it was directed at the venerable Freud, the real and actual enemy, . . . the great disillusioner, the seer and sayer of the laws of genius" (1942, p. 159). For that is the problem: this brother Hitler allows us to experience German genius in the form of moral and intellectual abjection, genius in the sense of exercising a magnetism which raises man above human limits, genius as the artistic ideal has always been depicted in the guise of Goethe. However much "moral mortification" we might feel about it, would it not be liberating to

recognize in Hitler the unconscious side of German genius? And to recognize ourselves in this *Künstler* [artist], a real *Gegenkünstler* [anti-artist]?
(Mann, 7 July 1938, 1984, p. 303). This is indeed what Goebbels claimed
when, on 16 April 1933, he wrote to the conductor Wilhelm Furtwängler:
"Politics too is an art, perhaps the highest and most comprehensive there
is, and we who shape modern German policy feel ourselves in this to be
artists who have been given the responsible task of forming, out of the
raw material of the mass, the firm concrete structure of a people" (letter
dated 11 April 1933 in *Deutsche Allgemeine Zeitung; The New York Times*,
vol. 82 (27), p. 476; cited by Lacoue-Labarthe, 1987, p. 93).

This was how Hitler annihilated the Goethean figure, the model of a
conception of education according to which each one turns the lot that
falls to him into a path oriented by the aesthetic creation of its significance. He reversed Pindar's precept "Become what you are", which that
man of genius had placed at the centre of symbolizing experience, and the
reversal assumed the form of a massacre. And yet, the art of deterioration
definitely helped him attain the state of a great man. This *Führer*, Mann
concludes, is the "trashing of the great Man" [*die Verhunzung des grossen
Mannes*] (Mann, 1974, p. 851).

The allusion to the man Moses is explicit;[2] his murder, far from devastating civilization, was its foundation. The murder of the primal father
placed crime at the origin of culture insofar as guilt can be a source of psychic work that is capable of curbing the destructive and self-destructive
compulsion of humanity. When the calls for the annihilation of ethical
obligations resounded, Freud and his contemporaries saw before their
own eyes the Nazi *Weltanschauung* doing much more than deviating from
prohibitions. It was the very foundation of codified renunciations that it
was dismantling. That is why Kertész speaks of a "crime against the contract in force" (Kertész, 1998, p. 58). Both "political dogma" and a programme for "the transmutation of an ideally true philosophical system
into a political community of faith and struggle", National Socialism, suddenly made *völkisch* [national/popular] the core "truth" of the "primitive
forces linked to race", while *das Volk* was no longer the people but the
original universality with which "human culture and civilization are inex-
tricably linked".[3]

Thus, the *völkische Weltanschauung* expresses "the most intimate wish
of nature", whereby "the unity of blood is the foundation of the German
people", whereby the State is considered as a means in the service of an
end – maintaining humanity in its original racial elements – and "the
creative forces of civilization are based on race". The Aryan "type" then
guarantees the "condition of the free development of all the faculties", the
free play of its forces once re-established: such is the basis of the struggle.
For the movement of nature and the movement of history become one,
the very idea of community eliminating any conflict between individual
interests. The large living organism of the troop makes any dissension an

anomaly. This is the "Nazi counterculture": the cultural conception of a natural and unifying force, hatred.

And the idea was no fantasy: it was translated directly into reality. "We must give up the idea that we can satisfy the masses with ideological concepts", Hitler proclaimed on 28 February 1926 before the "Nationalklub" in Hamburg, "their only stable feeling is hatred". A return of murder, then, exempt from repression and distortion. A return of murder built on an apparatus of identifications whose centre is the *Gestalt* [form] of the Aryan soul – and its axis would be soil and blood. A return of murder freed from the dramaturgy of the father of the horde, from forgetting, from the latency and reminiscence of the act – and one wonders if the thread of tradition, of its transmission, was not broken.

It was this fracture that *Moses and Monotheism* sought to come to terms with. Freud saw this task as an absolute necessity because, by making the *Führer* the very embodiment of the community, the Nazi emphasis founded civilization and its destiny on the power of the emotional rallying sustained by the soul of the leader. This soul had the capacity not only to *portray* but to *bring into being* the natural, that is to say mythical, underlying identity of collectivity. Mythical meaning here not that the civilizing movement was entrusted to politics, but rather to the "driving force", the *Triebkraft*, the power to gather up the soul of the people, of the Germanic soul: that which is embodied in the "primordial dreams" (see Rosenberg, 1982; see also, Lacoue-Labarthe & Nancy, 1991, pp. 53–56) which promote the foundations of identity, their own specifically Aryan "psychic style". This drive type is the lynchpin of the self-preservative drive, the *Selbsterhaltungstrieb*. How could Freud and his contemporaries fail to hear the echo of the terms of psychoanalysis and their deterioration, just as they were witnessing the disintegration of the notion of "society", the *Gesellschaft*, in favour of that of community, the *Gemeinschaft*, founded on unconditional loyalty to the *Führer*? Or, more exactly, for the benefit of the *Gefolgschaft*, the "troop" forged on the model of the blind adherence of the warriors of ancient Germany to their warlord.

Of course, one could say that Freud had seen the mechanism of this blindness coming from afar. When, in *Group Psychology and the Analysis of the Ego*, he considers in turn the "hierarchized" groups and "groups without leaders" – that is, groups with a visible leader and groups without an identifiable leader – this was to emphasize that ultimately the analysis of the libidinal structure of the group always refers to the intrapsychic interplay of the two agencies that are the ego and the ego ideal, and to their interaction within relations of identification. He further considers the case of those groups in which the "miracle" of the complete, albeit temporary, disappearance of any individual particularity, can be observed – the truly collective manic states at work in major festivals such as the Roman Saturnalia. But he did not see the situation arising of a lasting violation of prohibitions, elevated to the state of a social rule. And he did not suspect the role that *bios* [life] and the renewed conception of "vital necessities" could play in it, any more than he suspected the new function of *Gestaltung* [conformation]. In his eyes, a form of individuality remained, more or less guaranteed by the adherence of each individual to "several groups" – class, ethnicity, religion. This protected, through a variety of intersecting identifications, the diversity of the individuals within the same society.

Yet it is precisely in this connection that the Nazi *Gefolgschaft* theorizes a state of the social body which is no longer, strictly speaking, "society". From the moment the State is no more than the instrument of the popular "troop", the leader is no longer an institutional representative. As Schmitt (2013) writes:

> The Führer of the movement has a particular judicial duty whose inner justice cannot be realized by any other actor. . . . Yet in such a collective entity, one that is structured and divided into state, movement and *Volk*, there exists the proprietary inner right of those state-supporting life as well as communal institutions that are especially based on their sworn loyalty to the Führer, secured through the oath.
>
> (p. 66)

Reading Carl Schmitt, the paradox is perfectly clear: "The principle of the leader", the *Führerschaft*, does not consolidate the status of the leader; on the contrary, it destroys it, because the immediate adherence of the faithful members is no longer established on the basis of a principle of command, through which the legal representative is invested with his powers. The *Führerschaft* is in itself, by itself, the embodiment of the principle – all references to a third party disappearing – and the *Führer* "is", in his very being, the community. As Klemperer (2013 [1957]) points out, the political reality of the law of which the Führer becomes the living word is the "healthy sense of justice" (p. 245).[4] The essential element lies in the word "healthy" which does not even evoke a "sense of justice", but proclaims the sentimental spontaneity of unconditional fidelity. The will of the Führer is the general will; the general will lives in the will of the Führer. Heidegger, in his Rectorate speech commented: the *Gefolgschaft* is what gives rise to comradeship as a fundamental form of community, law and reality becoming one (Jouanjan, 2010, pp. 213, 218–219, 231).

They are also one because, as Werner Best stated in the legal journal *Deutsches Recht* in 1936: "The National-Socialist political principle of totality, which corresponds to our organic and indivisible vision of the unity of the German people, does not accept the formation of any political will outside our own political will. Any attempt to impose – even to preserve – another concept of things will be eradicated as a pathological symptom which threatens the unity and the health of the national organism" (cited by Chapoutot, 2017, p. 89). "German law" is therefore directly connected with sanitary considerations, carefully monitoring the state of political health of the German body, identifying and eliminating the germs of destruction, whether they came from internal degeneration or from contamination by the outsider. So vermin are a single political and physical element. This was, moreover, part of Hitler's programme in *Mein Kampf*: the laws of nature must be realized in the field of politics.

The hatred of civilization, explicit in the project of grounding culture on nature without mediation, ruins any emancipatory narrative as a consequence. But in the eyes of Freud and his contemporaries, it does much more. It dismantles the tragic place both as an ethical source of politics and as an enigma of fate. Now from Athens to Jerusalem, and ever since the reference to *Oedipus Rex* in the letter in which he informed Fliess of the abandonment of his *neurotica*, Freud had made the murder of the father a constitutive axis of "psychic reality" and at the same time a point of origin, capable of tying together individual morality and collective morality. First, under the aspect of the double crime – killing the father and sexually possessing the mother – with the punishment being turned round against oneself. Then, long before the agency of the superego was inferred, in the form of the bedrock of the first social alliance: when the murder of the primitive father – a figure passionately loved for his potency and protection, and furiously hated for this same potency and his unlimited power – led to the mutuality of a fraternal pact in which renunciations, expiations and totemic prohibitions governed by taboo-related moral conscience had their roots. This same mechanism became the basis for understanding religious illusion. It was once again this mechanism which, in *Moses and Monotheism*, underpinned the struggle of the mind to tear itself away from primitive animism, and finally to succeed in dematerializing the single God. Thus the path of *logos* made transgression both the essence of "tragic consciousness" and the source of access to deliberation and the law in a world which was gradually losing its sacred aura. This appeared one last time in "Analysis terminable and interminable", where Freud (1937) presents the Empedoclean struggle between unity and dislocation, between "Philia" and "Neikos" [love and strife], as the first philosophical form given to the struggle between the life drives and the death drive. It is then the pair formed by Ananké and Logos [necessity and reason] that has the task of dealing with the heterogeneity between instinctual drive demands, including destructiveness, and linking with words, including guilt.

With the irruption of National Socialism, it was as if this antinomy had become obsolete; as if the stranglehold in which the human order seemed inescapably caught – the freedom of our state of nature is, on the one hand, violently limited by the ferocity of the external world and, on the other, severely restricted by the instinctual drive renunciations necessary for social coming together – as if this shackle had been smashed to pieces under the weight of the mass, united organically, substantially and concretely. Yet, between the threat of chain murders and the foundation of social relations, it determined the heart of the cultural paradox formulated in *The Future of an Illusion*: "Every individual is virtually an enemy of civilization, though civilization is supposed to be an object of universal interest" (Freud, 1927, p. 6).

In fact, as early as 1927, Freud wondered whether "the assumptions that determine our political regulations" (ibid., p. 34) should not, like religious doctrines, also be called illusions. They were no doubt already changing colour in his eyes. Are the biological examples that he uses to distinguish a scientific error proper from that generated by belief simply a matter of chance? When Aristotle explains that vermin are developed out of dung, it is the doctor, according to him, who is venturing a hypothesis. On the other hand, "the assertion made by certain nationalists that the Indo-Germanic race is the only one capable of civilization" (ibid., pp. 30–31) is a belief based on wish-fulfilment and fortified by indifference to reality. Thus, from error to belief, and depending on a greater or lesser dissociation from reality, illusion can lead closer to delusional ideas. This continues until the moment when illusion takes on the garb of scientific assertions promoted by philologists, anthropologists and archaeologists, passionate consent then proves how much groups care little for the truth, how they constantly give "what is unreal precedence over what is real", and how they have a tendency not to distinguish between the two (Freud, 1921, p. 80).[5]

But the assault on tragic consciousness and the function of guilt did not stop there. For what happens to the identificatory function nourished by shared ideals when nothing distinguishes it from the identificatory base fuelled by shared criminality? What value did the words of language retain when on 1 August 1923 the leader made this declaration about radical political movements: "There are two things that unite men: common ideals and common criminality"? (Baynes, 1942, p. 75). When the mob took over this slogan, the idealization of the object would prove to be perfectly divorced from any disposition to sublimation: the drive was left with no other aim than the direct satisfaction of murderous wishes.

To take the measure of this dismantling, we must once again make a detour via the theses of Carl Schmitt for whom the opposition between friends and enemies determines not only the unifying antagonism of the community, but the very basis of politics. The essence of the latter resides in the faculty of the *socius* to dissociate itself radically from the other, the foreigner, the "substantial" enemy, the "absolute enemy". In the writings of this lawyer who justified the elaboration of the Nuremberg laws in 1934, the "decision of hostility", grounding a sovereignty rooted in the state of exception, is therefore based on an order that is not legal. On the contrary, the suspension of ordinary legality is closely linked to the theory of total war and the total State (Schmitt, 2003/1936, pp. 173–180; see also Zarka, 2009).[6] It directly echoes Hitler's declaration before the Congress of the Jurists of Leipzig on 3 October 1933, a declaration that was also of foundational significance: "The total State will not tolerate any difference between law and morality". In other words, the *Führer*, both as moral authority and supreme judicial authority, is the sole judge. He is the *nomos* [law] of the German people in a state whose unity resides primarily in "racial identity", *Artgleichheit*.

It was this actual destruction of the autonomy of the law, developed under the argument of concrete order that was witnessed by psychoanalysts who were contemporaries of the assertion of the "living ties" between the *Führer* and his *Gefolgschaft* [troop]. And culture itself was engaged in this active destruction. Éric Michaud (2008), who insists on the virtual synonymy of the words *Rasse* (race) and *Art* (the species, but also the way of being) in Nazi language, shows how the establishment of the *Führung* [leadership] was achieved through the excessive use of quotations – Luther, Bach, Kant, Goethe, Schopenhauer, etc. This usage sealed the Germanic cultural roots of the Nazi *Weltanschauung*. "When an ideologue or dignitary of the Third Reich quotes one of the "Great Germans" of the past", writes Éric Michaud, "it is always the same blood that flows, it is always the same substance that speaks, it is the race that speaks to itself, aware of itself and totally present to itself. It is the same blood that circulates in a great eternal body, of which the Führer is, as it were, the heart that pumps and irrigates this body in order to constantly renew its cells" (p. 5). The German *Volkskörper* [body of the people] has no history. It is a body which, in its very purity, constitutes its unique soul.

This had not escaped the notice of Levinas who, in 1934, took up the argument again concerning the ego's adhesion to the body, and the feeling of identity that it procures, to show how, in the National Socialist conception, this chaining or bondage to the body is the very essence of the spirit. "The biological, with the notion of inevitability it entails, becomes more than an *object* of spiritual life; it becomes its heart" (Levinas, 1990/1934, p. 69).[7] Since the self [*le moi*] is made up of the mysterious urgings of blood, the appeals of heredity and the past for which the body serves as an enigmatic vehicle, man's essence no longer lies resides in freedom. On the contrary, to be truly oneself means becoming aware of the original chaining to the body and accepting this ineluctable chaining. "A society based on consanguinity immediately ensues from this concretization of the spirit", Levinas continues – this new ideal bringing with it a convenience: "as a promise of sincerity and authenticity", it erodes the tragedy of freedom.

What has become of the tragic division – of this paradigm both of terror in the face of the unknown and of the work of culture, of this struggle between desire and reason, of the inner deliberation portrayed by the Greek tragedies at the dawn of democracy – when the "awakening of elemental feelings", race, the concretization of the spirit in the body, have become the breeding ground of a consensus, lawfully oriented towards the annihilation of the other? "Four years of continuous terror which had as its main target a single people, which would seek it out and exterminate it across an entire continent, from Denmark to Egypt via Ukraine: no commemoration, whatever its value, can give 'a real sense' of this work of death, which had no objective other than itself. The widespread and intensive scale of 'the destruction of the Jews of Europe' makes it unreal", writes Corinne Enaudeau (2013) of Claude Lanzmann's film, *Shoah*. "Making it touch the hearts of others requires much more than words: it requires a change in the regime of discourse".

Notes

1 According to Jacques Le Rider, the copy of *Moses and Monotheism* kept in the library that accompanied Thomas Mann in his Californian exile contains many underlined passages and several annotations.
2 Jacques Le Rider wrote about Joseph in Egypt (Mann, 1934): "The influence of *Moses and Monotheism* on the last volume of Thomas Mann's tetralogy *Joseph and his Brothers* Mann (1948) published in 1943 with the title *Joseph the Provider*, as well as on the short story, *The Tables of the Law*, published in 1944, has often been underlined. But it should also be noted that when he began writing *Moses and Monotheism*, Freud had not only been able to read the first three volumes of this tetralogy, but also discuss it personally with Thomas Mann (see Rider, 2005).
3 A. Hitler (1934) *Mein Kampf*, vol. II, pp. 414–422, pp. 429–433, pp. 440–444, p. 475 and pp. 506–509.
4 For details of the use of the term "Gefolgschaft" by the Nazis, see Schmitz-Berning (1998, pp. 252–254), in particular the speech by A. Hitler of 16 September 1935.
5 One only has to read *Mais où sont passés les Indo-Européens? Le mythe d'origine de l'occident* by Jean-Paul Demoule (2014) to be convinced of this.
6 On the relations between C. Schmitt and Heidegger, including their common membership of "The Commission for the Philosophy of Law", see Faye (2005, p. 249ff, 335ff).
7 This article was first published in 1934 in *Esprit* under the title "Quelques réflexions sur la philosophie de l'hitlérisme"; it was then republished by Payot & Rivages in 1997, accompanied by the essay of M. Abensour, *Le Mal elemental*.

References

Arendt, H. (1994). Politics and religion. In: *Essays in Understanding, 1930–1954: Formation, Exile, and Totalitarianism*. New York: Harcourt Brace & Co, pp. 368–390.
Baynes, N.H. (ed.).(1942). *The Speeches of Adolf Hitler (April 1922–August 1939)*. Oxford: Oxford University Press.
Chapoutot, J. (2017). *La Révolution culturelle nazie*. Paris: Gallimard.
Demoule, J.-P. (2014). *Mais où sont passés les Indo-Européens? Le mythe d'origine de l'occident?* Paris: Le Seuil.

Enaudeau, C. (2013). *Shoah,* filme de Claude Lanzmann, 1985. *Intersections,* Collège international de philosophie.

Faye, E. (2005). *Heidegger, the Introduction of Nazism into Philosophy.* Paris: Albin Michel.

Freud, S. (1912–1913). *Totem and Taboo. S.E.* 13. London: Hogarth, pp. 1–161.

Freud, S. (1921). *Group Psychology and the Analysis of the Ego. S.E.* 23. London: Hogarth, pp. 69–143.

Freud, S. (1927). *The Future of an Illusion. S.E.* 21. London: Hogarth, pp. 5–56.

Freud, S. (1937). *Analysis Terminable and Interminable. S.E.* 21. London: Hogarth, pp. 216–253.

Freud, S. (1939). *Moses and Monotheism. S.E.* 23. London: Hogarth, pp. 7–137.

Hitler, A. (1934). *Mein Kampf-Mon Combat,* trans. A. Calmettes and J. Gaudefroy-Demombynes. Paris: Nouvelles Éditions Latines.

Jouanjan, O. (2010). *Gefolgschaft et Studentenrecht*: deux gloses en marge du Discours de rectorat. *Les Études philosophiques,* 93(2): 211–233.

Kertész, I. (1998). *Ombre profonde,* ed. Kertész, 2009, pp. 53–62.

Kertész, I. (2009). *Holocauste Comme Culture.* Arles: Actes Sud.

Lacoue-Labarthe, P. (1987). *La Fiction du politique.* Paris: Ch. Bourgois, 1987.

Lacoue-Labarthe, P., Nancy, J.-L. (1991). *Le mythe nazi.* Paris: Aube.

Levinas, E. (1990/1934). Reflections on the philosophy of Hitlerism, trans. S. Hand. *Critical Enquiry,* 17(1): 63–71. [Quelques réflexions sur la philosophie de l'Hitlérisme, initially published in *Esprit,* republished by Payot & Rivages, Paris, 2002, accompanied by the essay of M. Abensour, *Le Mal élémental*: 27–108].

Mann, T. (1934). *Joseph in Egypt.* New York: Alfred. A. Knopf.

Mann, T. (1942/1938). A Brother. In: *Order of the Day: Political Essays and Speeches of Two Decades.* New-York: Knopf, pp. 153–161 [Frère Hitler. In: *Les Exigences du jour.* Paris: Grasset, 2003, pp. 301–310.]

Mann, T. (1944). *The Tables of the Law,* trans. Helen Lowe-Porter. New York: Alfred A. Knopf.

Mann, T. (1948). *Joseph and His Brothers,* trans. H.T. Lowe-Porter. New York: Alfred A. Knopf.

Mann, T. (1974/1939). Bruder Hitler. In: *Gesammelte Werke in XIII Bänden,* vol. XII. Fischer Verlag: Frankfurt/Main, pp. 845–852.

Mann, T. (1984). *Diaries, 1918–1939.* Seattle: Thrift Books.

Merlin, C. (1999). *Moïse et Aaron* de Schoenberg, opéra biblique. *Germanica,* 24(1999): 79–95, http://germanica.revues.org/2252.

Michaud, É. (1996). *Un art de l'éternité. L'image et le temps du national-socialisme.* Paris: Gallimard.

Michaud, E. (2008). Le nazisme, un régime de la citation. *Images re-vues, Histoire, anthropologie et théorie de l'art* [Online Journal], Special issue, 1/2008 (http://imagesrevues.revues.org/885).

Rider, J. (2005). Joseph et Moïse égyptiens: Sigmund Freud et Thomas Mann. *Savoirs et clinique,* 6: 59–66.

Rosenberg, A. (1982/1930). Personality and style. In: *The Myth of the 20th Century.* The Legion for the Survival of Freedom, pp. 252–277.

Rousseau, J.-J. (1762). *The Social Contract,* trans. H.J. Tozer.London: Swan Sonnenschein & Co, 1895.

Schmitt, C. (2013/1934). The Führer protects the law: On Adolf Hitler's reichstag address of 13 July 1934. In: *The Third Reich Sourcebook*, A. Rabinbach and S. Gilman (eds.). Berkeley: University of California Press, pp. 63–67.

Schmitz-Berning, C. (1998). *Vokabular des Nationalsozialismus*. Berlin/NewYork: de Gruyter.

3　The Freudian heresy

In an interview in July 2013, Kertész replied to Clara Royer: "In *Fateless-ness* [2004] what interested me the most was totalitarianism, and that's what I was studying in it. I pictured totalitarianism in the form of the father, and that is why I put a young boy at the centre of it – not to make the reader cry – but because, in my opinion, total dictatorship reduces a man to the state of a child, or more precisely, to a certain mode of infantile thought. That's why my character is a child. From this point of view, the Kaddish is its extension, it explores another dimension". "A Kaddish without a god?" Clara Royer asked him. "No", Kertész replied, "a Kaddish without a father" (Kertész, 2017, p. 27).

Much more than words, what Kertész was seeking was actually a change in the regime of the discourse. In search of the "language after Auschwitz", he wanted it to be "atonal". "If we look at tonality, the single tone, as a convention", he writes, "then atonality declares that this convention is no longer valid". (Kertész, 2009, p. 217). And in *Dossier K.* (2013) he again refers to this convention: "I am a nuisance in Hungary, in the organic extension of the Kádár regime, a dissonant voice in a convention of self-deception which by common consent is sustained through gritted teeth" (pp. 204–205). Tonality in literature was once "a system of values based on consensual morality" which determined the correlations of sentences and ideas. Today, atonal language must express the continuity broken by Auschwitz. This break is evidenced by the suicide of the intermediaries who were the survivors, whose consensuality could not take into account the rigorously coherent character of destinies. "Every language, every people, every civilization has a dominant "I" which perceives the world, orders it and represents it. This collective "I" in permanent action is a subject with which a large community – nation, people, culture – can generally identify, more or less successfully. But where is the homeland of Holocaust awareness, what language could claim to be the dominant 'I' of the Holocaust, the language of the Holocaust?" (Kertész, 2009, p. 224). The poet must therefore invent a language without a fundamental note, without basso continuo, because totalitarianism has deprived human beings of their solitude and the tragic dimension of their

DOI: 10.4324/9781003301660-4

destiny, and because ideals and imagination have been replaced by new ideological imperatives – including the conformism that robs "the Holocaust from its custodians and turns it into junk" (Kertész, 1992, p. 67 and pp. 176–177).

It is in this sense that the Holocaust should take on the proportions of a universal experience, in the sense that Freud linked the origins of monotheism to the original parricide. But, while parricide, the mark of the tragic and foundational fatality of the paternal function, made it possible to see the existence of man as the possibility that one day, a son might exist, the debacle of the tragic, equal to the collapse of the law, leads to the radical and necessary liquidation of the existence of the father: "your non-existence viewed as the necessary and radical liquidation of my own existence" (Kertész, 2005, p. 31, 1992, p. 11, 1990). Here again, the choice of the artist can only be radical. When, under the rule of the biological norm, adherence to the ideal of the leader led to the delegitimization of the place of the father and of the forbidden, words themselves must succeed, he says, in "breaking down the limits of language from the inside" (interview with Florence Noiville for *Le Monde des Livres*, 09.06.2005a).

But how can one succeed in breaking the straitjacket that encloses the very notions of war and conflict when, in Hitler's words, the disposition to sacrifice is likened to the noblest form of the drive of self-preservation? (Hitler, 1936, p. 325). And when, moreover, this greatness, stripped of all the traits of murderous ferocity, appears as the noble prerogative of the Aryan, while the Jews, led by their vulgar herd instinct, disperse once their attack as a pack of wolves has been completed? How, for instance, can we succeed in taking up again Freud's reflection, based on Hobbes – "man is a wolf for man" – that the state of war, inherent to the state of nature, and fear as a lever of social and political unity, are all of a piece? It is within this conflict, according to Hobbes, that a space of conditional reciprocity is created: by contract we give up our natural rights to everything because others agree to do the same – political unity proceeding from this pact of mutual renunciations.[1] However, while for Hobbes unlimited natural freedom (the correlate of which is murder) gives way to voluntary submission, what ultimately prevails under Freud's pen is the illusion that nourishes the hope of a rational assent to institutions. To what extent has racial naturalness, by invalidating any form of psychic conflict, disrupted the very theorization of such a transaction?

This, it seems to me, is the reason why Freud places "right" between inverted commas in *Civilization and its Discontents*. Admittedly, living together only becomes possible when a plurality of individuals manage to form a majority that is more powerful than each of its members. It is in this way that the power of the community is opposed as "right" to the violence of each individual. But this "decisive step of civilization", which opens out on to the following requisite, that of justice, in fact tells us nothing, writes Freud "as to the ethical value of such a law" (Freud, 1930, p. 95,

1933b, pp. 203–206, 209–211). All we can say is that it is "supposed" to be a law to which everyone has contributed and from which everyone benefits.

Freud expressed the same doubt and gave the same answer to Einstein two years later. While for Einstein (Freud, 1933b), "law and might inevitably go hand in hand" – judicial authority approaching more nearly ideal justice insofar as legislative authority possesses the "power" to ensure verdicts are respected – Freud, for his part, asks that "the word 'might' be replaced by the balder and harsher word 'violence'". For, as he points out, the very organs that have been created to oversee the observance of laws carry out "acts of violence in accordance with the law". This point of view is very similar to the notion of "legitimate violence" developed by Weber (2004, p. 78) in 1919 to define the domination of man over man that characterizes the modern state. Is this the breeding ground of political illusion? Freud's response to Einstein perhaps needs to be read from a Hobbesian perspective, but above all in the light of "Thoughts for the times on war and death' (Freud, 1915), that is to say of the disillusionment inflicted by war and the powerlessness of culture to prevent disorder. The indomitable return of the murderous ancestor has taught us that, even if "strength lies in unity", ideals are not able to resist the bankruptcy of civilization any more than the fabric of community can resist the dismantling of libidinal ties when faced with the passion of war. But, in reality, I think that in 1927, let alone in 1933, the illusion consisted in the fact that the very programme of nature had changed.

In *Totem and Taboo* (1912–1913), the universal event of death was considered as the first instigator of thought and the primary source of theoretical and moral creations. It was death that ordered the first recognition of *Anankè*, since the wound that it inflicts constantly returns in the fear resulting from murderous wishes, in sacred terror, in transgression, all motors of the work of culture. "Thoughts for the times on war and death" attests to the first reversal of this conception, consisting in the brutal transportation of psychic reality into reality. The reality of war is psychic reality enacted. Because the murderer of primeval times has never ceased to dwell in civilized man, the emotional excitement of war simply reveals this unconscious, but intact, disposition which shatters the constraints of morality along with the use of judgement. But with the introduction of the death drive, Freud released death from this very position. The internal activity of disorder is silent and only turns into murderous desire secondarily. As for culture, it has an identical function to that of the survival instinct of animals, namely, offering precarious protection against our compulsion to exterminate ourselves to the last man (1930, pp. 123, 144–145).

It was precisely at the moment when he introduced the death drive that Freud considered "the process of civilization" not only as the most general characteristic of life – "organic repression" – not only as analogous to the development of the individual, but as a "particular process which mankind undergoes" (ibid, p. 96 and p. 122). Freud described this process for the first time in *Civilization and its Discontents*, then for a second time in "Why war?" (1933b, pp. 213–215), and for a third time in his *35th Lecture* (1933a, pp. 178–180). In *Civilization and its Discontents*, Freud evokes this process after declaring that identificatory and libidinal ties are insufficient to ensure the coherence of societies in view of the tendency to self-destruction. In "Why war?" he writes: "We are pacifists because we are obliged to be for organic reasons" (1933b, p. 214), and the cultural programme, likened to the vital struggle of any species, is compared to the modifying effects of the domestication of animals. And in the *35th Lecture*, having weighed up the role of economic factors against the yardstick of Marxist theory, Freud does not hesitate to assert that this autonomous organic process is the real source of the work of cultural development and social evolution. No doubt influenced by all the other factors – economic conditions, but also psychic factors in the form of the primordial drive impulses, the self-preservative drive, the urge for aggression, the need for love, the longing for pleasure and avoidance of unpleasure – it is nonetheless "independent of them in its origin, being comparable to an organic process and very well able on its part to exercise an influence on the other factors" (1933a, p. 179).

Was this a response to the biologization of racial identity through the organic process of the drives? It is a question that we can seriously ask ourselves; for, according to Freud, not only are war and its murders, in accordance with human nature, "biologically well-founded", but the rejection of war and ethical requirements are also anchored in organic foundations. In making moral conscience the product of the turning round of destructiveness inwards (not projected outside in the form of aggression) and in establishing that the agency of the superego is capable of draining this portion of unbound energy originating in the death drive, Freud introduced a radical change of programme between the historical evolution of acts of aggression and their effects and the structure of the ethical agency, which, as the product of this inner reversal, is freed from any historical registration. He suggested that the process of cultural development, a strictly Darwinian programme, obeys the law that belongs to the deepest aspects of his animality, namely, the survival of the species. This was why Freud presented the second topography to Einstein as a "heresy", since it roots moral conscience in the death drive itself (1933b, p. 211). The fact remains that the Freudian heresy perhaps lay in the attack that Freud made on the biological version of self-preservation delivered by National Socialism, and in particular on its first clause: sacrificial self-destruction in combat.

Of course, this was not the first time that Freud had discovered the extent to which ideal motives placed in the foreground of consciousness can tap into destructiveness under the cover of the narcissistic gain procured by immersion in the masses. Ethics, indeed, can be recognized as the sorest spot of every civilization; whatever path is chosen, destructiveness, an inalterable feature of human nature, will always follow it (Freud, 1930, p. 142). But at the time of his exchange with Einstein, and faced with the question as to which force could still be put in the service of the law, he drew as far as possible the consequences of the introjection of destructiveness and of its turning round against the ego in the form of "moral conscience". He thus seems to literally turn upside down the "nature" of race promulgated by the Nazis, by replying: irrespective of the vagaries of history, "alongside" the satisfactions demanded, in spite of the proclaimed hatred, beyond the illusory promises held out by the "new order – this was in 1933 and Freud only mentioned the Bolsheviks – there will always be the natural programme of humanity which continues to work silently on the battlefield of the drives, where the life drive and the death drive confront each other, at the crossroads of life and survival. Furthermore, simply due to the drive conflicts that it constantly fuels, it constantly sets in motion new creations and new compromises which contribute to resolving the other discord, distinct from the "contradiction – probably an irreconcilable one – between the primal instincts of Eros and death" (ibid., p. 141), where the individual's claims to happiness and the limitation of pleasures by the civilized community are fought out.

Freud describes, then, a twofold movement which intertwines, without amalgamating them, the inclusion of the human community in the organic process with the clash between the imperative need for culture of every society and the hostility of each individual towards this culture; a double movement that grounds the interpretation of the "work of culture" proposed by Nathalie Zaltzman (2009). She suggests, in fact, that this work is carried out by transgressing taboos, acts of violence and cruelty, in short: evil, which depends on the drive economy, but is not, however, reducible to it. Cruel intentionality implies an inevitable reference to consciousness, a "dark consciousness", whether it be jubilant or numbed. For Nathalie Zaltzman, then, it is on this ground of consciousness that the process of cultural development imposes itself, operating by means of changes of representation that make it possible to gain access to the id opened up by transgressions. But for Freud, the cultural process, rooted in the organic, is concerned first and foremost with loosening our attachments to all progressive illusions, an essential aspect when the excitation of hatred undermines all discernment, and every critical position of understanding.

Where can thought find its impartiality if man's value-judgements, which "follow directly his wishes for happiness" (Freud, 1930, p. 145), are only an attempt to back up illusions with arguments? Clearly, the process of cultural development is not sufficient, since Freud immediately evokes the "dictatorship of reason". Nathalie Zaltzman does not mention this other than in connection with Freud's recourse to the taming of drive activity. According to her, the question has to be framed quite differently, particularly because nothing indicates that "the notions of primitive cruelty, hatred prior to ambivalence, the death drive, and the primal picto-gram of rejection fully grasp the reality of evil" (Zaltzman, 2009, p. 159; see particularly pp. 159–164). This is where the drive economy seems insuf-ficient. "Evil only exists", she writes, "insofar as it adds to impersonal drive destruction an intentionality, a qualification of destruction, the aim to harm" (p. 159). So it is not the animality of man that makes him bad; rather, it is "from the alliance of drive activity with the most developed psychic formations that evil acquires its characteristics" (ibid.). Technical rationality, morality, education and ideal constructions are the cultural conditions for hatred and destruction to be legitimized and disguised. It is therefore futile, according to Nathalie Zaltzman, to hope that culture "will ethically resolve its weak point by means of drive renunciation alone. A change in group psychology is also required, and this change must in turn influence phylogenesis. The progress of the psychic evolution of the spe-cies depends on the progress of its understanding of itself, running rather than on renunciations through successful repressions" (p. 160).

Moreover, in her view, the establishment of the legal category of "crimes against humanity" can be attributed to this kind of progress insofar as this category specifically transgresses two fundamental principles: the non-retroactive character of a law for crimes that had not hitherto been defined by jurisdiction, and the fact that every crime is subject to a stat-ute of limitations. Even so, the "evil thing" is elusive, the victim being the human race, while the perpetrator vanishes from the scene. "The eli-sion of the nature of evil and of the agents responsible for it, the relative indeterminacy of what makes crimes against humanity an evil that is not subject to a statute of limitations, its inadequate description by the term 'inhuman', even though a definition of humanity is promoted of which no one, even a monstrous criminal, ceases to be a part, all this gives rise to a movement of thought which advances only by eliminating the very thing that made it necessary" (p. 164). The fact remains that this legal construc-tion performed a considerable work of culture insofar as it offered a new interpretation of the human condition by bringing to the level of general common consciousness a psychic characteristic that had not been thought about previously. It founded a transindividual authority that gave every-one a basis of identification, independent of time and space, legally desig-nated by the term "humanity" and built on the perception of a collective determination of the individual. By opposing the erection of a "purified" humanity and by including the "inhuman", it works de facto in the direc-tion of consciousness, that which led Freud to write: "*Wo es war, soll Ich werden*" (1933a, p. 80).

In order to prevent war, "the ideal condition of things would of course be a community of men who had subordinated their instinctual life to the dictatorship of reason. Nothing else could unite men so completely and so tenaciously, even if there were no emotional ties between them" (Freud, 1933b, p. 213). Are we really to understand that, in writing this, Freud had come up against the problem of the erection of a "purified" humanity? Maybe things are more complicated than that. First of all, Freud was not unaware of the paradoxical function of consciousness. This is particularly clear when, in an aside in "Why war?", he asserts that, in matters of law, the two sources of disorder – attempts by certain rulers to revert to the rule of violence and the efforts of the oppressed to obtain equal rights – are also two sources of progress. "Paradoxical as it may sound", he wrote to Einstein, "it must be admitted that war might be a far from inappropriate means of establishing the eagerly desired reign of 'everlasting' peace, since it is in a position to create the large units within which a powerful central government makes further wars impossible" (1933b, p. 207). How can we not think that this *"ewige" Frieden*, this peace generally translated as "eternal", is an almost direct allusion to Kant's *Zum ewigen Frieden*, that is, to his 1795 essay *Perpetual Peace: A Philosophical Sketch?* Particularly as it was undoubtedly from Kant (following Hobbes) that Freud took up the idea that, although the state of nature is the state of war, it is nevertheless to be hoped that conflicts play a part in shaping social unity. Man desires concord; but his nature desires discord, writes Kant, who sees the "unsocial sociability" of men as the strategy by means of which nature pushes for the execution of the purposes of reason (Kant, 1795),[2] that is to say, to escape from a lawless state in order to enter a League of Nations in which each State, even the smallest, could obtain security and rights. The fact that it was precisely in connection with a League of Nations that Freud in turn reflected on the conditions for perpetual peace prompts me to think that Freud's "dictatorship of reason" echoes here with Kant's "supreme legislative reason", insofar as it is poses an obstacle to the disintegration of society, but includes the evils of war in the process. "Our best hope for the future," Freud writes in his *35th Lecture*, "is that intellect – the scientific spirit, reason, – may in process of time establish a dictatorship in the mental life of man" (1933a, p. 171) But on the same date, and for Einstein, he added: "But in all probability that is a Utopian expectation" (1933b, p. 213).

Still, the programme mankind undergoes resonates strangely. It is true that in connection with the Spartacist movements in Germany, Freud wrote to Lou Andréas Salomé on 17 February 1918: "What the human beast still needs above all is restraint. In short, one grows reactionary just as incidentally as the rebel Schiller did in face of the French Revolution" (Freud & Salomé, 1985, p. 75). But, when in 1930 and 1933, he ultimately linked the purpose of reason to the purpose of the survival of the species, the Darwinian hijacking of Kant which he sought to achieve – and this was not his first attempt[3] – resulted in the idea that the beast would somehow exercise restraint itself. Was this the ultimate disenchantment, once it is admitted that, under the control of a *Führer*, critical consciousness was effectively invalidated, the slavery of identification completed and relations to reality mutilated, as he had foreseen in *Group Psychology and the Analysis of the Ego.*

Moreover, everything was already indicating that the literalness of the *logos*, its petrification, a platform for mass murder, was capable of resisting any variation, every fertile metamorphosis. Just think of the "obedience of corpses" demanded by Eichmann in his defence. If, as Kertész writes, "reason failed" here, it was because the extermination of vermin and parasites had derailed the double meaning of words and the function of thought. Not only did the drainage of the death drive in the form of a cruel moral conscience fail, but the movement and erotic function of the demonic had lost their potential powers of creation. Sublimation was nothing more than disintegration. It had simply taken on the mask of prophylaxis.

And in fact, in the name of purity, language had implemented a biologizing semantics according to which, from the parasite to the bacillus, the Jew "as a ferment of decomposition" was henceforth "the absolute cause of the inner collapse of all the races, which he penetrates as a parasite" (letter from Adolf Hitler to Major Konstantin Hierl, cited by Miedzianagora & Jofer, 1994, p. 14). Hitler continued in this letter of 1920: "Just as I cannot blame a tuberculosis bacillus for an action which for men means destruction, but for it life, so I am obliged and justified, in my personal existence, to lead a fight against tuberculosis by exterminating its agents". As the Jew has become "by his actions a tuberculosis of the race of peoples", the "logical solution" is to eliminate radically the "lice of humanity" by exterminating them, as Himmler suggested in his speech at Poznań in October 1943, to the amazement of Goebbels. Indeed, inflicting death ceased to be a crime; it was a healthy way of handling prophylactic disinfection. It was necessary and sufficient, therefore, to turn the Jews into vermin. This is what Kertész (2004) would have liked to say to the soldier who was looking with disgust at his dilapidated body in the open truck that was taking him to the hospital at the Gleina camp: "Particularly upsetting to me, it was as if in his mind he had come to some opinion, deduced some general truth, and I would have liked to excuse myself: I was not entirely the only one at fault here, and in fact this was not the genuine me – but then that would have been hard for me to prove, naturally, I could see that" (pp. 174–175).

It would have been hard to prove, of course, because the erasure of the dividing line between culture and biological nature had been completed. For example, Alfred Rosenberg asserts that, in portraying his Mephisto in *Faust*, Goethe was undoubtedly depicting the Jew. The same Rosenberg states that Kant is a pure representative of the "Nordic spirit" and that the "'universality' of the judgement of taste can only be derived from an ideal of racial beauty and applies only to those who, consciously or unconsciously, carry in their hearts the same idea of beauty" (Rosenberg, 1986, p. 303 and 412).[4] The architect Schultze-Naumburg declares: "The artist, whether he likes it or not, *cannot* escape the conditions of his own body" (Schultze-Naumburg, 1928, pp. 74–77; cited by Michaud, 2008, p. 6, author's emphasis).

From Shylock to Siegfried, the artistic act and all its manifestations, in other words, all cultural solutions, are contaminated. In Kertész's view, it is this "denied spirit" to which Améry bore witness, and from which he died, when his *Unmeisterliche Wanderjahre* (1971) – a book whose title is untranslatable, a sarcastic play on *Wilhelm Meisters Wanderjahre* (1821) – calls directly on Goethe himself to give testimony. Améry "found no way out of culture; he went from culture to Auschwitz, then from Auschwitz back to culture as if from one camp to the other, and is if the language and intellectual world culture enclosed him like the barbed-wire of Auschwitz" (Kertész, 2011, p. 65).[5]

Did psychoanalysts have the means to fight against the bankruptcy of a humanism that had laid the groundwork for their first discovery? If we consider that Germany's "mental rearmament" preceded its military rearmament and that it was political myths "henceforth manufacture in the same sense and according to the same the same methods as any other modern weapon" (Cassirer, 1946, p. 282) that ensured its power, by what means could they confront the corruption of the symbolic framework by the concreteness of the "parasite"? The rejection of legal positivism, according to Olivier Jouanjan (2006) is basically a rejection of the law as a way of thinking about separation. The distance established by these "logical forms that make it possible to establish in the immediate density of a given situation ... an order that renders both action and reflection possible", is then banished, just as the place of the third party that situates the judge above the popular community is banished. "Such a separation is incompatible with the logic of incorporation. Incorporated, the judge belongs to the *Führer's* "troop", and is placed in a "personal relationship of fidelity" to him (p. 138). The total state says that what is "truly German" is a whole in which German blood and German spirit must not be differentiated. The fact remains that racial identity is clearly a fiction, a primary myth – a "myth of myths", or the myth of the formative power of myths" as Philippe Lacoue-Labarthe (1998, p. 136) writes – on which the Aryan *Gestalt* was built.

Notes

1 Th. Hobbes (2010/1651) *Leviathan*, ch. XI, "On the diversity of manners", and ch. XIII, "On the natural condition of men with regard to their happiness and their misery", as well as *De cive* (1983/1642), Book. I, chs. 1 and 2, and Book II, ch. 5.

2 See Kant (1795) *Projet de paix perpétuelle. Esquisse philosophique*, Paris, Vrin, 1999, supplements 1 and 2; see also Kant (1794) *Idée d'une histoire universelle au point de vue cosmopolitique*, Paris, Bordas, 1988, commented on by J.-M. Muglioni, propositions 4 and 7.

3 Freud had already practiced this method when, at the very end of *From the History of an Infantile Neurosis* (1918 [1914]), he borrowed from Kant the autonomy of the original "schemas", to make them "categories" allowing a pre-formation of the understanding of the world. This function, analogous to that of the transcendentals, was however compared, in a very Darwinian way, to the instinctive knowledge of animals (p. 120).

4 On Kant's usage and his neo-reading by the Nazis, see J. Chapoutot (2017) "A l'école de Kant?" in *La Révolution culturelle nazie*, pp. 110–131.
5 Améry's (1971) book (*Unmeisterliche Wanderjahre*) has not been translated into French; its title not only treats the *Meister*, the family name of Wilhelm in Goethe's title, *Wilhelm Meister's Wanderjahre* (Wilhelm Meister's Apprenticeship and Travels) as an adjective derived from the common noun *Meister* (master), but it negativizes as "unmasterly" ("The Unmasterly Apprenticeship").

References

Chapoutot, J. (2017). A l'école de Kant? In: *La Révolution culturelle nazie*. Paris: Gallimard.

Freud, S. (1912–1913). *Totem and Taboo. S.E.* 13. London: Hogarth, pp. 1–161.

Freud, S. (1915). *Thoughts for the Times on War and Death. S.E.* 14. London: Hogarth, pp. 275–302.

Freud, S. (1918 [1914]). *From the History of an Infantile Neuorosis. S.E.* 17. London: Hogarth, pp. 7–122.

Freud, S. (1930). *Civilization and Its Discontents. S.E.* 21. London: Hogarth, pp. 57–146.

Freud, S. (1933a). *New Introductory Lectures on Psycho-analysis. S.E.* 22. London: Hogarth, pp. 1–182.

Freud, S. (1933b [1932]). *Why War? (Einstein and Freud). S.E.* 22. London: Hogarth, pp. 199–215.

Freud, S., Andreas-Salomé, L. (1985). *Letters*, ed. E. Pfeiffer, trans. W. & E. Robson Scott. New York: W.W. Norton & Co.

Hitler, A. (1936). *Mein Kampf* (complete edition). Munich: Zentralverlag der NSDAP.

Hobbes, T. (1983/1642). *The Works of Thomas Hobbes, Vol 2, De Cive*. Oxford: Clarendon Press.

Hobbes, T. (2010/1651). *Leviathan. Revised Edition*, eds. A.P. Martinich and Brian Battiste. Peterborough: Broadview Press.

Jouanjan, O. (2006). Justifier l'injustifiable. *Astérion* [Online Review], 4/2006 (http://journals.openedition.org/asterion/643).

Kant, E. (1794). *Idée d'une histoire universelle au point de vue cosmopolitique* [Idea for a Universal History with a Cosmopolitan Purpose]. Paris: Bordas, 1988.

Kant, E. (1795). *Projet de paix perpétuelle. Esquisse philosophique* [Perpetual Peace: A Philosophical Sketch]. Paris: Vrin, 1999.

Kertész, I. (1990). *Kaddish for an Unborn Child*. London: Vintage Classics, 2004.

Kertész, I. (1992). *Journal de galère* [Galley-Slave's Journal]. Arles: Actes Sud.

Kertész, I. (2004/1975). *Fatelessness*, trans. T. Wilkinson. London: Vintage International.

Kertész, I. (2005/2003). *Liquidation*. London : Vintage.

Kertész, I. (2009). *L'Holocauste Comme Culture*. Arles: Actes Sud.

Kertész, I. (2011/1998). The Holocaust as culture. In: *The Holocaust as Culture*, trans. T. Cooper. London: Seagall, pp. 57–78.

Kertész, I. (2013/2006). *Dossier K.*, trans. T. Wilkinson. Brooklyn: Melville House.

Kertész, I. (2017). Entretien avec Clara Royer: "Il doit y avoir de l'Eros, il doit y avoir de l'humour dans l'art" [Interview with Cara Royer. "There must be Eros, there must be humour in art"]. *Lignes*, 53: 23–24.

Lacoue-Labarthe, P. (1998). *La fiction du politique*. Paris: Christian Bourgois.

Michaud, E. (2008). Le nazisme, un régime de la citation. *Images Re-vues* [Online]. Hors-série 1/2008(http://imagesrevues.revues.org/885).

Miedzianagora, G., Jofer, G. (1994). *Objectif Extermination*. Paris: Frison Roche.

Schultze-Naumburg, P. (1928). *Kunst und Rasse*. Munich: Lehmanns.

Weber, M. (2004). *The Vocation Lectures*, ed. D. Owen, T. Strong; trans. R Livingstone. Illinois: Hackett Books.

4   The parasite and identity: the *Gestalt*

Let us consider it a sinister historical fact that Jung celebrated in 1934 the strength and creative seeds of the Aryan unconscious, capable of developing new cultural forms – in contrast to the Jews, "relatively nomadic", who, it was claimed, had never succeeded in creating their own cultural form. At first this could be seen as the neo-cultural, that is to say counter-cultural, outcome of what was originally a major dissension concerning the function of "archetypes", were it not for the fact that, twenty-five years later, Jung's line of reasoning became the editorial line of the new *Zentral-blatt* – or more exactly of the *Journal for Psychotherapy and its Frontier Fields, including Medical Psychology and Psychic Hygiene* (Jung, 1934). What then did Jung write? He wrote that these typical creative forms, long hidden in the Germanic soul like an infinitely precious secret, had suddenly sparked a movement, National Socialism, which had taken hold of the German people to the great astonishment of the whole world. A creation that was all the more astonishing in that the Jewish categories of psychology, elaborated by a certain Freud who did not understand the Germanic soul, considered this psychic background as a banal childish swamp (*als kindisch-banalen Sumpf*). It was therefore in this very background that Freudian psychoanalysis was alleged to have neglected the primal mythical function, which clearly shows that "the Aryan unconscious has a higher potential than the Jewish unconscious".

So what is the nature of these myths? When Alexander Bein (1965, p. 147) emphasizes the "mythical-demonic" character of the representations arising from the semantic analysis of the Nazi vocabulary – bacilli, vermin poisoning, devouring, disintegrating the body of the people – he reminds us that, in every myth, greatness is metamorphosed infinitely. The little one becomes a giant, and the giant becomes a dwarf or even an invisible figure. But, when scientific concepts amalgamate biology and politics, the myth suddenly becomes reality, resulting in the "transfer" of microscopic or vegetable nature to culture. It is then able to frame a "hygienist" policy.

In fact, the Indo-Germanic mythology of the Nazis sought by every means to flesh out the picture of a conquering people by nourishing the

DOI: 10.4324/9781003301660-5

model of the warrior troop with a set of images depicting the virtues of a sedentary and creative peasant people. Otherwise, as Johann Chapoutot (2007, see also, 2012) shows, the warrior would only be a nomad and could not be distinguished from the Semite. It was therefore necessary to anchor him in the soil to differentiate them. "The Semitic spirit has never, at any time in the history of the world, possessed the least interest in the peasantry. A nomad is simply not capable of it since he revels in 'a parasitic existence'", wrote Richard Walther Darré, the theorist of the notion of "Blood and Soil" (Darré, 1929, p. 50; cited in Chapoutot, 2016, p. 215). This is how, when the SS launched the German divisions against the USSR, it was peasants who went into combat in order to regain the lands of Asia that the Jewish nomads, having infested the Slav populations, had usurped. The mythology of the Spartans, the Dorian conquerors who populated the Peloponnese, then did its work, adjusting the racial hierarchy to the framework of slavery in Sparta. But the real weapon of conquest was more explicitly than ever the *bios*. The living force of the conquering peasants was measured by the yardstick of death that threatened this army penetrating deep into hostile lands. Infected wells, contaminated food and poisoned water: the eradication of lice and germs had to be done with flamethrowers, from a distance, or else the carriers of typhus who threatened the health of the healthy and bright people with a widespread epidemic would be rounded up and placed in ghettos. Against the fatality of the scourge, methods and treatment procedures were drawn up. The SS were doctors of humanity. Pathogens are natural, and the need to reduce them is also natural: it is a matter of hygiene, not a question of ideology, said Himmler.

The biological operation is therefore two-sided. To make the Jew a natural parasite is at the same time to deprive him of any cultural form. Biologically, he only grafts himself onto the healthy plant to feed on it; culturally, as Jung writes, the Jew has never created and never will create a form of civilization of his own, his flourishing always requiring the existence of a host. The meaning of this is clear: in his verminous "concreteness", he is devoid of any proper form, of any *Gestalt*, unlike the great figures of mythology, which is the leitmotif of Alfred Rosenberg's (1982/1930) *The Myth of the Twentieth Century*. Kafka (1915) had sensed this, as evidenced by *The Metamorphosis*.

Gestalt and *Gestaltung* thus become the territory on which the concreteness of the state was shaped, both as a living whole and as a work of art. "The essential organicity of the political is in reality infra-political, even infra-social", wrote Lacoue-Labarthe (1987, p. 109). It is the organicity of the troop that is "fictionalized" in the form of a national aesthetic. "Politics is the plastic art of the state, just as painting is the plastic art of colour. Forming a People from the masses, and a State from the People, has always been the deepest meaning of genuine politics", wrote Goebbels (cited by Chaouat, 2011, p. 53). It is from this perspective – the subjugation of the law to an aesthetic of form – that the *Gestalt*, the product of the act of an artist, became the expression of the authentic Aryan figure, to which the sculptor from Germany subscribed. Conversely, the parasite is a "form-less" being, a nothing. The substantial thought of National Socialism thus sought by every means to desubstantialize the Jew. It exterminates him. But can it, asks Jouanjan (2009), really annihilate him? "What, in essence, is the *Vernichtung* of a *Nichts* [the reduction to nothing of a nothing]?" (p. 94).

In truth, the Jew is not quite a "nothing". He is a "mask". Thanks to this intermediate link, it is pointed out that the one who is ontologically face-less presents himself in the guise of a human. So, to unmask the Jew is to stare at him and discover that, under the semblance, no *Gestalt* allows him to be integrated into the "beautiful form", into the harmonious arrange-ment of all in one, the "one" of the community. To unmask the Jew is also – the path is more direct – to force him to wear the yellow star which denounces the masquerade. It is all the more necessary to lift the mask as the Jew is active under his disguise. Because he is indeed the defender of a legalistic moralism and a neutral legal positivism, he jeopardizes the efficacy of concrete thought, that is to say the legal-aesthetic configuration of the new order. An agent of abstraction, an accomplice of the speculation that distinguishes and separates concepts, the Jew is therefore the bearer of this chaos denounced by Nazi jurists when they dismantle the very notion of "legal person". The issue of identity is there, deeply rooted in the drive and the *bios*. Everything to do with the ability of culture to "rep-resent" is affected. Everything to do with identity will, more or less, bear the scar of this distortion. Everything that concerns the activity of *ego*, of the singular ego, will be marked by this.

There is no doubt that psychoanalysis suffered severely from this shock. It found itself directly confronted with what Adorno, taking up *Group Psychology and the Analysis of the Ego* (Freud, 1921) and *Civilization and its Discontents* (Freud, 1930), describes both as "the spectacular failure of cul-ture" (Adorno, 2001/1965, p. 129), the absurdity of a "resurrected culture" (1981a, p. 72) and the need to rise up against the "destruction of culture" (Adorno, 2001, p. 127).

"Even the most radical consciousness of doom" (1981a, p. 35) is then what leads him to dig the furrow of the antinomy into which the fracture of Auschwitz plunged humans. If barbarity not only triumphed in spite of culture but with this culture, if the disease of civilization was to be unable to escape from idealities and admit the stench, the first consequence is necessarily a paradox. Indeed, as Gerald Sfez (2016, pp. 31–35) writes, when one considers the ego as the last bulwark against annihilation, against the dissolution of singularities, the place which is allocated to it can only exasperate identity – which, in turn, constitutes the intrinsic peril of an exacerbated narcissism. The paradox holds true at the individual level, but the alliance promoted by the Nazis between self-preservation and identity indicates how much it holds true at the level of social unity as well. Hence the impasse for anyone who seeks to think about civilization after Auschwitz: "Anyone who pleads for the preservation of this culture [the resurrected culture] makes himself an accomplice of its untruth and of ideological illusion in general; but whoever does not do so and demands the creation of a *tabula rasa*, directly promotes the barbarism over which culture had elevated itself and which the mediations of culture had actually moderated" (Adorno, 2001, p. 119).

The reference to Freud is central here: "Freud, at every step of his theory, never forgot that what is internalized by the individual is violence" (Adorno, 2007, p. 33). Central again is the form that murder has acquired: it is a gentle, good-natured murder, which minimizes the "immemorial wound"; a murder by erasure, by repeated forgetting, of what "mutilation" means. "What in reality leads Freud to give particular weight to certain events which occurred in his childhood is, even if not expressly stated, the notion of the damage suffered, of *Beschädigung*, of 'mutilation'" (ibid., p. 21). This damage, continues Adorno, is due to the fact that social life occurs "in shocks, sudden and abrupt blows, due to the alienation of the individual from society". Such an experience is entirely fictitious, Adorno adds; its continuity is illusory, the shock structure of individual experience turning out to be "a system of scars" (ibid., p. 41).

But what happens to the consideration of these scars which do not heal, if in order to open the future to reconciliation, we "claim that despite everything we are all brothers, but only if the existing antagonisms are liquidated"? (ibid., p. 41). Where does the illusion of such a liquidation come from? In alienation by the *same*? For we are not all brothers and the antagonisms are not about to be eliminated. Against the zealots of identity, Freud, as much a psychoanalyst as a politician, is therefore called to account by Adorno with regard to the irremediable dissociation that he continually described. For example, in "Freudian theory and the pattern of fascist propaganda" (1951a), he states: "As a rebellion against civilization, fascism is not simply a recurrence of the archaic, but its reproduction in and by civilization" (p. 137, cited by Le Rider, 2007, p. 90). He realizes that social sublimation, the "cultural solution", does more than inhibit impulses as to "[their] aim" and replace them with a "non-sexual aim"; that identification, at the same time as it seems to accomplish the purposes of Eros by forming ever greater entities, "disposes of" instinctual drive relations to objects, thereby opening up the possible regression of narcissistic positions. As the collective has replaced the superego, "the ego hardly has any other choice than either to change reality, or to withdraw back to the id" (Adorno, 1968, p. 89), which is what is meant by 'regression'" (ibid., p. 90). He considers the role of the superego at the very heart of the issue of totalitarianism: this psychic agency "irrationally fuses the old anxiety of physical annihilation and, much later, that of no longer being part of the social group" (Adorno, 2011, p. 320).

We can understand, then, how "the pressure exerted by the prevailing universal upon everything particular, upon the individual people and the individual institutions, has a tendency to destroy the particular and the individual together with their power of resistance" (Adorno, 2005, p. 193). Self-preservation loses its ipseity, unless, going against the tide of the fiction of a rediscovered unity, we admit that we must leave the contradictions unresolved. Without doubt, this is one of the challenges of the fragmentary genre defended by Adorno, of defeating the hegemonic chimeras of theoretical totalizations.

More importantly, it is on this point that Adorno agrees with Beckett, an author to whom he constantly refers when he ultimately entrusts art with the political task of bearing witness to annihilation (1991a, pp. 261–262, 1951b, p. 50); or, more precisely, of this drying up of experience, this "vacuum between men and their fate, in which their real fate lies" (1951b, p. 55). Because the political scene is now built on the silent base of a murder – the murder of the other because he is "other" – the shock function of the work, including its power of silence, will have to bear the "consistent sense of non-identity" (Adorno, 1973, p. 5), a source of resistance against the pious images of culture. And because "the relation to history is expressed by means of a *taboo*", because "the shock is such that it cannot be talked about" (Adorno, 2010a, p. 165), "mutilated life" will demand the incompleteness of the infinitely small or Beckettian stammering. "One can only speak euphemistically about what is incommensurate with all experience", or by attenuation. If we cannot transform this dimension absolutely beyond experience, it will be necessary to find the formless form to speak of the reversal of transcendence, the return to point zero. A form, therefore, which will concede nothing to consumption, an anti-dialectical, anti-tragic, anti-metaphysical form.

Here we should reread in detail "Notes on *The Unnamable*" (Adorno, 2010b) and "Trying to Understand *Endgame*" (Adorno, 1991b). In particular this: "Instead of trying to liquidate the discursive element in language through pure sound, Beckett transforms it into an instrument of its own absurdity, following the ritual of the clown, whose babbling becomes nonsense by being presented as sense. The objective decay of language – which human being's words and sentences have swollen up into their own mouths – penetrates the aesthetic arcanum" (ibid., p. 262). If the position of bloody sarcasm or parody is not maintained, if the method of fragmentation is not defended, it will be impossible "to stand up to the worst by making it into language" (Adorno, 1981b, p. 253).

Reread them, but for the purpose of taking the measure of what these authors, Kertész included, make of survival, which led Adorno to write: "The situations in which men are forced to think 'positively' simply in order to survive are themselves situations of compulsion, which force people back on pure self-preservation and in thinking only what they need to in order to survive in such a situation, to a point where the *truth content* of what they think is hopelessly undermined and utterly destroyed" (Adorno, 2001, p. 124, (Adorno's emphasis). And which, thirty-five years later, led Kertész to write: "Finally, life in society rests on the tacit agreement according to which man does not have to realize that the simple fact of living matters more, much more, than all the values which were his until that point. But when he realizes this – because terror can put him in a situation where, every day, every hour, every moment, he is aware of nothing else – we cannot speak of culture, because all values give way to survival" (Kertész, 1995, p. 118).

Reread them because we can see how "the Holocaust as culture", that is to say the "extension" of the Shoah, has spread far beyond the two generations directly affected by this moment in history. In truth, writes Kertész, "at a given time the survivor must have fully understood what he would later call incomprehensible" (ibid., p. 120). The break is there; where "it is we who no longer understand ourselves" (p. 121). We no longer understand that the brutal existential low point that man had reached during this dreadful twentieth century constitutes a norm resulting from experience. However, during this century, let us admit that the masks have fallen; everything has become truer, the soldier has turned into a professional assassin, politics into a criminal enterprise, capital into a factory for the destruction of men, national sentiment into genocide (ibid., pp. 125–126). "Our age is one of truth, there is no doubt" (1999, p. 84, translated from the French).

How did psychoanalysts learn this truth? Take the example of Eichmann, who repeatedly apologized during his trial, saying that he had acted as a citizen who obeyed not only orders but the law. "I wanted to say about Kant", replied Eichmann to Judge Raveh, "that the principle of my will must always be such that it can become the principle of general laws" (cited by Chapoutot, 2017, p. 111; see also Arendt, 1981, p. 4). Eichmann, Hannah Arendt (1963, pp. 43–44) points out, was right when he claimed that administrative language was the only one he knew, incapable as he was of uttering a single sentence that was not a cliché, devoid of all thought. So it is not so much the fact that Eichmann could invoke Kant and the categorical imperative that remains astounding. It is the fact that Eichmann's unconscious distortion agrees with what he himself called Kant's version of "the household use of the little man" (ibid., pp. 135–136[1]). The Nazi appealed to "practical reason" under the heading of a reformulation proposed by Hans Frank in *Die Technik des Staates* [The Technique of the State] (1942, pp. 15–16): "Act in such a way that the *Führer*, if he was aware of your action, would approve it" (cited by Chapoutot, 2017, p. 116).

As for what concerns us, it is even more astounding that psychoanalysis has partly responded to "Kant's adaptation 'to the household use of the little man'" by renouncing the theoretical framework of metapsychology. When the victim's speech, combined with the power of emotion, leaves out the "manic monotony" (Kertész, 2011/1988, p. 47; Mesnard, 2007, 2008) of the camp experience, when the imagination, in the very rhetoric of the description of the supposedly unrepresentable, pushes towards what Philippe Mesnard (2007) calls "the pathetic configuration" – to be precise, the "compassionate, contemporary vision" against which Kertész and Lanzmann fight – when, finally, we see the theory of intrapsychic agencies and in particular the highly complicated interaction between the id, the ego and the superego gradually replaced by a theory of putting lived experiences into images and narrative form, under cover of the argument of the benefits of dreaming and of the gains in identity, yes, it is possible to wonder what sort of damage Nazism inflicted on psychoanalysis. What did psychoanalysis do with the alteration of the very image of murder that shook the metapsychological framework of prohibition and of ethics? What "atonal language" were analysts able to invent? To what extent did the argument of the non-scientific nature of psychoanalysis not conceal the surrender to the magnitude of the task? And what does the new sequestration of the ego correspond to in the exacerbation of issues of identity?

It is to be noted in any case that the turning point of the discussion – and it is not only a question of Rorty and his version of the unconscious, but also of what happened to the radicalism of the Frankfurt School with the "communicational" turning point (see Enaudeau, 2017; Assoun, 2001) – was more or less contemporaneous with the work which oriented the attention given to the Shoah in the direction of listening to the survivors. Arguing from an interior space where our individual identities are thought to take shape, empathy and its use were employed to tighten the analytical field around a dialogue which, once its inclusion in the assembly of common ideal and superego-related agencies had been abandoned, was supposed to be roughly enough to provide access to the private experience of the catastrophe. This movement spread far beyond the investigations which focused on collecting testimonies and helping survivors. But the gradual extension of this way of looking at things, which ultimately led many analysts to consider that they were now confronted with unprecedented clinical configurations, did not dwell on the fact that, more than the pathologies of our patients, it was perhaps a question of a theoretical gloominess resulting from the upheaval undergone by psychoanalysis and its theory. Kohut's statement, made in 1980 to a reporter of the *New York Times Magazine*, bears witness to this; the fact that the trauma of his flight from Austria was decisive in his later conception of narcissism and borderline pathologies indicates how much the empathic turn he introduced was the personal consequence of an experience which profoundly affected analytical theory itself (Marcus & Wineman, 1985).

Conversely, consider the tribute that Max Horkheimer paid in 1948 to the memory of Ernst Simmel, a member of the Berlin Psychoanalytic Institute, who had participated alongside Freud, in 1918, at the International Congress of Psychoanalysis devoted to wartime neuroses, and who later emigrated to California (Horkheimer & Ernst, 1948). In this commendation, Horkheimer emphasized this analyst's stated opposition to the adaptation of the practise of psychoanalysis. Simmel's strength was his refusal to give up the "philosophical and abstract" part of Freudian doctrine and his resistance to any simplification when it came to reflecting on what was at the origin of "mass delusions". In this eulogy, it is as if Horkheimer had surmised in 1948 what might happen in the post-Holocaust period. To abandon the complexity of the theory of the drives and the apparent fragility of metapsychological hypotheses meant giving up the ethical core of psychoanalysis. But perhaps it was also to close once and for all the door to abstraction: henceforth analysts would have to stick to clinical, practical, concrete, non-speculative thinking.

In this sense, the Nazis, who immediately recognized psychoanalysis as their worst enemy, making it "a Jewish science", were not mistaken. Simmel, like Adorno, Horkheimer and Fenichel – contributors to the symposium on anti-Semitism held in San Francisco in 1944 – refused to separate theoretical abstraction from clinical practice. Their project – and it is remarkable that they were very concerned at that date with the evolution of anti-Semitism in the United States, whose propaganda through the voices of Henry Ford, Pelley or Winrod was extremely virulent[2] – their project consisted of thinking about sociology and psychic life together. Furthermore, the relationship between industrialization, cultural pauperization, rupture with reality and the direct promise of the fulfilment of prohibited desires, forbade in their eyes the continued use, on the one hand, of the expression "mass hypnosis" and, on the other, the diminution of "subjects to the narrowest definition of their selves" (Adorno, 2011, p. 328). In short, at that date, these thinkers, with Freud in their hands, were reflecting on the sleight of hand between the "unconscious psychological desire for self-annihilation", supported by the totalitarian horde, and the direct consequences of political disappropriation, caught up in the values subservient to *bios* and its scientificity. They were therefore taking up the crux of Freudian reflection: the confrontation with what, in terms of "outlook on the world", of *Weltanschauung, Civilization and its Discontents* called in 1930 "mass delusion" (Freud, 1930, p. 81 and pp. 84–85).

Notes

1 "The household use of the little man" is Eichmann's phrase.
2 It is interesting to consult the Archives of the "Conference in the Field of Antisemitism" as well as volume 3 of the *Studies on Prejudice (Anti-Semitism and Emotional Disorder)* edited by Nathan W. Ackerman and Marie Jahoda: http://www.ajcarchives.org/ajcarchive/DigitalArchive.aspx

References

Adorno, T.W. (1951a). Freudian theory and the pattern of fascist propaganda. In: *The Culture Industry: Selected Essays on Mass Culture*, J.M. Bernstein (ed.). London: Routledge, 1991, pp. 132–157.

Adorno, T.W. (1951b). *Minima Moralia*, trans. E.F.N. Jephcott. London: Verso, 1974.

Adorno, T.W. (1968). Sociology and psychology. *New Left Review*, 2(47): 79–97.

Adorno, T.W. (1973). *Negative Dialectics*. New York: Continuum, 2007.

Adorno, T.W. (1981a). *Prisms: Cultural Criticism and Society*. Cambridge, MA: MIT Press.

Adorno, T.W. (1981b/1967). Notes on Kafka. In: Adorno, 1981a, pp. 245–271.

Adorno, T.W. (1991a). *Notes to Literature*, vol. 1, ed. Rolf Tiedemann, trans. Shierry Weber Nicholsen, New York: Columbia University Press.

Adorno, T.W. (1991b). Trying to understand *Endgame*. In: Adorno, 1991a, pp. 241–275.

Adorno, T.W. (1994). Antisemitism and Fascist propaganda. In: *The Stars down to Earth and Other Essays on the Irrational in Culture*. Routledge, pp. 162–171.

Adorno, T.W. (2001/1965). *Metaphysics: Concept and Problems*, ed. R. Tiedemann; trans. E. Jephcott. Stanford, CA: Stanford University Press.

Adorno, T.W. (2005/1969). Education after Auschwitz. *Critical Models, Interventions and Catchwords*. New York: Columbia University Press, pp. 191–204.

Adorno, T.W. (2007). *La Psychanalyse révisée*, followed by J. Le Rider, *L'Allié incommode*. Paris: L'Olivier.

Adorno, T.W. (2010a). Notes on beckett*, trans. by Dirk Van Hulle and Shane Weller. *Journal of Beckett Studies*, 19(2): 157–171. www.euppublishing.com/toc/jobs/19/2

Adorno, T.W. (2010b). Notes on *The Unnamable*, trans. Shane Weller. *Journal of Beckett Studies*, 19(2): 172–178.

Adorno, T.W. (2011). À propos du rapport entre sociologie et psychologie. In: *Société, intégration, désintégration*. Paris: Payot, pp. 317–361.

Arendt, H. (1963). *Eichmann in Jerusalem: A Report on the Banality of Evil*. New York: Viking.

Arendt, H. (1981/1978). *The Life of the Mind: The Groundbreaking Investigation on How We Think*, ed. Mary McCarthy. San Diego: Harcourt Brace Javanovich.

Assoun, P.-L. (2001). Psychanalyse et théorie critique. Généalogie d'un lien. *Tumultes*, 17–18: 129–146.

Bein, A. (1965). Der jüdische Parasit; Bemerkungen zur Semantik der Judenfrage. *Vierteljahrshefte für Zeitgeschichte*, 13: 121–149.

Chaouat, B. (2011). La clameur originaire du politique. *Cités*, 45: 45–58.

Chapoutot, J. (2007). La charrue et l'épée. Paysan-soldat., esclavage et colonisation nazie à l'Est (1941–1945). *Hypothèses*, 1(10): 261–270. Reprinted in Chapoutot (2017), pp. 239–266.

Chapoutot, J. (2012). Les Nazis et la 'nature'. Protection ou prédation? *Vingtième siècle. Revue d'histoire*, 113: 29–39.

Chapoutot, J. (2016). *Greeks, Romans, Germans: How the Nazis Usurped Europe's Classical Past*, trans. R.R. Nybakken. Oakland, CA: University of California Press.

Chapoutot, J. (2017). *La Revolution culturelle nazie*. Paris: Gallimard.

Darré, R.W. (1929). *Das Bauerntum als Lebensquell der nordischen Rasse*. Munich-Berlin: Lehmann.

Enaudeau, C. (2017). L' 'oubli' de la reconnaissance: psychanalyse et critique sociale chez Axel Honneth. *Revue française de psychanalyse*, 81(2): 464–480,

Frank, H. (1942). *Die Technique des Staates*. Vienna: Burgverlag.

Freud, S. (1921). *Group Psychology and the Analysis of the Ego. S.E.* 18. London: Hogarth, pp. 65–144.

Freud, S. (1930). *Civilization and Its Discontents*. *S.E.* 21. London: Hogarth, pp. 57–146.

Horkheimer, M., Ernst, M. (1948). Simmel and the Freudian philosophy. *International Journal of Psychoanalysis*, 29: 110–113.

Jouanjan, O. (2009). 'Pensée de l'ordre concret' et ordre du discours 'juridique' nazi : sur Carl Schmitt. In: *Carl Schmitt ou le mythe du politique*, Y.-C. Zarka (ed.). Paris: Presses Universitaires de France, pp. 71–119.

Jung, C.J. (1934). Zur gegenwärtigen Lage desder Psychotherapie. In: *Zentralblatt für Psychotherapie und ihrer Grenzgebiete einschließlich der Medizinischen Psychologie und Psychischen Hygiene*, vol. VII, p. 1–16 [viewed online at archiv.org]. Also in: *Zivilisation im Übergang, Gesammelte Werke*, vol. X. Olten, Switzerland: Walter-Verlag, 1974, pp. 190–191.

Kafka, F. (1915). *The Metamorphosis*, trans. A.L. Lloyd. London: Faber & Faber, 1937.

Kertész, I. (1999). *Un autre*. Arles: Actes Sud. [(2004) *Someone Else: A Chronicle of the Change*, trans. T. Wilkinson. *Common Knowledge*, 10(2): 314–346].

Kertész, I. (2001). *Le refus*. Arles: Actes Sud.

Kertész, I. (2009). Ce malheureux XXe siècle. In: *L'Holocauste comme culture*. Arles: Actes Sud, pp. 113–136.

Lacoue-Labarthe, P. (1987). *La Fiction du politique*. Paris: Ch. Bourgeois.

Le Rider, J. (2007). *L'Allié incommode*. Paris: L'Olivier.

Marcus, P., Wineman, I. (1985). Psychoanalysis encountering the holocaust. *Psychoanalytical Inquiry*, 5: 85–98.

Mesnard, P. (2007). *Témoignage en résistance*. Paris: Stock.

Mesnard, P. (2008). *L'ambivalence du vide, entre Giorgio Agamben et Binjamin Wilkomirski*, ed. M. Rinn (2008).

Rinn, M. (2008). *Emotions et discours. L'Usage des passions dans la langue*. Rennes: Presses Universitaires de Rennes [new edition online: http://books.openedition.org/pur/30405).

Rosenberg, A. (2017/1930). *The Myth of the Twentieth Century*. Black Kite Publishing.

Sfez, G. (2016). *Logique du vif*. Paris: Hermann.

5 Psychoanalysis and *Weltanschauung* in 1930

Weltanschauung has more than one meaning. Without going into the *Weltanschauung/Weltansicht* debate (its English counterpart would be conception of the world/outlook on the world), let us say, to be brief, that the notion really took shape with Humboldt [1769–1859] and his comparative study of languages. Because thought is not solely dependent on language in general but is closely linked to the singular specificity of each language, Humboldt (1974) developed the hypothesis of an "indivisible intertwining of human consciousness and language" (pp. 80, 85, 199 and 203). The link between the specific form of each language and the construction of the world that it engenders determines a specific *Weltanschauung* – on the crest line between sensitive perception and intellectual conceptualization, at the interface between subjectivity and objectivity. The concept then evolved in the course of the nineteenth century to refer more generally to the philosophical systems.

The definition that Freud gives of *Weltanschauung* testifies to this evolution. The "conception of the world", he writes, "is an intellectual construction, which resolves all the problems of our existence uniformly on the basis of one overriding hypothesis, which accordingly leaves no question unanswered and in which everything that interests us finds its fixed place" (Freud, 1933a, p. 158). Associating ideology and *Weltanschauung*, Hannah Arendt (2017/1951) gives a definition that is ultimately quite close to Freud's:

> Ideologies always assume the postulate that one idea is sufficient to explain everything in the development from the premise, and that no experience can teach anything. . . . The danger in exchanging the necessary insecurity of philosophical thought for the total explanation of an ideology and its *Weltanschauung* . . . [is] of exchanging the freedom inherent in man's capacity to think for the strait jacket of logic, with which man can force himself almost as violently as he is forced by an outside force.
>
> (p. 617)

Freud, for his part, refers to the necessarily insecure situation in which psychoanalytic thought operates. Unlike religion and philosophical

DOI: 10.4324/9781003301660-6

systems, it cannot form a conception of the world which is proper to it. In search of coherent explanations, the only one that psychoanalysis can adopt is that of science, on the condition of carefully verifying its data and accepting the incompleteness of its models.

Thus, between 1927 and 1939, there was a proliferation in German-speaking countries of psychoanalytic texts relating both to the relations between analysis and the various "conceptions of the world" then in vogue, and to the scientific value of its theories. The debate included religion and its critique, largely taken up by Freud in the *35th Lecture*, but it involved other *Weltanschauungen*, ranging from socialist and Marxist positions to the "new conception" initiated in 1924 by National Socialism. Although psychoanalysis immediately abandoned "energy" as conceived by *Naturphilosophie* in favour of the thermodynamics of the physicalists, we must undoubtedly see in the power that it continued to grant to the "magic of words" the motivating force underlying these questions.

Nevertheless, between the threat of a return to supernatural beliefs and the risk of a simplistic materialism implied by "naturalistic" determinism, the focus of the debate was indeed deeply marked by the political violence of the period. With the destructiveness of positivism and the return of obscurantism, all the thinkers of the time – Paul Valéry, Ortega y Gasset, Thomas Mann – knew that the status of rationalism was under the spotlight. The conclusion of "Philosophy and the Crisis of European Humanity", a lecture given in 1935 in Vienna by Edmund Husserl (1970), testified to this. "The 'crisis' could then become distinguishable as the *apparent failure of rationalism*. The reason for the failure of a rational culture, however, as we said, lies not in the essence of rationalism itself but solely in its being rendered superficial, in its entanglement in 'naturalism' and 'objectivism'" (p. 299). That is why Husserl saw only two outcomes: either its fall into hostility to the spirit and into barbarity; or the rebirth of Europe from the spirit of philosophy, "thanks to a heroism of reason which definitively overcomes naturalism". This "heroism of reason" resonates strangely with the "dictatorship of reason" to which Freud appealed in 1932 (Freud, 1933b, p. 171, 1933a, p. 213).

In either case, dictatorship or heroism, the rise to power of Adolf Hitler had turned all data upside down, especially under the effect of a complete blurring of what should now have been entrusted to science. Which science was it? Which nature did they claim to adhere to? And which determinism was being called on? Opposing science to the obscurantism of religion no longer seemed to be enough when the territory of words, piece by piece, was being contaminated by the forceful entry of nature into the political field. Nature, that is to say what we, late readers of the translation of *Mein Kampf* into French, group together under the haunting repetition of the term "instinct";[1] but which they, over there, in their time, understood well as it was said to them: Hitler and Alfred Rosenberg spoke to them about "drive", about *Trieb*. And it was indeed the dimension of the "demonic", a term Freud had been using from the first hour, and its energy, that were invoked.

This was the paradox that the analysts of the day faced. But "paradox" is not the right word, since early on the trap took the form of an abyss. An abyss whose edges we cannot grasp, precisely because the confusion described by Victor Klemperer (2013) was doing its work:

> Nazism permeated the flesh and blood of the people through single words, idioms and sentence structures which were imposed on them in a million repetitions which were taken on board mechanically and unconsciously. . . . Words can be like tiny doses of arsenic: they are swallowed unnoticed, appear to have no effect, and then after a little time the toxic reaction sets in after all.

(p. 15)

The toxic effect would soon take on the appearance of a struggle to the death, with the result that, under the suitable mask of its official name, "Psychoanalysis and *Weltanschauung*", this was arguably one of the most formidable episodes of what Nazism succeeded in doing to psychoanalysis. It was not only in the form of the destruction of the psychoanalytic institutes of the central empires, but because it was realized that, in order to fight, some analysts had to relinquish whole sections of theory and to bend others in order to find or to rediscover the theoretical axes based on which the dyke of consciousness was in a position to thwart drive activity. The resistance of the ego, its libidinal autonomy, an overarching ethic reintroduced by means of a superego capable of challenging mass identificatory subjugation, were already apparent in a veiled form in the texts of Heinz Hartmann published before his emigration – texts which in some respects formed the basis of ego psychology. But let us take a closer look.

Between 1930 and 1933, no less than four texts appeared under the title "Psychoanalysis and *Weltanschauung*": a lecture by Carl Müller-Braunschweig (1931) – then a member of the Berlin Psychoanalytic Institute, before he became a prominent Nazi collaborator of the Göring Institute, and before he founded in 1951 the German Psychoanalytic Association [DPV] – a lecture, therefore, delivered on the occasion of the congress of the German Psychoanalytic Society [DPG] and published in the *Almanach der Psychoanalyse* in 1931;[2] in 1933, Freud's *35th Lecture*; on the same date, a second text by Müller-Braunschweig (1933), published under the same title in the *Reichswart, Organe de l'Alliance Raciste Européenne* on 23 October 1933;[3] finally, still in 1933, a text by Heinz Hartmann (1933) also entitled "Psychoanalyse und Weltanschauung".[4] Why such a proliferation? What was at stake?

Müller-Braunschweig's lecture in 1930 began by asking the question: What is the relationship between the notion of *Weltanschauung* and the scientific position? Science, he wrote, explores reality, uncovers facts, and from that data "abstracts" a number of recurring and logical relationships.

The notion of *Weltanschauung* is of a completely different nature: it not only recognizes reality as it is, but transforms it, intentionally and reasonably, according to ideas of what it should be. In other words, it is not a "view" of the world, which the tenor of the word would suggest. What, without exception, *Weltanschauung* designates are decisions concerning the way in which one wants to act on the world and in life, in other words, it designates a shaping[5] of external reality.

Throughout this text, Müller-Braunschweig pursues, then, the comparison between science and conception of the world in order to contrast them in the clearest way. While the first only has the accuracy value of "knowing about what is", the second takes into account a whole set of values and standards according to which it seeks to "shape" what is given – such as education, the "culture of personality", artistic conceptions, the moral and legal order (*Ordnung*), and the political and economic order (p. 103). Now, in order to be able to function while taking reality into account, *Weltanschauung* needs the knowledge provided by empirical science; and yet it cannot wait for a complete body of scientific knowledge to be delivered to transform this reality. It therefore uses other means to carry out its task, and in particular the fact that the material on which it acts participates in the very determination of the process of shaping (*Gestaltung*) (pp. 104–105). It is the same here as with statuary, where the material is a factor in its shaping. Its own qualities, adds Müller-Braunschweig, partly determine the use that can be made of it, that is, the "tone" of the work. There is therefore nothing in common between the influence of the material on the shaping of the model and the scientific purposes of the chemical analysis of this material.

Within this opposition, on which side does psychoanalysis position itself? Is it a science? Or should we consider it as a *Weltanschauung* oriented towards the modelling of determined norms and values? If the question arises, continues Müller-Braunschweig, it is because psychoanalysis has considered certain forms of instinctual drive life and character as slippages, as pathological deviations from a development which is seen as normal. From diffuse autoeroticism to the subordination of the part-drives under the primacy of genital functioning, from early narcissism to the full object-love of adults, from the infantile predominance of destructive tendencies to a state in which these tendencies are rendered harmless thanks to their erotic connections, thanks to reaction formations or thanks to a fruitful competition at work – which allows for their sublimation – in every case, the conquest by the ego of the territories of the id implies a development in man which goes from submission to the drives to control of the drives. Such lines of development, writes Müller-Braunschweig, seem to have "a normative character". But this norm in fact corresponds to an "ideal-type" (*Idealtypus*) (p. 105) which is only found in reality to an infinitesimal degree. In other words, it results from a process of abstraction and in no way relates to the normativity of the practical ideals involved in *Weltanschauung* and in the realization of actions. And as a matter of fact, psychoanalysts do not give directions to the patient. The difference between their theoretical knowledge concerning the normality of drive life, with its ideal colouring, and its erection in the form of goals to be achieved is therefore great.

However, it must be admitted, continues Müller-Braunschweig, that psychoanalysis as a practice may seem to set the norm as a requirement: the primacy of genital functioning, access to mature object relations, the overcoming of primitive destructive tendencies, in short, these therapeutic "goals" could be mobilized very directly and very actively by the analyst. But the "specificity of psychoanalysis" is precisely that at the same time as it establishes norms which could be part of a *Weltanschauung*, it avoids treating the result of this research as practical ideals for development. When Freud writes: "The patient should . . . be educated to liberate and fulfil his own nature"[6] this formulation is not oriented in the direction of utopian perfection. We are just happy when we are able to help a patient rediscover his strength to work again and to enable him to free himself from unconscious drive compulsion, from the sense of guilt, from his symptoms, in short to help him accept the world as it is and to bring about a modification of the drive economy that works in favour of the ego. And Müller-Braunschweig concludes: knowledge and standards are like the constellations which guide the walker; albeit essential practically and theoretically, they are never goals to be attained (p. 109).

Müller-Braunschweig copied here in part Freud's lecture presented in September 1918 at the Budapest Congress and published under the title "Lines of advance in psychoanalytic therapy" (Freud, 1919). This is easily noticeable when he refers to the analogy between psychoanalysis and chemical analysis; or when he draws implicitly on Freud's remark about Putnam,

> our honoured friend . . . who must forgive us for not being able to accept his proposal – namely, that psycho-analysis should place itself in the service of a particular philosophical outlook [*Weltanschauung*] on the world and should urge this upon the patient for the purpose of ennobling his mind.
>
> (ibid., p. 165)

He copied the Freud of 1918 but omitted what Freud says about his position with regard to the "outlook on the world": "I have been able to help people with whom I had nothing in common – neither race, education, social position nor outlook [*Weltanschauung*] upon life in general, without affecting their individuality" (ibid.). Moreover, if Putnam is mentioned in this text, it is because in "On the history of the analytical movement", Freud (1914) had already recognized that this man, in protecting psychoanalysis so courageously from the denunciations of it in America, had in doing so "yielded too much to the strong ethical and philosophical bent of his nature" (p. 31), setting psychoanalysis an "impossible demand" whereby he expected psychoanalysis to "place itself at the service of a particular moral-philosophical conception of the universe" (ibid.).[7] In other words, if the moral *Weltanschauung* enabled Putnam to hold his own against attacks from his colleagues, any intervention by a *Weltanschauung* in the conduct of analyses was, in Freud's eyes, a departure from the method itself. In 1918, Freud was even firmer: "In my opinion, this is only after all to use violence, even though it is overlaid with the most honourable motives" (Freud, 1919, p. 165).

Is this the reason why Müller-Braunschweig, after having differenti-ated the Freudian position, did not hesitate in 1930 to put "the materialist conception of the world" under the spotlight, one to which some ana-lysts thought that psychoanalysis could refer? And besides, what sort of materialism was it? Müller-Braunschweig's point suddenly became pro-digiously convoluted when he attacked those who considered that psy-choanalysis legitimized above all the power of "economic factors" over the mind. In the reciprocal relationship between instinctual drive forces and the activity of the mind, the strength of the latter plays its part. This was why, according to him, it was all the same legitimate to consider a conception of the world advocated by psychoanalysis, based on ideals, "on condition that it is confined to practical idealism and abstains from any metaphysical conception" (p. 114). This, Müller-Braunschweig added, is what Freud (1923) suggests in *The Ego and the Id* when he protests against the unjustified reproach made against psychoanalysis of neglecting what is elevated in man. The fact that the superego and ideals have their ori-gin in instinctual drive conflicts and infantile processes does not detract from their "value". Just as, conversely, psychoanalysis unmasks certain allegedly ideal allegations as fallacious covers for much less ideal motives. By keeping to the sphere of strictly empirical research, psychoanalysis in reality offers the best that it can offer, concludes Müller-Braunschweig: a *Weltanschauung* which is not terrified by new views on reality, which does not tremble in the face of unknown abysses, and which allows us to conquer "a sincere love of reality" (p. 115). Why should "everything in the world and in life" (pp. 115–116) be different from what happens with individuals, our neighbours? Does not the recognition of their weaknesses and their baseness lead us to show them more love and trust, to feel more deeply something like a "destiny", "a shared guilt" which brings us closer to them? So we can hope that we show for "the whole of the world and of life a new confidence and a new love" (p. 116).

It is probable that we owe in part the efflorescence of texts on the rela-tionship between psychoanalysis and the conception of the world to Pfis-ter's (1993) publication of his pamphlet "The illusion of a future". The debate between Pfister and Freud, as friendly as it was, left no room for doubt. Freud did not yield anything to Pfister concerning the scientificity of psychoanalysis and did not hide from him that the "pastor of souls" that he was had inspired the figure of the opponent who appears in *The Future of an Illusion* (Freud, 1927). In a letter to Pfister dated 16 October 1927 (in Meng & Freud, 1963, p. 110), he wrote: "When you have read it you must let me know what measure of toleration and understanding you are able to preserve for the hopeless pagan" (see also Freud, 1927, pp. 41–42).

Ungodly, since, for him, religion was dependent on illusions created by desire, involving a denial of reality, and was in all points akin to obsessional neurosis. According to Freud the acceptance of a universal religious neurosis exempted the individual from creating a personal neurosis. It was therefore in the name of an "education to reality" (Freud, 1927, p. 49, Freud's emphasis) that scientific work must fight against this *Weltanschauung* which rejected any rational basis for cultural and moral prescriptions.

On the other hand Pfister did not give up either: "I cannot have things out with you properly on the subject of religion because you completely reject philosophy, approach art in a way that differs from mine, and regard morality as something self-evident". And he continues: "Your substitute for religion is basically the idea of the eighteenth century Enlightenment in proud modern guise" (letter from Pfister to Freud dated 24 November 1927 in Meng & Freud, 1963, pp. 114–115).

Pfister denounces this "scientism", this "positivism", on the grounds that "there is no science without metaphysics. There never has been and never will be", that "our categories of thought, whether one thinks of them in Kant's sense or otherwise, always play a part", and that "therefore, we must practice a critique of knowledge" (cited in Boyd, 1994, p. 204). And he did not hesitate to question Freud about the metaphysical foundations of what the latter called "experience": "Each experience contains an elementary, childish metaphysics" (Pfister, 1993, p. 33) – expressions like "force", "cause", "law" overriding the empirical nature of the natural sciences, as well as the concepts of physics such as "matter", "substance", and "energy". Even the opposition between *Sein* und *Schein*, between being and appearance, implies a reference to philosophy and its metaphysical reflection. As for the evaluation of values, it does not depend on "sensibleness" since "the degree of sensibleness is not necessary the measure of value" (Boyd, 1994, p. 194), and it is on this point, that of ethics and morality, that Pfister's attack – however affable it may be – seeks to undermine analysis: "It is very doubtful", he writes, "whether, taking everything into account, scientific progress has made men happier or better" (letter from Pfister to Freud dated 24 November 1927, in Meng & Freud, 1963, p. 115). And so, he concludes, "you must not be surprised if I plead on behalf of retaining the religious doctrinal system as the basis of education and of man's communal life. This is a practical problem, not a question of reality-value. (Freud, 1927, p. 52).

But in matters of reality, if the debate was so intense, it was because the discussion initiated by what would later be called the "the Freudians of the left" had been added to the critique by Pfister's Christian *Weltanschauung*, in particular the publication by Wilhelm Reich in 1929 of "Dialectical materialism and psychoanalysis" (Reich, 1929a) and "Psychoanalysis in the Soviet Union" (Reich, 1929b), followed in 1931 by Fromm's text, "Politics and psychoanalysis" (Fromm, 1931).[8]

From this current, in addition to Reich and Fromm, both of whom were subsequently excluded from the International Psychoanalytic Association, let us recall the names of Ernst Simmel, Otto Fenichel, Siegfried Bernfeld, Edith Jakobson and Paul Federn. These were people who were initially trained in the closest Freudian circle, either in Vienna or in Berlin, who all belonged to the socialist movement, but who, in some cases, were very close to the communist movements. A number of them, linked to the Frankfurt School, were to meet in San Francisco during the symposium devoted to anti-Semitism organized by Horkheimer and Simmel in 1944. Let us say that these names punctuate the publications of the period 1928–1934, which constantly raised the question of reality in the form of the link between social development – the ideological dimension included – and analytical contributions.

This was the case for Fenichel's (1932) text, "Psychoanalyse der Politik" [Psychoanalysis of politics] which returned to the problem of "value" at the level of capitalist economy and at the libidinal level, and also for Bernfeld, a psychoanalyst and pedagogue, and a friend of Aichhorn, who had published four years earlier "Ist Psychoanalyse eine Weltanschauung? [Is psychoanalysis a Weltanschauung?]" (Bernfeld, 1929). For him, psychoanalysis is a scientific discovery whose effects touch on our conceptions of the world, just as Darwin or atomic physics had done. This was based on Freud's own hypothesis, according to which psychic processes derive from physiological sources – a hypothesis which had helped the development of "materialism", even if this materialism no longer had much weight in "modern" circles of philosophy. Bernfeld, who attended Moritz Schlick's seminars, was undoubtedly referring here to the Vienna Circle's criticism of pseudo-scientific theories as well as to his own research on the anchoring of psychoanalysis in the hard sciences. On the other hand, in his article "Ist Psychoanalyse eine Weltanschauung?" (Bernfeld, 1929, p. 30), he noted that materialism continued to be important as a social fact in proletarian circles – and in fact, four years later, he was to create in the company of Anna Freud, August Aichhorn and Willi Hoffer, a study group on "psychoanalytic pedagogy" open to analysts in training as well as social workers and teachers. But in 1928, it was the hour of politics and its mysteries, especially when assumptions, theories and facts that were in themselves of great importance were considered as unimportant, while facts of little importance could acquire considerable social significance. And Bernfeld gives the example of the differentiation between brachycephalic and dolichocephalic types, a harmless theory as such but which, as a "conception of the world" built on cranial measurements, proved to be essential in German anti-Semitic and racial nationalism. The relationship between scientific value and impact in terms of *Weltanschauung* is therefore never direct. If we consider, for example, Freud's discoveries concerning sexuality, one could find in them, continues Bernfeld, an argument against bourgeois sexual morality and a rehabilitation of sexuality as a powerful natural force against Christian asceticism. In reality, the practical consequences that can be drawn from analytical findings are quite diverse. This is why detractors of psychoanalysis, whatever side they come from, can finally agree on one point: it is above all destructive. Hence Bernfeld's conclusion: apart from its strictly scientific contribution, what psychoanalysis can bring to a larger view of the world is the kind of enlightenment it promotes. To do so, it should no longer be confined to the space reserved for "cultivated people". If it was integrated into social education in general, it could work in the direction of freedom.

In 1928 – when the Communist Party and the Social Democratic Party together again won forty per cent of the votes in the legislative elections – Bernfeld's text still resonated with the hope that had animated Freud in 1910 when he addressed the analysts gathered together at the Nuremberg Congress: "We must be able to wait. . . . The harshest truths are heard and recognized at last, after the interests they have injured and the emotions they have roused have exhausted their fury. . . . [W]e must be able to wait" (Freud, 1910, pp. 147–148).[9] Freud's argument was based, at that time, on the fundamental interdependence of time and the values generated by progress, and Freud concluded his address by insisting on the prospects of an enlightened social future. In 1933, the situation was quite different. The education of the masses had taken the form of "a new love" according to Müller-Braunschweig, while the sounds of the boots of the new order were resounding. How could the Nazis come to terms with the "Jewish science"?

Notes

1 Thus *Instinkt* and *Trieb* were translated indiscriminately in the only French translation of *Mein Kampf* that was available at that time by Calmettes and Gaudefroy-Demombynes (Hitler, 1934).
2 This lecture was delivered on 29 September 1930, two weeks after the elections which gave 107 seats to the National Socialist Party.
3 Historical documents relating to this period were made available to the French public thanks to the bilingual edition, published by Alain de Mijolla and his team, of the volume by K. Brecht et al. (1987) *Hier geht das Leben auf eine sehr merkwurdige Weise weiter . . .* [henceforth cited as *Ici, la vie . . .*; the references in this volume are given according to the pagination of the texts in German, followed by that of the French translation]: for this text by Müller-Braunschweig, p. 97 (French trans., pp. 245–246). This text was unearthed by Dahmer (1933); it gave rise to a very violent conflict during the first IPA congress which returned to Germany (Hamburg) in 1985. See also Dahmer (1984).
4 H. Hartmann (1933) Psychoanalyse und Weltanschauung. *Psychoanalytische Bewegung*, V, reprinted in *Almanach für Psychoanalyse*, Vienna, 1936, pp. 96–113. [both the Almanach texts and journal texts from this period can be viewed on archive.org]

5 *Gestalt, Gestaltung,* and *gestalten* appear thirteen times in the first six pages of this short text.
6 Müller-Braunschweig does not give the reference: Freud (1919 [1918]).
7 This, moreover, is what he had written to Putnam himself in a letter dated 8 July 1915 (see Jones, 1953–1957, Vol 2., pp. 472–473).
8 Texts published respectively in (Reich, 1929a) *Pod Znaméniem Marxisma* (Under the banner of Marxism), III, 1929, (Reich, 1929b) in *Psychoanalytische Bewegung,* I/4, 1929, p. 358–368 and (Fromm, 1931) in *Psychoanalytische Bewegung,* III/5, special book devoted to the *Psychoanalysis of politics,* 1931. In 1930, returning from the USSR, Reich presented at Freud's house an oral account of his position, the title of which seems to have been "Psychoanalyse und Weltanschauung". According to F. E. Hoevels (1996), this manuscript has not been preserved as is but partly integrated into "Dialectical Materialism and Psychoanalysis".
9 This was the project implemented with the creation of the Berlin Polyclinic in 1920.

References

Arendt, H. (2017/1951). *The Origins of Totalitarianism.* London: Penguin.

Bernfeld, S. (1929). Ist Psychoanalyse eine Weltanschauung? *Almanach für Psychoanalyse,* 4: 28–37. First published in *Zeitschrift für psychoanalytische Pädagogik,* II, 1927–1928, pp. 201–208.

Boyd, J.H. (1994). *Affirming the Soul: Remarkable Conversations between Mental Health Professionals and an Ordained Minister* (Appendix A: "The illusion of a future – a friendly Discussion with Prof. Sigmund Freud", pp. 177–215). Connecticut: Soul Research Institute, Cheshire.

Brecht, K., Friedrich, V., Hermanns, L., Kaminer, I., Jülich, D. (eds.). (1987). *Hier geht das Leben auf eine sehr merkwürdige Weise weiter. . .* Hamburg: Kellner Verlag.

Dahmer, H. (1983). Kapitulation vor der 'Weltanschauung'. Zu einem Aufsatz von Carl Müller-Braunschweig aus dem Herbst 1933. *Psyche,* 37: 1116–1135.

Dahmer, H. (1984). Psychoanalyse unter Hitler; Rückblick auf eine Kontroverse. *Psyche,* 38: 927–942.

Fenichel, O. (1932). Psychoanalyse de Politik [Psychoanalysis of politics]. *Psychoanalytische Bewegung,* 4(3): 255–268.

Freud, S. (1910). *The Future Prospects of Psychoanalytic Therapy. S.E.* 11. London: Hogarth, pp. 141–151.

Freud, S. (1914). *On the History of the Psychoanalytic Movement. S.E.* 14. London: Hogarth, pp. 7–66.

Freud, S.(1919 [1918]). *Lines of Advance in Psychoanalytic Therapy. S.E.* 17. London: Hogarth, pp. 157–168.

Freud, S. (1923). *The Ego and the Id. S.E.* 19. London: Hogarth, pp. 13–66.

Freud, S. (1927). *The Future of an Illusion. S.E.* 21. London: Hogarth, pp. 5–56.

Freud, S. (1933a). *New Introductory Lectures on Psycho-analysis. S.E.* 22. London: Hogarth, pp. 1–182.

Freud, S. (1933b [1932]). *Why War? (Einstein and Freud). S.E.* 22. London: Hogarth, pp. 199–215.

Fromm, E. (1931). Politics and psychoanalysis, trans. Mark Ritter. In: *Critical Theory and Society: A Reader,* S.E. Bronner and D. MacKay Kellner (eds.). New York: Routledge,1989, pp. 213–218.

Hartmann, H. (1933). Psychoanalyse und Weltanschauung. In: *Psychoanalytische Bewegung*, V, pp. 416–429; reprinted in *Almanach für Psychoanalyse*, Vienna, 1936, pp. 96–113.

Hitler, A. (1934). *Mein Kampf-Mon Combat*, trans. A. Calmettes and J. Gaudefroy-Demombynes. Paris: Nouvelles Éditions latines.

Humboldt, W. von. (1974). *Introduction à l'oeuvre sur le kavi et autres essais*. Paris: Seuil.

Husserl, E. (1970). Philosophy and the crisis of European humanity. In: *The Crisis of the European Sciences and Transcendental Phenomenology*, trans. D. Carr. Evanston: Northwestern University Press, pp. 269–300.

Jones, E. (1953–1957). *The Life and Work of Sigmund Freud (Vols. 1–3)*. London: Hogarth.

Klemperer, V. (2013 [1957]). *The Language of the Third Reich. LTI – Lingua Tertii Imperii: A Philologist's Notebook*, trans. M. Brady. London: Bloomsbury.

Meng, H., Freud, E.L. (eds.). (1963). *Psychoanalysis and Faith: The Letters of Sigmund Freud and Oskar Pfister*, trans. E. Mosbacher. London: Hogarth.

Müller-Braunschweig, C. (1931). Psychoanalyse und Weltanschauung. In: *Almanach für Psychoanalyse*. Vienna: Internationaler Psychoanalytischer Verlag, pp. 102–116.

Pfister, O. (1928). *Psychoanalyse und Weltanschauung*. Leipzig: Internationaler Psychoanalytischer Verlag.

Pfister, O. (1993/1928). The illusionof a future: A friendly disagreement with Prof. Sigmund Freud. *International Journal of Psycho-Analysis*, 74: 557–559.

Reich, W. (1929a). Dialectical materialism and psychoanalysis. In: *SEX-POL: Essays, 1929–1934*, L. Baxandall (ed.). New York: Vintage Books, 1966, pp. 1–74.

Reich, W. (1929b). Psychoanalysis in the Soviet Union. In: *SEX-POL: Essays, 1929–1934*, L. Baxandall (ed.). New York: Vintage Books, 1966, pp. 75–88.

6 Purifying psychoanalysis scientifically

This is not the place to return to the details of the terrible negotiations that took place within the German Psychoanalytic Society when Hitler arrived at the Chancellery, or to the destruction of the Viennese Psychoanalytic Society and its publishing house during the annexation of Austria. German-speaking psychoanalysts and researchers have gone into this question at length, as have historians. Both the numerous and detailed articles in the *International Dictionary of Psychoanalysis* edited by Alain de Mijolla (2004/2002, 2013) and the more controversial texts published by Bernd Nitzschke (2003) have made it possible to complete the irreplaceable collection of documents, *Ici, la vie continue de manière fort surprenante* (Mijolla et al., 1987, see Chapter 5, note 3).

To these must be added the book by Regine Lockot (2003), *Die Reinigung de Psychoanalyse* [The Purification of Psychoanalysis], and, among others, the works of Geoffrey Cocks (1992) and Volker Friedrich (1989). Let us say that the facts are now fairly well established. In a word, under the direction of M. H. Göring, a policy of Aryanization of the German Psychoanalytic Society, in which certain analysts collaborated, including Boehm, Schultz-Hencke, Kemper and Müller-Braunschweig, led to the creation of the Göring Institute, long chaired by Jung. Jewish psychoanalysts were excluded and, for the most part, went into exile to Britain, the United States and Argentina. Others were murdered, such as John Rittmeister and Karl Landauer. Jones, who is criticized by some for his contacts with the Nazi authorities, was the chief craftsman behind this mass emigration.[1] After the fall of the Reich, the German Psychoanalytic Society [DPG] remained excluded from the International Psychoanalytic Association for reasons of collaboration, while Müller-Braunschweig managed to create the German Psychoanalytic Association [DPV] which was recognized by the IPA in 1951. Let us add that, in the post-war period, the role played by Alexander Mitscherlich, the founder in 1947 of the journal *Psyche*, was decisive in this intellectually devastated country. He was the co-author in 1949 of *Wissenschaft ohne Menschlichkeit* ["Science without humanity"] (Mitscherlich & Mielke, 1949) on the participation of German physicians in the eugenics policy of the Nazis, and in 1959 he founded the Sigmund Freud Institute

DOI: 10.4324/9781003301660-7

in Frankfurt, where Adorno and Horkheimer had resettled, and was one of the first to unearth documents concerning the Nazi period.

One can easily guess that the polemics that run through the previously mentioned texts do not only involve the position of Jones. As Thomas Aichhorn (2007) has shown very well, Freud's position in 1933 was: "No provocations, and even less, concessions" (see also letter from Freud to Eitingon dated 17 April 1933, in Schröter, 2009, p. 789; Anna Freud & Aichhorn, 2012) – the idea of a possible survival of psychoanalysis dominating against all odds the powerless diplomacy of the period. This is clearly evident in the correspondence he maintained with Eitingon and Jones, the former fighting to the last ditch against the new masters of the Berlin Institute, the latter advocating sufficient contact with them to gain time, obtain visas and look for places of welcome abroad, hoping that the analytical cause might survive the disaster. Note that it is in this context that, having agreed to see Boehm during an impromptu visit of the latter to Vienna – Federn attended the meeting – Freud asked him to "free him from Reich". In addition to wanting this expulsion for "scientific reasons" – in particular sexual reductionism and the social-psychic views on the authoritarian character – he had feared for some time that Reich's notoriety as a communist militant would be detrimental to the German Psychoanalytic Society (on this point see Fallend & Nitzschke, 2002). "I started the battle against the Bolshevik aggressors, Reich and Fenichel", he wrote to Jeanne Lampl-de Groot on 17 January 1932 (cited by Paul Roazen, 2003, p. 8). Similarly, it was Freud who made the exclusion of Schultz-Hencke, a virulent critic of Freud's theory of the libido, a condition for the acceptance of Müller-Braunschweig and of Boehm as presidents of the DPG.

But today it is Müller-Braunschweig's position that I want to focus on. Not because of the terrifying sleight of hand which had allowed him, in the eyes of Anna Freud, Jones and participants in the IPA Congresses of 1949 and 1951, to appear for the second time as "the saviour of psychoanalysis ", at the head, this time, of the German Psychoanalytic Association [Deutsche Psychoanalytische Vereinigung, DPV] newly founded by him, while the DPG was excluded because it had been integrated into the Göring Institute,[2] but because of his active participation in "bringing into line" both the administrative and theoretical aspects of psychoanalysis during the period.

In October 1933, Müller-Braunschweig again published a text, this time in the *Reichswart, Organ of the European Racist Alliance*, whose title "Psychoanalyse und *Weltanschauung*" indicated the wish to be in continuity with the previous debates (Müller-Braunschweig, in Mijolla et al., 1987, pp. 96, 245–246).

Except that the love for what is new had indeed taken an entirely new turn! Everything suggests, on reading the first part of the text, that it is really a defence and illustration of Freudian psychoanalysis, torn between the enthusiastic admiration of some and the stubborn rejection of others. Freeing psychoanalysis from "primary misunderstandings" such as pansexualism, insisting on the emphasis placed by Freud on the conflict between the ego and instinctual drive life, in particular because of destructive tendencies, Müller-Braunschweig (1933) explains how the neurotic is a person "who has failed to resolve such conflicts, who has failed to submit his inner impulses to the ordering and dominant power of his spiritual self" (p. 97).

Explaining that the "repression" of this instinctual drive life and its proliferation in a zone henceforth inaccessible to the ego are the cause of the symptoms, he argues that the psychoanalyst helps the patient to resolve in a fully responsible manner what he has previously avoided, quoting Freud (1923[1922]): "It can more truly be said that analysis sets the neurotic free from the chains of his sexuality" (p. 252). To which he hastens to add that the criticism made against analysis of starting from "materialistic, non-spiritual assumptions" is unjustified: the ego synthesizes, regulates, balances the psychic economy and, in particular, tends to control the id, and is helped in this by the demands and the ideal values of the superego. It is a difficult fight in which the ego, quick to allow itself to be corrupted or seduced, always seems ready "for lazy compromises"; a "dramatic fight" between spiritual and instinctual drive forces, in which Müller-Braunschweig (1933) sees a "heroic image which can only honour [man]" (p. 97).

It is here, with heroism, that the first turn of the screw comes; because in this way he rehabilitated psychoanalysis against the accusation "of being disintegrative and un-German". On the contrary, it works, according to him, towards restoring an "intact, constructive and creative will". Its effect is therefore salutary, liberating and uplifting. And then comes the second turn of the screw. Of course, it must be admitted that psychoanalysis is a dangerous instrument in the hands of a destructive mind and that it is therefore of the utmost importance to be sure of the hand that is using it. But fundamentally, by "striving to transform those who lack enthusiasm and capability into capable and strong people, those who are inhibited in their instincts into instinctually assertive people, whimsical people estranged from life into human beings capable of looking reality in the face, those who are subjugated by their drive impulses into people who are able to dominate them, egotistical individuals, incapable of loving, into individuals capable of love and sacrifice, those who have lost interest in everything into people capable of serving a common cause" (ibid.), it [psychoanalysis] can, in the first instance, play a role in the formidable work of education, and serve "a heroic conception of life turned towards reality, something constructive, whose lines have just been newly established" (ibid.). Let us be clear: psychoanalysis can be German, German in the sense of the Nazi *Weltanschauung* with which it is, yes, quite able to collaborate.

How can one not think that, from the 1931 conference, when Müller-Braunschweig defended the role of *Weltanschauung* in action, love of reality and the possible "conformation" [Gestaltung] of humanity according to the structure of living matter, the heroism of German nationalism was already on the prowl, including in the form of sublimated tendencies and of the political and moral order? And particularly if we add that in 1935 this same Müller-Braunschweig wrote another text, this time entitled "Psychoanalyse und Deutschtum", [Psychoanalysis and Germanness"] (Müller-Braunschweig, 1935), in which he unambiguously proclaimed that, as the teaching staff of the Berlin Institute was of international composition, it had been "very difficult for the German members to give [this] Society a specifically German character" (p. 167). Hence his wish that psychoanalysis now be allowed to contribute to "German psychotherapy" and, perhaps more strangely, the apparent change of course; since, in addition to the pioneering character of psychoanalytic discoveries, Müller-Braunschweig this time valued psychoanalysis as a science: "a quest without concessions for truth and nothing else". The moral obligation of unshakeable firmness and disinterestedness would alone render the German people "authentic and valid services" (ibid.).

I say strangely, but the word is incorrect because, in truth, it is evident that the scientific *Weltanschauung* turned out over time to be the underlying basis of the supposed "rescue" of the Berlin Institute within the Göring Institute. And that is why we must speak here of a fight to the death which, moreover, was not visible. Thus, during the meeting that was held on 30 November 1935 in the presence of Jones – its urgency being linked in particular to the crisis situation created by the arrest of Edith Jakobson who was imprisoned for 28 months because she was Jewish and resisted the Nazis – we see that Boehm constantly insisted on the fact that psychoanalysis was not a *Weltanschauung* and that, for this very reason, the resignation of the German Psychoanalytic Society from the IPA would be like an admission of guilt: it would confirm the accusation made against psychoanalysis of being associated with some political "conception of the world". Hence the obvious but devious solution, namely, the wish that the "*nicht-Reichdeutsche*" members (non-German-Reich, euphemism for Jewish members without specifying their "Jewishness") should not be expelled but should "voluntarily resign".

We have two reports of this meeting. The first is a letter from Jones to Anna Freud (dated 2 December 1935, in Mijolla et al., 1987, pp. 114–115, 251–252), who writes of Müller-Braunschweig: "He flirts with the idea of combining a philosophy of psychoanalysis with a quasi-theological conception of National Socialist ideology, and as you can imagine, it really preoccupies him a lot" (translated from the French). But the man was not just a collaborator of the Nazi regime in his spare-time. If one examines the minutes of the same meeting written by Boehm on 4 December 1935 (ibid., pp. 116–127; 251–255), one sees that he was preoccupied by an identical concern: in a conversation with Werner Achelis and Kurt Gauger, psychotherapists and members of the SA (*Sturmabteilung*), he says that he had argued that psychoanalysis was not antagonistic to the Nazi

Weltanschauung. So that, when his interlocutors reminded him of the *"welt-anschauliche Reinigungsaktion"*, the "ideological cleansing action" carried out by the Gestapo, he paradoxically saw in the warning a real chance to avoid dissolution. The argument, in fact, is only valid if one understands that the strictly scientific orientation of psychoanalysis, its autonomy from any *Weltanschauung*, guaranteed above all that it had nothing to do with Marxism: evidence that was immediately brought forward by Boehm when he evoked the exclusion of Wilhelm Reich in 1933. To Gauger again, he stated that "he had never experienced any destructive influence of psychoanalysis on the love of the fatherland" (ibid., pp. 116–117; p. 253).

Likewise, in confidential talks with Professor von K., a Nazi dignitary and *Gauleiter* [district chief] of the Union for Struggle for German Culture,[3] about the future of the German Psychoanalytic Society, Boehm drew attention to Freud's anti-Marxist positions, which Müller-Braunschweig also highlighted without Eitingon's knowledge in the note written for the Nazi authorities. As a result, von K. backed Müller-Braunschweig's approach in front of Achelis, then in office at the Ministry of the Interior, with the effect that no action was taken against the DPG and that the Berlin Institute continued under his presidency and that of Boehm. Von K. undoubtedly did not have to regret his gesture if we consider the organization of the theoretical training programme proposed in 1939 by Müller-Braunschweig: in terms of love of the great whole, we find there the study of the "body-soul" unity, the theory of heredity and race, a course on biology and endocrinology, another on the differential diagnosis between organic and psychic disorders, and some lectures on "the maintenance of the hereditary patrimony" and "the psychology of races" (ibid., p. 149; 264).

Researchers unanimously point out that the separation of "German psychotherapy" from "Jewish psychology", which obviously includes "Jewish-Bolshevik" cultural theories, is essential. Gauger made this clear in May 1934, in his opening speech of the Nauheim Congress, one he gave in his uniform as an SA member (Gauger, 1934; cited by Nitzschke, 2003). The materialism of Freudian psychoanalysis was extremely close to the economic materialism of Marx; however, it was not necessary to discuss the value of Freud's "quasi-scientific" formulations; it was enough to ensure that they were not a weapon in the hands of the anti-religious communist organizations. The recommendation was therefore imposed that the members of the Institute should have made a "thorough scientific study" of Adolf Hitler's book, *Mein Kampf*.

What other path was there? Only one, that which was built on the deepest aspects of German culture, in which Freud was very much embedded and from which he had to be successfully extracted. M. H. Göring, on behalf of the Institute, made this very clear in the columns of the *Völkische Beobachter* in May 1939: "Someone like Freud as a Jew could not grasp the unconscious as such; he therefore had to try to explain it somehow in terms of the strict orientation of the natural sciences. A German doesn't need this at all. The purely instinctive rejection of Freud's doctrine, constructed from the history of the development of the sexual apparatus, began decades ago. We owe the knowledge of the forces that lie dormant in the unconscious to our very own Leibniz, to Dr. Carus, Goethe's friend, and to Feuchtersleben (1838) who, a hundred years before, in his little text "Zur Diätetik der Seele" [Dietetics of the *soul*] wrote: "The unconscious, the creative forces of feeling and fantasy, are the basis of life" (Mijolla et al., 1987, p. 141, 260). And on which subject did Göring speak? "*Weltanschauung* and psychotherapy".

Thus the strategy of maintaining the Göring Institute within the IPA may be seen as the Nazis' wish to obtain international recognition, even if this association was pure "Jewish-Marxist filth" (Nitzschke, 2003). With Jung, who became director of the *Zentralblatt für Psychotherapie* in 1933, all the currents previously excluded were now gathered together, while all Jews were excluded, and the Institute found its unity in the care given to the mental health of the *Volk*, the spearhead of the policy of war and conquest. It was therefore sufficient to integrate the work of the institute under one of the combative disciplines of the Reich. In this "new" discipline, however, the "values" of German culture weighed as heavily as the values of "science".

We have to appreciate the bottleneck in which German and Austrian analysts were caught. The dose of arsenic lay in the fact that the Nazi psychotherapists (but this went far beyond the circle of the Göring Institute) referred to what had been the in-between situation in which psychoanalysis was born: think for a moment of Freud's double heritage; on the one hand, he was inspired by Goethe's poem "*Natur*" and the primal phenomenon of creative energy to which it refers, and, on the other hand, he adhered to the "physicalist oath" of his masters, Brücke, Helmholtz and Du Bois-Reymond, who espoused a strictly scientific method based on the energy of forces revealed by physics; except that the Nazi psychotherapists shifted energetics into the field of "liberating the living forces" of individual egos. In the same vein, the struggle against "materialism" rejected any form of "economy", the status of "value" being purely and simply related to ideal values.

The discussion around value was all the more heated as it stood at a crossroads. On the one hand it implied what Freud understood by value in psychic dynamics – that is to say, the postulate of a qualitative "indifference" of drive energy, converted into "cathexis-value", which determines the "transvaluation" of psychic values. It was a question, then, of the kingpin of displacements, condensations and over-determinations at work in the structures of the unconscious. But the discussion also involved what Marxists were trying to develop at the junction of psychic value and value in a capitalist economy. And finally it implied the relationship between "value" and "norm" which, in a gradual slide, ended up becoming one – the reference to the moral and social norms of the people in combat being used to discredit the "materialists". It was therefore up to "relations to reality" to legitimize the twists that the regenerated scientificity of the Nazis praised. However, ever since *Group Psychology and the Analysis of the Ego* (Freud, 1921) we have known what happens to the confiscation of reality-testing, when the masses yielded the place of critical authority to the Führer, giving preference to what is unreal over what is real.

This is where the arsenic was poured, and its toxic effect was operative when the unreal was proclaimed as reality itself and psychoanalysis summoned as one of its guardians. Müller-Braunschweig completed the *Reichswart* text by defending analysis in the name of a heroic conception of life turned towards reality, putting it in the service of the "common" cause; he was no doubt hoping in doing so to echo the pages devoted by Freud (1920) to the reality principle in *Beyond the Pleasure Principle* – and in particular to the fact that the therapeutic effort makes an appeal to the reality principle to allow unpleasure to enter the field of consciousness, which is opposed by the resistance of the ego against the liberation of repressed impulses (ibid., p. 20). Unless, that is, Müller-Braunschweig sought to refer to the *31st Lecture* according to which the aim of psychoanalysis is "to strengthen the ego, to make it more independent of the superego, to widen its field of perception and enlarge its organization, so that it can appropriate fresh portions of the id" (Freud, 1933, p. 80); with the difference that, in the altered version of the draining of the Zuider Zee, the emphasis by Müller-Braunschweig was less on the relationship between the id and the ego than on the ego's contribution to strengthening the task of the *Volksgemeinschaft*, of the "community of the people" united by soil and blood, if its natural energy is organically channelled thanks to the new *Weltanschauung*.

Göring was right: Leibniz, Carus, and many, many others were employed in the machine for twisting words and thoughts, whilst – and this was the ultimate paradox – adaptation to reality was ultimately based on the "creative" and "combative" motive forces of the irrational. Heine had seen this coming as early as 1835 when, in *De L'Allemagne*, he wrote: "However, do not worry, my dear compatriots, the German revolution will be neither more debonair nor softer because Kant's critique of reason, Fichte's transcendent idealism and the philosophy of nature have preceded it. These doctrines have developed revolutionary forces which are only waiting for the right moment to explode and fill the world with dread and admiration". The most frightening will be the philosophers of nature, he continued, who, putting themselves in communication with the primal powers of the earth, evoking the forces of the whole of Germanic pantheism,

> will perpetrate in Germany a drama compared to which the French Revolution will be but an innocent idyll. It is true that today everything is calm, and if you see here and there a few men gesticulating a little sharply, do not think that these are the actors who will one day be in

charge of the performance. They are simply yapping little dogs flying around the empty arena, barking and baring their teeth, before the hour when the troop of gladiators must enter who will fight to the death.

(Heine, 1835, translated from the French)

This is what Thomas Mann affirmed when he denounced the Nazi desire "to break the primacy of reason and to re-establish in triumph, in their primitive vital law, the forces of darkness and abysmal depths, the instinctive and the irrational" (Mann, 1929, p. 127, translated from the French]).

If, between the irrational foundations of our being and the rational treatment of this instinctual dynamism, psychoanalysis was in the eyes of Thomas Mann in a position to oppose the contemporary prostration in the face of the demonic forces in the psyche, it is because the humanism which it conveys is based, according to him, on "scientific exactitude" "modesty", and a "taste for understatement" (Mann, 1936, p. 115).

But what exact knowledge was there in 1933, or in 1936? Let us remember that Achelis, author of the text "Das Problem des Traumes" [The problem of dreams] which he sent to Freud[4] – earning him a solid clarificatory statement on the "metaphysical nuisance" and a severe lesson in Latin translation – was not only involved in the Göring Institute but also in teaching at the polyclinic of Berlin. Let us add that, among his objectives, the taking into account of the healthy instinct, the fight against the "ghost" of reason as a single principle, and "the research and development of the forces of nature in us through depth psychology", in short the alliance between nature and culture integrated into "the organization" and "psychic conduct" were to be powerful weapons in the fight against the damage to civilization (Roelcke, 1996, pp. 6–8). We then see how Hitler's absolutely constant appeal to instinctual drive activity faced psychoanalysts with an even more dizzying hijacking than the purity of the race; the entanglement of civilizing values in biological material was backed up by a scientific discourse presented in the garb of the German academicism of the time. The interweaving of pan-Germanism and anti-Semitism, the knotting of raciology and archaeology in the search for "Indo-Germans" (the Nordic race), the summoning of linguistics under the rule of anthropologists and "geneticists", the pure and simple identification of race and culture by the yardstick of the "identity" of the Aryans all lead, under the pen of Alfred Rosenberg (1982/1930), in *The Myth of the Twentieth Century*, to the wish for the constitution of an *organic racial state*. Leibniz, Herder and Nietzsche, but Kant as well, are invoked by him, while Hitler continuously states that the masses are a part of nature, and their feelings its driving force. But feeling is not enough, nor is the inner will. It is only when the ideal push for independence and the aspiration for freedom are given the form of an "organization" that the ideals of *Weltanschauung* can be realized. Organization and the organic are therefore necessarily confused, while the State is the incarnation of the people's "self-preservative drive", this being based on the participation of man "in the great totality of life": acting thus therefore implies respecting the laws of life (Graupner, 1941; cited by Chapoutot, 2014, pp. 37, 66, 118–121).

There is a curious resonance here with "the totality of the world and of life" as Müller-Braunschweig called it in his conference of 1930, if we think that for everyone, and Himmler in particular, "the people are a living, organic unit" whose development dominates the political scene and decision-making. Law and "the feeling of what is just", its correlate, simply serve this organic dimension, the "biological unity of everything" requiring that we give up separating culture and the *bios*.[5] Together, they proceed from a conscious thought of "community" – a universalism revisited and which is claimed to be legitimized by Kant himself, in the words of Otto Dietrich, Secretary of State at the Ministry of Propaganda. This was a Kant who could no longer differentiate between general legislation – that which Eichmann appealed to in Jerusalem – and universal legislation, and who could no longer distinguish between a will subjectively subject to an empirical maxim aimed at immediate action, and free will instituting moral law as universal legislation. A Kant who, albeit "Nazified", nevertheless resisted.

Notes

1 On the details of the *Realpolitik* led by Jones during these years, see the article by Steiner (2011).
2 Schultz-Hencke was excluded at the same time as the DPG. Regine Lockot strongly underlines the aberrant nature of these decisions, since Müller-Braunschweig had collaborated with the Nazis in an infinitely more active way than Schultz-Hencke, but Freud's criticism before the war was decisive after the war, it seems. The literature on this point is very abundant.
3 Boehm mentions this in his account of the "events of 1933–1934" (Mijolla et al., 1987, *Ici, la vie . . .* pp. 99–109, 246–249).
4 To Achelis, who accused him of having neglected philosophy by asserting the sexual source of dreams, Freud replied: "You translate *'acheronta movebo'* as 'moving the citadels of the earth'. But it means 'to stir up the underworld'. . . . The wish rejected by the higher mental agencies (the repressed dream wish) stirs up the mental underworld (the unconscious) in order to get a hearing. What do you find "Promethean" about this?" (letter dated 30 January 1927, in Freud (1960, pp. 374–375).
5 "The closer a law comes to the natural order, the better. It is only in this way that it can fulfil its role and illustrate the sacred laws of nature and of life" wrote K. Schmidt-Klevenow (German jurist and head of the Waffen-SS), quoted by Chapoutot (2017, p. 186).

References

Aichhorn, Th. (2007). "No provocations and even fewer concessions" (panel at the 45th International IPA Congress in Berlin, 25–28 July 2007 on the theme "Remembering, repeating and working through in Psychoanalysis and Culture today").

Bögels, G.F. (ed.).(2017). *Sigmund Freud- Briefe an Jeanne Lampl-de Groot 1921–1939* [Sigmund Freud, Letters to Jeanne Lampl-de Groot 1921–1939]. Gissen: Psychosozial Verlag.

Chapoutot, J. (2014). *La loi du sang. Penser et agir en nazi*. Paris: Gallimard.

Cocks, G. (1992). Repressing, remembering, working through: German psychiatry, psychotherapy, psychoanalysis, and the 'missed resistance' in the third reich. *The Journal of Modern History*, 64: 204–216.

Fallend, K., Nitzschke, B. (eds.). (2002).*Der "Fall" Wilhelm Reich* [The Reich "case"]. Giessen: Psychosozial Verlag.

Feuchtersleben, E. von (1838). *Diätetik der Seele* [Dietetics of the *Soul*]. Vienna: C. Armbruster.

Freud, A., Aichhorn, T. (2012). *Die Psychoanalyse kann nur dort gedeihen, wo Freiheit der Gedanken herrscht, Briefwechsel 1921–1949* [Psychoanalysis Can Only Prosper Where There is Freedom of Thought], edited and commented on by Th. Aichhorn.Frankfurt: Brandes & Apsel.

Freud, E.L (ed.). (1960). *The Letters of Sigmund Freud, 1873–1939*, trans. T. and J. Stern. New York: Basic Books.

Freud, S. (1921). *Group Psychology and the Analysis of the Ego. S.E.* 18. London: Hogarth, pp. 65–144.

Freud, S. (1923[1922]). *Two Encyclopaedia Articles. S.E.* 18. London: Hogarth, pp. 235–259.

Freud, S. (1933). *New Introductory Lectures on Psycho-analysis. S.E.* 22. London: Hogarth, pp. 1–182.

Friedrich, V. (1989). From psychoanalysis to the 'great treatment': Psychoanalysts under National Socialism. *Political Psychology*, 10(1): 3–26.

Gauger, K. (1934). Psychotherapie und politisches Weltbild. *Zeitschrift für Psychotherapie*, 7: 158–168.

Graupner, H. (1941). Die Einheit alles Lebendigen. In: *Das naturgesetzliche Weltbild der Gegenwart*, L. Stengel von Rutkowski (ed.), pp. 271–301.

Heine, H. (1835). *De l'Allemagne, Œuvres V.* Eugène Renduel: Paris, 1835/1853, pp. 180–183 [consulted on line: https://archive.org/streamdelallemagne05heingo og#page/n195/mode/2up].

Lockot, R. (2003). *Die Reinigung der Psychoanalyse. Die Deutsche Psychoanalytische Gesellschaft im Spiegel von Dokumenten und Zeitzeugen (1933–1951).* Giessen: Psychosozial Verlag.

Mann, T. (1929). Freud dans l'histoire de la pensée moderne. *Sur le mariage. Lessing, Freud et la pensée moderne.* Mon temps. Paris: Aubier, 1970, pp. 108–149 [for the English translation see Mann(1933) Freud's position in the history of modern thought, trans. H.T. Lowe-Porter, *The Criterion: A Literary Review* 12 (49) (July), 549–570].

Mann, T. (1936). Freud and the future. *The International Journal of Psychoanalysis*, 1956, 37: 106–115.

Mijolla, A. (de) Renz,V., Brech, K., Friedrich, V., Hermanns, I.M., Julich, D. (eds.). (1987). *"Ici, la vie continue de manière fort surprenante . . .", Contribution à l'histoire de la psychanalyse en Allemagne.* Paris: Association internationale d'histoire de la psychanalyse.

Mijolla, A. de.(ed.). (2013). *Dictionnaire internationale de psychanalyse*, revised and enlarged edition. Paris: Fayard/Pluriel.

Mitscherlich, A., Mielke, F. (1949). *Wissenschaft Ohne Menschlichkeit: Medizinische und Eugenische Irrwege Unter Diktatur Bürokratie und Krieg*. Heidelberg: Lambert Schneider.

Müller-Braunschweig, C. (1933). Psychoanalyse und Weltanschauung. *Reichswart, Organe de l'Alliance Raciste Européenne*, 22 October, 1933. Also in: Mijolla et al., 1987, pp. 98, 245–246.

Müller-Braunschweig, C. (1935). Psychoanalyse und Deutschtum. Taken from *Nationalsozialistische Idee und Psychoanalyse*, published in Mijolla *et al.*, 1987, pp. 167–270.

Nitzschke, B. (2003). Psychoanalysis and National Socialism. Banned or brought into conformity? Break or continuity? *International Forum of Psychoanalysis*, 12: 98–108.

Roazen, P. (2003). *Cultural Foundations of Political Psychology*. New Brunswick & London: Transaction Publishers.

Roelcke, V. (1996). 'Zivilisationsschäden am Menschen' und ihre Behandlung: Das Projekt einer 'seelischen Gesundheitsfuhrung' im Nationalsozialismus. *Mediz-inhistorisches Journal*, 31: 3–48.

Schröter, M. (ed.).(2009). *Eitingon,Correspondance 1906–1939*, ed. S. Freud-M. Paris: Hachette.

Steiner, R. (2011). In all questions, my interest is not in the individual people but in the analytic movement as a whole. Itwill be hard enough here in Europe in the times to come to keep it going. After all, we are just a handful of people who really have that in mind. *International Journal of Psychoanalysis*, 92(3): 505–591.

7   Hartmann: *logos* against *bios*

Was Adorno wrong when, in 1927, he saw in psychoanalysis "a sharp weapon . . . against every attempt to create a metaphysics of the instincts and to deify dull organic nature"? (Müller-Doohm, 2005, p. 105).[1]

No, if you consider the battle that was waged by the analysts of the day on the side of *logos* against the onslaught of *bios*; and yes, judging by the price paid to pull psychoanalysis out of the theoretical ambush represented by the entanglement of the living with the question of values. By the living, I mean energetics, that is to say the drive energy which, as Hartmann (1948) was to emphasize in the immediate post-war period, has nothing to do with the "*élan vital*" and which, under Freud's pen, was only an "operational concept" (p. 373). He then openly regrets that the English translation makes no difference between *Instinkt*, as used in biology, and *Trieb*, with its correlates in the form of the drive reserve of the id, the self-regulating systems of the mental apparatus, the role of self-preservation and the diversification of the drives linked to the differentiation of the agencies.

In truth, in "Psychoanalysis und *Weltanschauung*" Hartmann (1933), taking up again Freud's *35th Lecture,* was fighting on two fronts: on the one hand, the rejection of any "psychoanalytic *Weltanschauung*" amounted to a refusal to include analysis in any political orientation whatsoever; and, on the other, if one ventured to speak of "norms", these had to be rigorously restricted to what can be scientifically demonstrated insofar as the very notion of *Weltanschauung* involves the irrationality of personal positions and judgments. It was therefore more necessary than ever to question the formation of value systems: not only from a global point of view, as Nietzsche (2010) had previously done in *On the Genealogy of Morals,* but from the point of view of the individual ontogenesis of morality, with the complex interplay of repression, reaction formations, identification and the superego.

This is precisely where the problem lies. In the "battle of opinions" that was then raging, in the midst of what Hartmann modestly called "the current transitory setbacks" of psychoanalysis, the question was one of knowing what place could be ascribed to the rational elucidation of psychic life. Of course, he conceded, every man advances in the search

DOI: 10.4324/9781003301660-8

for facts with a "pre-scientific image of the world", the empirical position being initially impregnated with the conceptions of the moment, the
preconceived expectations and subjective positions which nourish strictly
scientific research. The problem raised by such interference is all the more
acute in that *logos*, that is to say the very foundation of psychoanalysis, can
turn out to be dependent on ideological systems. This was the reason why
psychoanalysis was being criticized on all sides for having only one purpose, that of devaluing things of the mind out of revenge on the grounds
that it was the product of conservative or revolutionary *Weltanschauungen* in turn. However, describing the "genesis" of the determining factors
of a moral position, that is to say their modes of construction, can in no
way be equated with the negative or positive evaluation of the values that
it implements. Psychoanalysis only provides tools and not a diagram of
values; tools which also make it possible to ask questions concerning, for
example, practical ethics in pedagogy, or those relating to social problems.
But what *needs* to be done is not within its purview.

It is as if Hartmann were responding point by point to the suspect ambi-
guities of Müller-Braunschweig. This response becomes even more severe
when Hartmann returns to the late Nietzsche and his reference to "the ethics of vital values". By considering that the truth or falsity of a judgment is
determined by its biologically inhibiting or facilitating effect, the thinker
gave supremacy to the laws of *bios* over the laws of *logos*. "Freud", Hartmann insisted, "is most strongly opposed to this aspect of Nietzschean
philosophy – such thoughts, such as contempt for reason and idolatry of
instinct, have become very common today. He does not simply approve
of life, but a certain orientation in the development of the living" (p. 105),
that is to say what is stated in the words "where id was, there ego shall
be".[2] The ego, that is to say, precisely the element in the human being that
is the seat of the imperatives of *logos*, and not simply the organ of energetic
action; the agency that, from this point of view, ensures the possible con-
cordance of representations with the real outside world.

There is no room, therefore, for intuition, metaphysical solutions, relativism or scepticism. The sole value system is that of *ratio*; ethics is related
to the values of knowledge and the ideal position is that of the primacy
of intelligence. By defending *logos* against the vital forces, Hartmann was
attacking head-on the aberrations in respect of the biological foundations
of the drive: either we let it drift towards instinct with its biologico-racial
component, or we apply the word "scientism" to it, which is intended to
refer Freud's scientific *Weltanschauung* to the "narrow views" of an out-
dated nineteenth century.

It should be noted that as early as 1928, in "Psychoanalyse und Wertproblem" [Psychoanalysis and the problem of values], Hartmann (1928)
posed the problem of the ways that subjectivity, contaminated by desire,
can confuse the correct evaluation of the data of reality. The forefront of
the struggle at that time concerned the distinction between a scientific

position and the evaluation of ethical goals. But in 1933, the front was, as it were, split in two, as if, in addressing Müller-Braunschweig, he had to respond, in anticipation, to Husserl's (1970) criticism that the cause of the failure of a rational culture lies in the swallowing up of rationalism by "objectivism", which necessarily provokes hostility to the spirit and barbarity (p. 299). Hartmann (1927) had, however, already unravelled this question in *Die Grundlagen de Psychoanalyse* [The Fundamentals of Psychoanalysis],[3] when he became an informed reader of phenomenology and defended the distinction between immediate knowledge, acquired by means of lived experience, and knowledge constructed thanks to the extraction of causal laws, deduced from recurrences. He then deepened the distinction between "psychological understanding", based on subjective experience and the meaning attributed to it by consciousness, and "psychoanalytic knowledge", implying the need to take into account mechanisms which alone can explain the fact that meaning escapes subjective consciousness. This distinction, which aimed at linking analysis to the field of natural sciences, did not, however, ignore the contradiction inherent in the notion of explanation in psychoanalysis: specific to knowledge, it nevertheless requires time for understanding the other person, which cannot be dissociated from empathetic perception.

But in 1933, the tone changed towards those who were not terrified by new views on reality, who did not tremble at unknown abysses and who advocated a *Weltanschauung* that opened out on to "a sincere love of reality". As Johann Chapoutot (2017) writes, they clearly "distinguished between law (*Gesetz*), a written, abstract and dead norm, a heritage of Jewish formalism, and law (*Recht*), which is living, dictated by nature, always oral, instinctual and concrete" (pp. 84–85). And they made the distinction all the more energetically since, on this horizon where norm and life come together, *Vernunft* (reason) and *Intellekt* or, worse, *Intellektualismus* must also be held in respect. "If the Enlightenment inaugurated the time of debate, the anti-Enlightenment sanctioned that of combat" (ibid).

One thing is certain: it was in this context of combat that Hartmann put forward the notion of the "ego's adaptation to reality", presented not as a value in itself, but as "a means to an end". What end? One that should make it possible to extract the ego from instinctual drive activity. One that ensures that, once the development of the child is completed, it will have the means to fight against the powerful attraction of fantasy and the ideal, and their narcissistic benefits – the same attraction that Freud describes with regard to the power exerted by the Führer over the masses. One that, despite the constant threat of hallucinatory fulfilment, and despite the propensity for denial, sustains the capacities for reality-testing. "Ego psychology and the problem of adaptation", a lecture given by Hartmann in 1937 to the Vienna Psychoanalytic Society four years later (that is to say, very shortly before his exile), perfectly explains the dilemma (Hartmann, 1939). Although Freud started by building his theory of the psychical apparatus on "biological" concepts (ibid., p. 77 (Hartmann's inverted commas)), the consequences of this usage could not be equated with an adaptation to reality as conceived for example by Darwin: psychoanalysis does not speak to us of natural "selection" (which was what the racial biology of the time was constantly talking about), but rather about *alloplastic* or *autoplastic* transformations that allow humans to modify either their environment or themselves in their adaptation to this environment. Furthermore, the Freudian model emphasizes the real danger of the drives coming from the id, especially if one includes the role of the death drive in intrapsychic economics – which Hartmann did. The fact that the compulsion to repeat plays a role in adaptation in the case of traumatic neuroses, and that the development of the superego makes it possible to overcome the internal danger, does not tell us which mechanism, in the struggle to maintain an internal equilibrium, enables the ego and thought to accept unpleasure. In Hartmann's eyes, the hypothesis of postponing pleasure and obtaining it later by other means, as well as the Ferenczian hypothesis of masochism, are insufficient to explain the acceptance of reality and the cohort of deprivations and disappointments that it inflicts.

The question therefore that haunts Hartmann is that the differentiation id/ego-superego, owing to the very fact that the superego has its roots in infantile experience – and the reference to Freud here is solid – can at any time lead to phenomena of "de-differentiation". We then witness totally "regressive" forms of adaptation to reality, driven by affects and judgments of reality that are put in the service of destruction – Hartmann refers to the "free aggression" which is linked to the death drive by Freud. The status of consciousness and the stability of the ego, preconditions for thought, must therefore be reconsidered in the light of the relationship between the death drive and desexualized libido concerning which we discover that, from being an opponent of the id, it can become its ally.

Whatever criticisms one makes of what was to become ego psychology, it is clear that the orientation of one of its founders was determined by a crucial question in the turmoil of dark times: how could one ensure that reason, logic, a system of thought capable of holding fast the links of causality, a line of reflection seeking the path of objectivity, in short "the primacy of intelligence", regained their dignity and, above all, their supports in the psychic life of individuals? At a time when "the dictatorship of reason" was pushing for a theoretical shift towards strengthening the ego and its autonomy in relation to the drives, the political disaster of triumphant Nazism was bearing down with a weight that I had not previously suspected. It is in this sense that I see here one of the most formidable episodes of what Nazism succeeded in doing to psychoanalysis.

This is especially so since psychoanalysts, and intellectuals more generally, try to think of the cultural ruin in terms of "mass psychosis". This was a term used by Einstein in July 1932, in his letter to Freud inviting him to reflect on the question "Why war?: "Is it possible", he asks Freud, "to control man's mental evolution so as to make him proof against the psychoses of hate and destructiveness?" (Freud, 1933b [1932], p. 201). It was a term that Freud in turn used in the *35th Lecture* (1933a, p. 160, 16), that is to say, at the same date, since, according to Strachey, this last lecture took place at the end of May 1932. The use he makes of it is in line with the divergence he establishes between the conceptions of the world and the scientific position. The former meet an emotional need and are made from the dough of illusion, fuelled by unconscious wishes. Even if wish-fulfilment undoubtedly contributes to artistic achievements and to the creation of religious and philosophical systems, in no case can the "transference" of psychic demands to the sphere of scientific knowledge be allowed. "For", Freud continues, "this would be to lay open the paths which lead to psychosis – whether to individual psychosis or group psychosis" (ibid., p. 160). And he adds that the truth cannot be tolerant, that it admits of no compromises or limitations. Indeed the consequences of this psychosis have nothing to do with "the harmless dream psychosis", which is a momentary turning away from the outside world. It results from the way in which the subject turns away from reality, either because the repressed unconscious has become too powerful and crushes the conscious portion attached to reality, or because reality has become so intolerably painful that the threatened ego rushes headlong, in a desperate revolt, into the arms of unconscious drive activity.

As Jacques André (1998) has pointed out, the notion of "group delusion" had appeared previously in *Civilization and its Discontents* (Freud, 1930) – a single occurrence of the term, which takes up what Freud had put forward ever since "Narcissism: an introduction" (1914) and "Instincts and their vicissitudes" (1915) on the subject of narcissism and distress associated with the loss of the love object. "The ego hates, abhors . . . all objects which are a source of unpleasurable feeling for it" (p. 138), which is why what is bad, what is alien to the ego, what is external to it, are at first identical for the original pleasure-ego. Thus, the psychic act of "spitting out" is the precursor of negation, before language has asserted its capacity to fragment instinctual drive charges into small quantities (Freud, 1925, p. 237). But, according to Jacques André, Freud takes a further step in *Civilization and its Discontents* when he attempts to grasp in the collective order the combination of unlimited narcissism, the associated hatred and the transformation of infantile distress into omnipotence. "The misfortunes of civilization", he writes, "those that Freud knew, and even more those that followed, give the expression "pure pleasure-ego" its full *political* significance" (André, 1998, p. ix). Purity, purification and purge speak of primary hatred, which is no longer a matter only of sadistic-anal aggression; they belong to the quest for an original unlimitedness, a flawless narcissism, more than to the sphere of castration anxiety. In *Civilization and its Discontents*, Freud makes guilt a "topographical variety of anxiety" (Freud, 1930, p. 135; André, 1998, pp. xvii–xiii), thereby situating the child upstream in relation to oedipal guilt. He is a child in distress, threatened not with castration but with losing the love of the all-powerful protector; a child who will rush into the arms of the Führer who is able to delude him with phantasmagorical promises and appease his desperate revolt against the world.

Does this mean, however, that sadism is now out of play? Not at all, judging by the discussion conducted by Freud (1926) in *Inhibitions, Symptoms and Anxiety*, when he returns to the relationship between aggressiveness, regression and the death drive: "The aggressive impulse flows mainly from the destructive instinct; and we have always believed that, in a neurosis, it is against the demands of the libido and not against those of any other instinct that the ego is defending itself" (ibid., p. 124). In other words, while regression and its points of fixation had hitherto been identified in terms of libidinal stages (oral or sadistic-anal), it was necessary, with the introduction of the death drive, to take into account the fact that sadism now appeared as the representative of the instinctual drive opposed to Eros. Would this explode the previous construction of successive libidinal phases? Freud answers in the negative, arguing that there are no pure instinctual drive impulses, that the two impulses, libidinal and aggressive, are mixed in various proportions, and therefore, that the destructive sadistic cathexis can also be treated as a libidinal cathexis.

The sadism of the superego was its beneficiary, and was undoubtedly closely linked with social ferocity when it was not individuals but men in crowds who subsequently shared the psychotic delusion that had become a mass doctrine. Certainly, "each one of us behaves in some one respect like a paranoiac, corrects some aspect of the world which is unbearable to him by the construction of a wish and introduces this delusion into reality" (Freud, 1930, p. 81). But, as a rule, the delusional subject does not find a companion in misfortune with whom to share the delusion. However, when "the attempt to procure a certainty of happiness and a protection against suffering through a delusional remoulding of reality is made by a considerable number of people in common" (ibid.), then mass delusions – of which religion is one model – intimidates reason, and even destroys all powers of criticism.

Religion maybe, but not just religion. So when Robert Wälder (1935) wrote in the autumn of 1934, "Etiology and course of mass psychoses" with an appendix "On the historical situation of the present",[4] he placed in the forefront the desertion by the ego and the superego from the role they play in reality-testing, the defusion [*Entmischung*] of Eros and the death drive, the "total splitting" of love and aggression with the disappearance of ambivalence, the role of projection and delusion, and the libidinal satisfaction of uninhibited hatred. Wälder draws on *Group Psychology and the Analysis of the Ego* – not on *Civilization and its Discontents* – and on a careful study of the crisis of capitalism in the 1930s. After studying the eruption and development of psychotic positions in healthy individuals, and in particular the fact that mass psychosis protects them from insanity, his conclusion concerns the orientation of Western civilization, which, through technical progress and all forms of mechanization, has systematically turned to "alloplastic" adaptation programmes. What becomes of the autoplastic ego resources of these citizens remains an open question.

Hartmann quotes Wälder, just as he quotes Karl Mannheim on the conflict between the rationality of production mechanisms and individual rationality, to stress how the huge growth of industrialization had contributed to the expansion of the irrationality of the masses. In the immediate post-war period, Ernst Simmel also took up the notion of mass psychosis in his contribution to the colloquium on anti-Semitism in San Francisco. Unlimited destructiveness, in line with a frenzy that totally denies reality, is a syndrome which in psychiatry is known as the paranoid form of schizophrenia – the difference being that in this case the anti-Semite does not feel ill. On the contrary, his anti-Semitism gives him a considerable advantage: his "inflated" ego feels "superior" by virtue of belonging to the community of non-Jews (Simmel, 1944, p. 58ff).

Admittedly, they do not feel ill. But the loss of reality indicates that the pathology is the result of a rupture with the outside world, the latter restricting itself to the group of "like-minded" people, who together "have autocratically created a new world, external and internal at the same time", a world "built according to the desires of the id". How can we not think about the impact of the texts, "Neurosis and psychosis" (1924a) and "The loss of reality in neurosis and psychosis" (1924b), written by Freud immediately after *The Ego and the Id*? These texts are rarely cited, but they are present when it comes to the creation of a "neo-reality". The expression of the rebellion of the id against the outside world – or, adds Freud, "if one prefers, its incapacity to adapt itself to the exigencies of reality, to, *Ananké* [Necessity]" (1924b, p. 185) – appears only in the differentiation between autoplastic modification and alloplastic modification. In this reference to the Freudian texts, one aspect remains in the dark: the psychotic task of creating new perceptions corresponding to the new reality; is not the world of fantasy the storehouse from which the material or the models are taken for the construction of the new reality, generating illusions of memory and hallucinations?

In the dark, maybe. But everything suggests that, faced with the delusional wall of the time, the inclination which tended towards a theory giving precedence to the ego and its faculties for judging reality was rooted in the fight to the death in which *Weltanschauung*, the very word of *Weltanschauung*, had de facto become the theatre.

Mein Kampf was published in 1925 and 1926. It was stated very clearly there what the National Socialist movement meant by drive, biology, selection and value. "Its publication", writes Victor Klemperer (2013), "literally fixed the essential features of its language" (p. 19). In addition, intuition, the obviousness of affect, melded into the "feeling of truth" of the masses, in short, everything that "organically" justified the unity of the "national community" placed "organic growth" inherited from romanticism in the forefront. It was all this, made up of the constant mixture of three currents – biologization, technicization and myth-ification – which entered individual psychic lives by way of the com-mon language. And it was in this context that *Weltanschauung* took on an everyday colour, familiar, intimate and public all at the same time; that it took the place of philosophy, which was now ignored; and that "intelligence" become despised (p. 165). And further that "system" was replaced by "organization" – the foundations of the latter being "organic truth" which as opposed to logical truth (pp. 103–104). A truth that was contained in the first religious myth, the mysterious centre of the soul of the people. The very notion of *Reich*, writes Klemperer, became a *Weltan-schauungsgedanke* [ideological thinking], which as such "transcends real-ity" (p. 120).

So, with the LTI, the Language of the Third Reich, the *Weltanschauung* really changed meaning at the same time as reality was becoming the product of old words suddenly endowed with new meanings. Psycho-analysis, faced with the metamorphosis of its own working tool, did not escape this deleterious effect. As for what happened to the defence and illustration of the scientific values of psychoanalysis, once the Jewish ana-lysts had gone into exile in the United States, we learned about this on discovering the fate that they suffered at the hands of the logicians and positivist philosophers. Everything suggests that Ernst Nagel (1959) and Arthur Danto (1959) – architects of the symposium held in New York in 1958 under the title "Psychoanalysis, scientific method and philosophy" – had no idea of the struggle to the death which these Freudian psycho-analysts had survived.[5] Calling on psychoanalysis to explain itself over the causal "illusions" maintained by its pseudo-logic and its instinctual drive metaphysics, concluding that it was incapable of claiming the slight-est scientificity, "demonstrating" the illegitimacy of statements incapable of squaring with reality, they did not even consider in their debate with Hartmann the fact that he had experienced the very worst of logical confu-sion, of distortion of reality, of the disorder of instinctual drive processes that had become a support for delusion.

In 2002, the debate had not yet been settled when Yecheskiel Cohen (2002), a member of the Israeli Psychoanalytic Society, spoke as part of a panel organized by the European Federation of Psychoanalysis on the topic: "Psychoanalysis in Germany after the Shoah". He contested with the utmost vigour the idea that one could consider the position taken by Müller-Braunschweig as "courageous, and even admirable"[6] – a man who, in a letter to Jones, had demanded in 1936 that the Jewish psychoanalysts who had fled Berlin should pay their outstanding membership fees to the German Psychoanalytic Society. Quoting Anna Antonovsky (1988), Cohen pointed out that when Nazi Germany was defeated, Müller-Braunschweig made sure he persuaded the IPA that the main question was not the Göring Institute, but rather the disagreement with the "new psychoanalysis" of Schultz-Hencke, the man whose exclusion Freud had demanded in 1933, in return for the acceptance of Boehm and Müller-Braunschweig as head of the DPG. Thus Müller-Braunschweig was reinstated in the IPA, along with a few colleagues, dropping Schultz-Hencke not only because he was a neo-Freudian – which he was, being considered today by some to be a pioneer of "empirical psychoanalysis" – but also because he was the sole agent of the grievance – which he was not, many others having collaborated as much, if not more, with the Nazis.

Was it along this path – that of a so-called orthodoxy validated by Freud – that the "new psychoanalysis" became involved in the debate without anyone noticing it? At the end of the war, in the general chaos, it certainly appeared in turns as traitor and victim.[7]

Notes

1 Extract from Adorno's habilitation thesis, completed in 1927.
2 Hartmann's allusion probably relates to texts such as paragraph 4 of *Beyond Good and Evil*: "The falseness of an opinion is not for us any objection to it: it is here, perhaps, that our new language sounds most strangely. The question is, how far an opinion is life-furthering, life-preserving, species-preserving, perhaps species-rearing" (Nietzsche, 2003/1886, p. 14).
3 See in particular chapter I [Psychoanalysis as a science of nature] and chapter III [Understanding and Explaining], in particular pp. 54–58 [consulted online].
4 Consulted online. It was initially a memoir that came within the same international framework, the League of Nations, as "Why war?"
5 These are the debates that took place around H. Hartmann's lecture "Psychoanalysis as a Scientific Theory". On this point, I would like to refer the reader to my book, *Psychoanalysis, Apathy, and the Postmodern Patient* (Kahn, 2018)
6 It was about Ludger Hermann's intervention at the fiftieth anniversary of the Deutsche Psychoanalytische Vereinigung (DPV).
7 On this point, see G. Cocks (2001) and the antagonistic positions of E. and J. Goggin (2001).

References

André, J. (1998). *Préface à Le malaise dans la culture*. Paris: Presses Universitaires de France, pp. v–xviii.
Antonovsky, A.M. (1988). Aryan analysts in Nazi Germany: Questions of adaptation, desymbolization, and betrayal. *Psychoanalysis and Contemporary Thought*, 11: 213–231.
Chapoutot, J. (2017). *La Révolution culturelle nazie*. Paris: Gallimard.

Cocks, G. (2001). The devil and the details: Psychoanalysis in the third reich. *Psychoanalytical Review*, 88(2): 225–244.

Cohen, Y. (2002). Panel on psychoanalysis after the shoah. European psychoanalytic federation. *Bulletin*, 56. www.epf-fep.eu/eng/article/contribution-to-the-panel-on-psychoanalysis-in-germany-after-the-shoa

Danto, A. (1959). Meaning and theoretical terms in psychoanalysis. In: *Psychoanalysis, Scientific Method and Philosophy*, S. Hook (ed.). New York: University Press, pp. 314–318.

Freud, S. (1914). *Narcissism: An Introduction. S.E.* 14. London: Hogarth, pp. 73–102.

Freud, S. (1915). *Instincts and Their Vicissitudes. S.E.* 14. London: Hogarth, pp. 117–140.

Freud, S. (1924a). *Neurosis and Psychosis.S.E.* 19. London: Hogarth, pp. 149–153.

Freud, S. (1924b). *The Loss of Reality in Neurosis and Psychosis. S.E.* 19. London: Hogarth, pp. 183–187.

Freud, S. (1925). *Negation. S.E.* 19. London: Hogarth, pp. 235–239.

Freud, S. (1926). *Inhibitions, Symptoms and Anxiety. S.E.* 20. London: Hogarth, pp. 87–174.

Freud, S. (1930). *Civilization andIts Discontents. S.E.* 21. London: Hogarth, pp. 57–146.

Freud, S. (1933a). *New Introductory Lectures on Psycho-analysis. S.E.* 22. London: Hogarth, pp. 1–182.

Freud, S. (1933b [1932]). *Why War? (Einstein and Freud). S.E.* 22. London: Hogarth, pp. 199–215.

Goggin, E.J. (2001). *Death of a "Jewish Science": Psychoanalysis in the Third Reich.* West Lafayette, Indiana: Purdue University Press.

Hartmann, H. (1927). *Die Grundlagen de Psychoanalyse* [The Fundamentals of Psychoanalysis]. Leipzig: Thieme.

Hartmann, H. (1928). Psychoanalyse und Wertproblem. *Imago*, XIV: 421–440 [consulted online].

Hartmann, H. (1933). Psychoanalyse und Weltanschauung. *Psychoanalytische Bewegung*, V, pp. 416–429; reprinted in *Almanach für Psychoanalyse*, Vienna, 1936, pp. 96–113.

Hartmann, H. (1939). Ichpsychologie und Anpassungsproblem [Ego psychology and the problem of adaptation]. *Internationale Zeitschrift für Psychoanalyse und Imago*, XXIV(1–2): 62–135. Consulted online.

Hartmann, H. (1948). Comments on the psychoanalytic theory of instinctual drives. *Psychoanalytic Quarterly*, 17: 368–388.

Husserl, E. (1970). The crisis of European humanity and philosophy. In: *The Crisis of European Sciences and Transcendental Phenomenology*, trans. D. Carr. Evanston: Northwestern University Press.

Kahn, L. (2014). *Le Psychanalyste apathique et le patient postmoderne.* Paris: l'Olivier.

Klemperer, V. (2013 [1957]). *The Language of the Third Reich. LTI – Lingua Tertii Imperii: A Philologist's Notebook*, trans. M. Brady. London: Bloomsbury.

Le Rider, J. (2007). *L'Allié incommode.* In: *La Psychanalyse révisée*, T.W. Adorno (ed.). Paris: L'Olivier.

Nagel, E. (1959). Methodological issues in psychoanalytical theory. In: *Psychoanalysis, Scientific Method and Philosophy*, S. Hook (ed.). New York: NY University Press, pp. 38–56.

Nietzsche, F. (2010/1887). *On the Genealogy of Morals*, trans. Ian Johnston. Arlington, VA: Richer Resources Publications.

Nietzschze, F. (2003/1886). *Beyond Good and Evil.* Fairfield, IA: Ist World Library.

Simmel, E. (1944). Antisemitismus und Massen-Psychopathologie. In: *Antisemitismus.* Frankfurt-am-Main: Fischer Taschnbuch, 1993.

Wälder, R. (1935). Atiologie und Verlauf des Massenpsychosen [Etiology and course of mass psychoses]. *Imago,* 21(1): 67–90.

8 Extreme trauma: which unconscious?

"The *Shoah* is an event because it has given annihilation something other than images, namely, a tangible consistency. The witnesses that Lanzmann draws into the process of recollection do not speak about it. They relive their lives in the death that the film inflicts on us without crushing us. There is no "identification" there, which would require identificatory figures on to whom one could project oneself. There is no hero, no Christ-like figure, no example to follow, no promise for the future. It all took place. It is this fact alone that we must recognize and yet we forget it again and again. Reluctantly", writes Corinne Enaudeau (2013).

However, in 1998, in a text entitled "The primitive scene of atrocity", Nanette Auerhahn and Dori Laub (1998) (see also Laub, 1988) explained how Claude Lanzmann's film is the exemplary work of a man who, haunted during childhood by the fate of the Jews sent to the East, succeeded as an adult in overcoming the specific defence mechanisms of the survivors and their children. While the majority of them, grappling with the "chaos" and the destruction of any form of internal representation, had often abandoned the project of reconstructing memories of the event that had befallen them, Lanzmann succeeded in creating the setting of a primary scene thanks to the "interactive matrix" of interviews. Penetrating into the heart of the "empty circle" of the atrocity, he gave shape to his obsession with the camps which had occupied his youth. Thanks to the interviews, he found that being at the original scene of destruction itself – reference is made, in particular, to the testimony of Philip Müller, a member of an Auschwitz *Sonderkommando* – being in the presence of the "black hole" left by the indescribable nature of massive trauma would be a way of defending himself from the memory gap engendered by the dissolution of the *Self* caused by traumatic experience. For the authors, Lanzmann's work is an attempt at reparation.

Their approach does not stop there: apart from the fact that the film-maker deals with infantile fantasies that act as a protective shield against the horrifying reality of facts, there is more. Not only is Lanzmann's preoccupation – another supposedly defensive aspect of his approach – seen as a way of diverting attention from the task of mourning, but furthermore

DOI: 10.4324/9781003301660-9

the use of the film and its images reflects the impossibility of having access to a developed associative process, as required by "authentic memories" and "authentic narratives". In this sense, Lanzmann's film participates in a process that affects the survivors as well as their children: in order to defend themselves from the "empty circle" of representations, they employ visualizable "screen memories" which are actualized metaphors of what would otherwise remain outside the bounds of thought. In short, there was not a word in this psychoanalytic commentary of the "nerves of steel"[1] that it took for Lanzmann to think of the cold passion of mass murder, to "embody" the abiding crime in his construction, to refuse in particular memory sequences by obstinately pursuing the quest for a long form made up of moments, which conceded nothing to the haste of the images, of the "non-place" in short which is the very subject of the work.

In fact, this text by Dori Laub and Nanette Auerhahn was the culmination of a long series of articles published, together or separately, by the two authors beginning in 1983 – texts in which they return to the absolutely specific character of the traumatic experience of the camps, and in a way that seems exemplary to me. Indeed, according to the authors, far from being comparable to the usual analytical model of trauma, the extreme traumatic situation with which the historical event of the concentration camps confronts us requires that we abandon any theoretical reference to the notion of après-coup. It is in terms of psychic "fragmentation", in terms of the destruction of internal links under the impact of the destruction of external links, that the effects of such an experience should be approached clinically. The traumatic desolation generated, along with the rupture of the internal coherence of the individual, an almost irreparable collapse of the temporal network, thereby destroying the "representational matrix" (Auerhahn & Laub, 1989, pp. 386–387, 390). This is why what is traumatic for the survivor is not the fact that a past trauma, by recurring in the present, is now made operative. Rather, it is much more the fact that the present trauma is constituted by the very loss of all internal connections, by the disappearance of any possibility of historicization of the experience thanks to the network of memories which normally make it possible to link associatively, through the process of après-coup, the two periods of the past and the present. The life of the survivor is composed of a non-integrated material, an assemblage which cannot be symbolically bound by the permanence offered by the historical narrative about oneself; the "black hole" left by the traumatic state having abolished any hope of gaining a vision of what took place. In this world invaded by affect, but affect that is as unrepresentable as the experience itself is unthinkable, in a world so devastated that it has become silent – and the model of appalling silence is related to the silence of the "Muslim" – the confirmation of the nightmare by reality has destroyed the boundary between reality and fantasy. Because the horror of the camps lies in a perceptual, physical, concrete and unmediated experience which engendered a process of desymbolization, the only path that remains for the survivor – or indeed for his children, because the traumatic experience, due to its indelible character, is necessarily transgenerational – is therefore that which is partially opened by the use that the latter makes of "screen memories" or "screen narratives" (see Laub & Lee, 2003).

It will therefore come as no surprise to learn that such screens – which, moreover, can take the form of "screen transferences" when, in analysis, sexual fantasies invade the relationship between the patient and the analyst and everything suggests that the figure of an exciting father is present in the process of reliving induced by the treatment – are not the distorted product of wishes impelled by desire or infantile sexuality. They are subsequent, "mythical" creations, whose "narcissistic skin" value is essentially defensive.

Let us be quite clear: between the "screen identifications" which present themselves in sexual and sadistic scenarios, and the unrepresentable dimension of traumatic experience, there is no place in the theorization of the authors for repression, distortion, or the return of the repressed. There is just room for an attempt to form an idea of the unthinkable thanks to its "contextualization" by sexual fantasies, which somehow make it possible to gain access to the brutality of the event through fantasies about origins. Dreams, metaphorization thanks to the primal scene and artistic creations are all protective screens and edifices erected around a void that has totally or partially destroyed the normal functioning of the psychic apparatus. The treatment tool will therefore be to mobilize screen re-enactments opening the way, in dialogue, to the restoration of the destroyed symbolic processes.

The primal scene of the atrocity should not therefore – I continue my reading – be interpreted as a sexual scene despite its appearance. It would be a profound misunderstanding of what the "sexualized version of the Holocaust" is. Just as there can be no question of granting a strictly fantasy-based function to the belief of certain patients, the children of survivors, that, for example, their mother prostituted herself in the camp in order to survive, or that, for the same reason, their father was a ruthless kapo or a willing slave. These beliefs would merely be the product of the contamination of sexual life by trauma. These are "legends" that allow survivors to face the terror of the empty circle of memory and the unmediated violence of the event. Milton Jucovy (1985) has called them "romanticizations of memories", particularly when the pathological variants of "family romances" are identified as "presumed secrets" intended to fill in the impossible narration of the camps.

The primal scene proper is organized by the longing to see and know. But, here, the primal scene of the atrocity relates rather to the erasure of knowing, to the loss of an organized universe. The misunderstanding of taking one for the other has, moreover, generated two types of "errors" among therapists who have cared for survivors and their children. The first is that committed by "those psychoanalysts who, taking into account the fictional nature of these stories, treat reality as a fantasy and the actualized metaphor as a simple metaphor. They aestheticize the experience and focus only on what the mind creates, losing sight of the frightening external reality" (Laub & Auerhahn, 1989, p. 363, 396, 1984, 1987, 1993). Conversely, the other error is made by those who insist unduly on the reality of the horror scenes, thus missing the nature of the impact of the parental experience on the experience of the children, an impact that is revealed in the obliteration of the void by such fictitious creations. In any case, these therapists reinforce the rupture of contact that these people have made with their fragmented internal reality, with their memories and their needs. This rupture serves to fight against the pain, since these individuals are completely oriented towards achieving for themselves the best possible adaptation to a "false life".

A detailed account of this series of hypotheses would only have an anecdotal and edifying value, were it not for the fact that they are representative of a deep and continuous movement in analytical theory over the last thirty-five years. Let us take as a starting point the work of the group led by Mortimer Ostow and supported by the *Psychoanalytic Research and Development Fund*. For nine years starting in 1981, this group brought together sixteen analysts, Jews and non-Jews, and a historian, Yosef Yerushalmi. The participants sought, from a detailed study of nineteen analytical cases, to identify the psychic constants at the root of anti-Semitic positions. The work, published in the volume *Myth and Madness* (Ostow, 1995), was presented in the *International Journal of Psychoanalysis* (Ostow, 1996). However, one of the conclusions of this research was that few "recognized anti-Semites" were in analysis. As for anti-Semitic "attitudes", they were more a matter of passing feelings or comments, corresponding to moments and manifestations of negative transference. But what strikes one above all, on reading this report, is the difficulty that exists in approaching the subject, which extends to total avoidance. From anti-Semitic "mythology" to the methodical extermination of six million Jews, the obstacle formed by the improbable gap between imaginary conceptions and reality was reinforced through the reduction of collective and cultural clinical dynamics to individual clinical dynamics.

In fact, by summing up the "myths" which, from the Old Testament to Tacitus, from the Gospel of Matthew to medieval accusations of kidnapping and sacrificing Christian children, from the *Merchant of Venice* to the *Protocols of the Elders of Zion*, have treated the Jews as the chief cause of all the woes of the community, and by making anti-Semitism a disguised return of polytheism in the form of the materialization of the demon, the study seems to add little to *Christians and Jews: A Psychoanalytic Study*, written between 1941 and 1952 by Rodolphe Loewenstein (1951).[2] And little, compared to what Nathan Ackerman and Marie Jahoda (1948) published. In the immediate post-war period, these texts attempted to take up the disaster of the Holocaust in analytical terms within the framework of a long history in which religious education had collaborated in reversing superego hatred towards the father against the figure of the Jewish scapegoat, where "possession of gold" had been associated with the cruelty, disgust, shame and sexual arousal involved in anal fantasies; and where "social mental illness" was seen as the delusional solution offered to the masses to resolve intrapsychic as well as intercommunity and economic conflicts. The struggle against depression through the frenzied adaptation of the individual to the dominant group in order to participate in its power, the attempt to turn passivity into activity, the "self-enlargement" obtained by identification with the masses, the function of the ideals and the position of the Führer were seized upon as an individual solution adopted collectively to counter narcissistic suffering and castration anxiety. And already projection appeared to be one of the key words of anti-Semitic psychopathology.

However, although the work of the "Ostow group" falls within the same theoretical lineage, also making the projection and theorization of defence mechanisms the springboard for a madness which seemed to refuse to enter the nets of psychoanalytic models, and though, in the same way as the work of the post-war period, except that of Saul Friedländer (1971, 1975), it fails to review the legacy left by Freud concerning primary destructiveness and the death drive – an astonishing piece of negligence, in truth – on the other hand it clearly reveals the emergence of a new kind of model to describe the "homeostatic regulation of affect" in psychic life. In this model, where affect oscillates in phases between two poles, the system can malfunction in two directions, that of euphoria and that of depression, with the rapid alternation between the two states resulting in the psychic disorders of borderline personalities, or even dissociative experiences leading to psychosis. When the ego is overloaded with libidinal energy and this overload creates a state of exuberance, or when, for internal or external reasons, the ego is depleted in energy, a spontaneous adjustment generally takes place, making it possible to find a sort of constant level of mood. But in cases of violent and profound changes, we see a succession of fantasies of death and rebirth, quite similar to what religions describe in terms of the apocalypse. By linking these "individual apocalypses" to the Apocalypse as it appears in religious belief – both a threat of punishment by destruction and a prelude to rebirth – we would come to understand how individual psychic movements in which the punitive agent presents itself in the guise of the Jewish demon and the cataclysm, had become bound up with the collective movement of massive destruction accompanied by the promise of a triumph to come.

Regarding this model, I will provisionally note two features: the first is the pure and simple equation of affect with psychic energy; the second, whose consequences are no less significant, is that the anti-Semitic group is thought of as a "homogeneous group". The constitution of this group allows the individuals within it to create the illusion of a "reunion with the mother", thus taking possession of her in a hallucinatory manner. While individual megalomania finds its fulfilment in the extension of each ego to the whole group, narcissistic pathology is described in terms of regression to a state of primary fusion. Between the omnipotent ego of each individual and the colossal body of the masses, the concept which suddenly dominates is that of the mother group. But the authors leave in the shadows the link between this "mother group" and the mythical figure of the demon – a demon whom Ostow nevertheless says is the inverted replica of God and the watermark of a father figure.

Why dwell on this work? First of all, because it is as if the actual implementation of mass extermination, accomplished by Nazi barbarism, no longer allowed the Ostow group to refer in depth to Freud's work, prior to the war. *Totem and Taboo, Group Psychology and the Analysis of the Ego* and *Civilization and its Discontents* are seldom cited, and when they are, it is not with regard to the inaugural function of the murder of the father in the building of civilization. As for what Freud elaborates concerning the renunciation that reinforces hostility to civilization and the "surprising" alliance of progress and barbarism (Freud, 1939, p. 54), I have found no trace of it.

In addition, the Ostow group met during a period when there was a real change in the point of view on the "Jewish question". Henry Krystal's (1968) book *Massive Psychic Trauma* (see also Krystal, 1984), Judith Kestenberg's survey undertaken in 1970 which, in 1974, became the subject of a research group on "survivor parents" and their children,[3] the publication in 1982 of this research in a volume, *Generations of the Holocaust* put together by Bergmann and Jucovy (1982), which includes several contributions by Kestenberg, the work of Des Pres (*The Survivor: an Anatomy of Life in the Death Camps* (Des Pres, 1976)) responding in 1976 and 1979 to that of Bettelheim are all milestones in the reflection on the consequences of the Holocaust. One of the culmination points was the congress of the International Association of Psychoanalysis held in Hamburg in 1985. They all promoted the "clinical study of survivors", which seemed to them to be the only way to think about the disaster. From 1980, the "Holocaust" appeared as the new face of the Jewish question in so far as it had the physiognomy of catastrophe. A new face whose very name expressed the sacrificial perspective, which seems to exempt thought from the formidable task of conceiving of modern-day anti-Semitism while, instead, the group of victims was formed.

As Giorgio Agamben (2003) points out in *Ce qui reste d'Auschwitz*, it was Bettelheim who paved the way. In "Individual behaviour and mass behaviour in extreme situations" (Bettelheim, 1943), he made the "Muslim" the man on the verge of an ineluctable death, having lost his humanity in the experience of absolute terror, a psychically dead shadow before meeting physical death, a paradigm for his analysis of childhood autism; he restated and developed this in his (1967) book *The Empty Fortress*. But by 1963 the "survivor syndrome" had already become a "clinically recognizable entity". A convergence had taken place between the clinical definition of the "extreme situation" and the total withdrawal it causes and its relatively univocal theoretical basis: trauma.

One of the players in this convergence was Niederland who, in 1961, clearly argued that the diagnoses hitherto made on the lasting pathologies of camp survivors – involutional depression, general asthenia, etc. – did not allow the victims to have their rights recognized and to obtain compensation from post-war Germany. The lack of proper specifications made it impossible to establish a link between the harm of the camps and the illness that subsequently resulted. It was therefore up to psychoanalysts to clinically reconsider the very numerous and varied complaints the victims suffered (headaches, back pain, asthma, hypertension, ulcers, gastrointestinal disorders, extreme fatigue) and to recognize under the "somatic mask" the traces of psychic damage that would have no other means of expression than through bodily manifestations. It was consequently the use of the *historical context* that enabled them to unite the extreme diversity of these sufferings within a single territory, while the conceptual unification of these somatic pathologies led to the creation of the "group of victims".

I have spoken of "traces" of psychic damage. But the term is undoubtedly inadequate, because the psychoanalytic debate criticized here revolves precisely around the question of knowing whether traces of the catastrophic experience could only have been registered in the unconscious. Moreover, evoking the notion of the unconscious is probably also inadequate. Because what Niederland (1964) describes – and many others would subsequently rely on his conception – is a body which manifests experience in an actuality that does not and will not find its words. It is therefore in the area of silence without memory that anxiety, the loss of any form of pleasure, anxiety dreams which are said to be "recurrent" – but never "repetitive" – and the alteration of the very notion of identity affect the body-image and the self-image, all this being subjectively felt as lasting damage to the Self. This damage is so long-lasting that Niederland (1968) considers the survivor syndrome as irreversible, while the subsequent effects of these traumas seem to remain inaccessible to any treatment.

According to this view of "extreme trauma", any work of mourning is impossible, especially since, among the defence methods used by the survivors, repression has lost not only its place but all meaning. The dead haunt the memory of the living, and the guilt for having survived can only be dealt with by denial and splitting, mechanisms that are clinically dissociated from the theorization of perverse organizations which are the pure products of an extreme experience. The evaluation of psychic damage, on account of annihilation and in relation to the propensity to somatization, often results in the observation that there is a lack of psychization which ultimately relates to an unconstituted state of psychic life, a pre-psychic state prior to the Self. For the same reason, pain, shame and guilt can in no case be treated as the psychic consequence of unrecognized death wishes or the product of a primary hostility which has not found expression in an intrapsychic formation. Certainly, Niederland admits, it is true that masochistic tendencies are at work in some cases. But more often than not, it is the very fact of surviving that constitutes the core of the internal conflict. "Survival is unconsciously felt to be a betrayal" (Niederland, 1981, p. 419).

But then which unconscious are we talking about here? Is it even legitimate to speak of the unconscious when the "magnitude of the trauma" was so strong that it shattered the psychical apparatus and the memory apparatus, when the real event has forever taken the place of any intrapsychic events, and when the approach to this "unintegratable" experience cannot be achieved by any other path than that of subjectivity? A subjectivity so altered that the restoration of the Self is the only possible way of healing, the only therapeutic tool available being remembering *as such*. In this context – at the least, paradoxical, if we consider that subjectivity is conceived here precisely as a feeling described subjectively, which at minimum presupposes a psychic apparatus that is capable of describing – in this context, therefore, it is clear that so-called "orthodox" psychoanalysis was unable, both because of its practice and its theoretical tools, to face these new pathologies.

Because the Nazis created a reality far more frightening than any fantasy, because terror and horror were the only possible reactions in these situations of absolute passivity and dereliction, because guilt itself was meaningless in a chaotic world where choice – the one thing that might explain the survivor's guilt – did not exist, and because guilt essentially had a commemorative function, as an expression of loyalty to the dead, and was the only way to maintain a sense of belonging, there was no other solution than to deviate from the "orthodox" position of many analysts who only knew how to use theoretical rationalizations, powerless as they were to contain their intense emotional reactions. And this orthodoxy, denounced by Yael Danieli (1984), was in the name of the very use of the traditional tools of analytic treatment.

Questioning the "conspiracy of silence" that has so far surrounded the process of listening to those who have returned from the camps – and the pact of silence only exists because the inability of survivors to talk and think is linked to the wish in society that nothing be said about the horror, a wish for which analysts have made themselves the voluntary or involuntary spokespersons – Danieli maintains that, in these treatments, the therapist reacts much more to the scraps of stories reported by survivors than to their behaviour during the session. The notion of countertransference therefore ceases to be relevant. Or, more exactly, if there is a countertransference, this does not occur under the effect of what the patient makes the analyst experience within the treatment itself. It is a countertransference reaction to the Holocaust itself. That would explain why the transference is null and void: the "real" trauma would require specific help which takes into account the "real experience" of the victims.

A step beyond the trauma, a step beyond the explosion of the Self under the "emotional shock", a step beyond the generalization of any production in terms of screen, in the remeshing of the memory of an event that is at once indelible but devoid of trace, the theory of empathy imposed itself as the main theoretical and clinical tool, in situations where the complexity of psychic operations had vanished into thin air, giving way to post-traumatic disorder. It is remarkable, moreover, that the integration in the DSM III[4] of "post-traumatic" pathologies (Post-Traumatic Stress Disorder, Chronic or Delayed) as independent pathologies dates back to the same period: 1982.

Henry Krystal wrote explicitly in 1984 that, in surviving patients, the "trauma makes repression impossible", and that very often the "super-ego functions are more disturbed than the ego functions" (p. 471). Some authors attempt to state the reasons leading them to reject the psychic operation that is sometimes able to account for the power of amnesia. But their rejection of repression is based on the argument of a theory of intra-psychic explosion marked by "black holes" embedded in the psychic life of these *borderline* states, or by a somatic illness acting as a silent solution. Likewise, more than one wonders, more or less fleetingly, how the patient makes the almost total abrasion of memory coexist with its persistence intact in mental life, sometimes even at the conscious level. But no one dwells on the relevance of the hypothesis "with high pressure resistance" – to paraphrase Freud – in other words, with high pressure psychization, of an anti-cathexis by forgetting, such that both partners of the analytic situation might initially have the feeling that the door to memory is closed forever. Yet, we have to admit, the survivors survived, and they often remember.

"We can forge a memory but we cannot refuse forgetting, for the good reason that memory, reminiscence, remembering and commemoration are conscious and voluntary acts, even if this is not always the case", writes Rachel Ertel (2015).

> Forgetting, on the other hand, is an unconscious force, over which we have no control. Yet it is a strength, it is a mental activity. . . . To forget is an active and transitive verb. There would be no memory if there was no forgetting. Forgetting works on the memory. We can say that memory is built on forgetting. . . . The involuntary erasure creates the need for remembering.
>
> (p. 17; author's emphasis)

Notes

1 These are his words, used in the interview he gave to François Gantheret (1986).
2 Joshua Trachtenberg's (1943) book *The Devil and the Jews: The Medieval Conception of the Jew and its Relation to Modern Antisemitism* provides a remarkable review of the subject.
3 The project was called "International Study of Organized Persecution of Children" (ISOPC) and was followed by the publication by Judith Kestenberg (1988) of *Child Survivors of the Holocaust.*
4 DSM III: Common abbreviation for the *Diagnostic and Statistical Manual of Mental Disorders*, published by the American Psychiatric Association.

References

Ackerman, N., Jahoda, M. (1948). The dynamic basis of anti-Semitic attitudes. *The Psychoanalytic Quarterly*, 17: 240–260.

Agamben, G. (2003). *Ce qui reste d'Auschwitz. L'archive et le témoin*. Paris: Rivages Poche.

Auerhahn, N., Laub, D. (1989). Failed empathy – a central theme in the survivor's Holocaust experience. *Psychoanalytic Psychology*, 6: 377–400.

Auerhahn, N., Laub, D. (1998). The primal scene of atrocity. *Psychoanalytic Psychology*, 15: 360–377.

Bergmann, M.S., Jucovy, M.E. (eds.). (1982). *Generations of the Holocaust*. New York: Columbia University Press.

Bettelheim, B. (1943). Individual and mass behaviour in extreme situations. *Journal of Abnormal and Social Psychology*, 38: 417–452; reprinted in Bettelheim, B. (1979). *Surviving and Other Essays*, New York: A.A. Knopf, pp. 48–83.

Bettelheim, B. (1967). *The Empty Fortress: Infantile Autism and the Birth of the Self*. New York: Free Press.

Danieli, Y. (1984). Psychotherapists' participation in the conspiracy of silence about the Holocaust. *Psychoanalytic Psychology*, 1(1984): 23–42.

Des Pres, T. (1976). *The Survivor: An Anatomy of Life in the Death Camps*. Oxford: Oxford University Press.

Enaudeau, C. (2013). *Shoah* (1985) film by Claude Lanzmann. *Intersections*, Collège international de philosophie.

Ertel, R. (2015). "Nous sommes les souvenants qui refusons l'oubli". Pouvoirs de la poésie. *Le Coq-héron*, 221(2): 14–19.

Freud, S. (1939). *Moses and Monotheism. S.E.* 23. London: Hogarth, pp. 7–137.

Friedländer, S. (1971). *L'antisémitisme nazi, Histoire d'une psychose collective*. Paris: Le Seuil.

Friedländer, S. (1975). *Histoire et psychanalyse*. Paris: Le Seuil.

Gantheret, F. (1986). Les non-lieux de la mémoire. *Nouvelle Revue de Psychanalyse*, 23: 11–24.

Jucovy, M. (1985). Telling the Holocaust story: A link between the generations. *Psychoanalytic Inquiry*, 5: 31–49.

Kestenberg, J. (1988). *Child Survivors of the Holocaust*. New York: Guilford Publications.

Krystal, H. (1968). *Massive Psychic Trauma*. New York: International Universities Press.

Krystal, H. (1984). Review of *Generations of the Holocaust. The Psychoanalytic Quarterly*, 53: 466–473.

Laub, D. (1988). The empty circle: Children survivors and the limits of reconstruction. *Journal of the American Psychoanalytic Association*, 46: 507–529.

Laub, D., Auerhahn, N. (1984). Post-traumatic memory as pathway and obstacle to recovery. *The International Review of Psycho-Analysis*, 11: 327–344.

Laub, D., Auerhahn, N. (1987). Play and playfulness in Holocaust survivors. *The Psychoanalytic Study of the Child*, 42: 45–58.

Laub, D., Auerhahn, N. (1993). Knowing and not knowing massive psychic trauma; forms of traumatic memory. *International Journal of Psychoanalysis*, 74(2): 287–302.

Laub, D., Lee, S. (2003). Thanatos and massive psychic trauma: The impact of the death instinct on knowing, remembering, and forgetting. *Journal of the American Psychoanalytic Association*, 51(2): 433–464.

Loewenstein, R. (1951). *Christians and Jews: A Psychoanalytic Study*. New York: Dell Publishing Co, Inc.

Niederland, W. (1961). The problem of survivor. *Journal of the Hillside Hospital*, 10: 233–247.

Niederland, W. (1964). Psychiatric disorders among persecution victims. *Journal of Neurological and Mental Disease*, 139(5): 458–474.

Niederland, W. (1968). Clinical observations on the survivor syndrome: Symposium on psychic traumatization through social catastrophe. *International Journal of Psychoanalysis*, 49: 313–315.

Niederland, W. (1981). The survivor syndrome: Further observations and dimensions. *Journal of the American Psychoanalytic Association*, 29: 413–425.

Ostow, M. (1995). *Myth and Madness: The Psychodynamics of Anti-SEMITISM*. Piscataway, NJ: Transaction Publishers.

Ostow, M. (1996). Myth and madness: A report of a psychoanalytic study of anti-semitism. *International Journal of Psychoanalysis*, 77: 15–31.

Trachtenberg, J. (1943). *The Devil and the Jews: The Medieval Conception of the Jew and Its Relation to Modern Antisemitism*. New Haven: Yale University Press.

9 Mother, child and empathy

No one dwells on the function of forgetting because, in response to the question of repression, one text was frequently cited at the time of these debates as a reference: "Trauma and repression" by Jonathan Cohen (1985). It is cited but not read sufficiently closely. However, apart from the extremely confused thinking, its reading holds more than one surprise. I will try to give an account of it because the line of thinking is instructive.

Starting from the observation that the theoretical link between trauma, "which refers to events in the external world", and repression, "which refers to purely mental phenomena", has been little or inadequately examined since Freud's work on trauma in 1920, and emphasizing the difference between the compulsion to repeat and mere repetition, Cohen draws on the fact that the refutation of wish-fulfilment as the sole aim of dreams led Freud to describe a "new level of psychic organization 'beyond the pleasure principle' that could be produced or activated by trauma" (Cohen, 1985, p. 166; Cohen, 1980; Cohen & Kinston, 1984). Certainly, he adds, many analysts have rejected this radical revision of mental functioning. However, taking up from the structural point of view the psychopathology corresponding to the alteration or complete destruction of the function of repression, insofar as this is at the centre of neurotic functioning, would make it possible to understand how the permanence of identity, forged by stability over time, and the function of transforming wishes into new wishes, ensured by the dynamic of new interactions, might fail. His hypothesis explicitly criticizes the positions of ego psychology that make neurotic functioning and internal conflict the paradigm of psychic functioning. And no less explicitly, he argues that *Beyond the Pleasure Principle* manages to spin the quantitative metaphor of the excess of traumatic excitation but misses the clinical observation of this destructive excess, leaving out the picture the clinical gap between the effects of repression proper (secondary repression) and the effects of primary repression.

According to Cohen, the effect of primary repression, "considered from a clinical rather than an abstract point of view", corresponds to events that are lived through but not experienced as a part of the self, and so are not representable in the overall wish-organized construction of personality.

DOI: 10.4324/9781003301660-10

This absence of structure and representable experience in a region of the self, which is the outcome of the traumatic state, is primary repression, the author emphasizes. Such primary repression leaves the individual grappling with primitive self-protective operations, aimed only at avoiding stimuli. These operations – encapsulation, cocoon, encystment, shell and so forth – are not ego defences but simply provide an armour against retraumatization, and have been termed variously as schizoid personality (Fairbairn, 1952), false-self (Winnicott, 1960) and narcissistic personality organization (Kohut, 1971). Cohen specifies that if, in spite of everything, repression proper develops laterally, it modifies the defence systems, which are primarily those of denial, splitting and projective identification. However, primary repression itself cannot be modified by the defensive formation because it is devoid of representation. This is why, according to him, the metaphor of "holes" is appropriate: holes from which all psychic structuring, all forms of representation are absent, while the direct, immediate clinical manifestations of primary repression spare all the detours of the return of the repressed. But there is no mention of the productions resulting from secondary repression, of the meanderings that are inevitable when thinking about the object of forgetting. As the direct path is wide open, it is the disintegration of the primary object itself which, in doing so, is observable. Such a pathology, one suspects, can only lead – this is one of the pseudo-psychic outcomes – to somatic disorders.

If I say that Cohen's article is quoted but not read sufficiently closely, it is because no one seems to be moved by the fact that one of Cohen's major references is Abram Kardiner's (1941) study on war neuroses. This work, written when Kardiner had already been forced to leave the International Psychoanalytic Association, stemmed directly, in his own words, from his orientation towards the social sciences. In this study, Freudian concepts are deemed deficient by the author and criticized accordingly, in favour of a "physioneurosis" in which the adaptability of the whole organism replaces Freud's conceptualization (ibid., pp. 12–13, 266, 338–343).

The reader will have recognized in this model – even though it varied during the twenty years that followed – the model of borderline states, of "boundaries" on which psychoanalysis has been moving in recent times. The unknowable, the unthinkable, the unrepresentable, and the unintegratable come to the fore here, accounting for a post-traumatic pathology that was first circumscribed by the context of events. For the paradox is indeed that the category of survivor – a category which gave rise to, if not a new, at least a very broad theorization in psychoanalysis – is the direct product of a determination made by the use of the diachrony of events. By relying on the "historical" knowledge of events which are no longer associatively available to the subject, and by considering that psychic silence is commensurate with the direct impact of an experience of terror that the subject is unaware of but of which we have knowledge by virtue of external testimony, written or oral, the clinical determination of these new pathologies refers to the context as cause, while semantically saturating the description of the psychic situation with the reasoned introduction of "objective" facts. From this point of view, the procedure for investigating the children of survivors, described in 1985 by Milton Jucovy, leaves no room for doubt. "In order to maintain a spirit of scientific objectivity" Jucovy states, the researchers began, during each case study, by considering the overall pathology of the patient before questioning the relevance of referring to the Holocaust to understand its genesis. Did this make it possible to establish its specificity? Not really since, according to the author himself, it is always very difficult to disentangle the "private pathology" from what is due to the effects of the Holocaust. Although the "symptoms seen in the second generation [are] neither unique nor exclusive", researchers nevertheless came to an agreement that being exposed to the Holocaust through the parents' past experience may have served as a significant organizing experience for later developmental conflicts in their children. According to Jucovy, this is because, when the symptoms are considered as a conglomerate, they "form a complete clinical picture which is palpable and recognizable" (Jucovy, 1985, p. 32).

Thus the catastrophe of mass death, with, as a corollary, the prevalence of pain – an affect which, even if it is absent, is deemed to be inevitably present – leads to treating the "Holocaust" as the one fact that makes it possible to describe both the event and its consequences. For the notion of "extreme limit" brings together under one umbrella the extreme limits of reason that mass extermination represents for culture, the individual extreme pathologies characterized by narcissistic failures, the destruction of the universe of representations and the rout of the psychic scene itself.

There is a considerable paradox here affecting the notion of representation as much as the event that should be represented. And it increases when one has just finished reading *Liquidation* by Imre Kertész, because this text, as brief as it is profound, written in the same language, devoid of emphasis, as *Fatelessness*, aims precisely to grasp the event independently of the pathos that had covered it in order to pose the major question: What sort of event is it? And how can we grasp it without immediately framing it in terms of the semiology imported by historical discourse? For anyone who plays the "game" of camp names – and Kertész repeats here, as in *Kaddish for an Unborn Child*, how much he knows that in this game of names that is the game of nomenclatural heroization, he has from the outset the trump card: "Auschwitz" – how can thought be taken any further except by making it turn on itself in a void, a void that is perhaps not the one left by experience but, more probably, the one promoted by a simplified theory of trauma? In any case, it is as if psychoanalysis – but is it still psychoanalysis? – anchored to the identity-based conception of the individual, had not succeeded here in breaking away from a vision of the subject and his "formation" as inherited it from the Age of Enlightenment.

Confronted with the collapse of representations emancipated from a destiny endowed with meaning, it abdicates in the same movement any claim to support the hypothesis of a complex psychic life by removing language from its power of shaping tirelessly – due precisely to repression, to the erasure of the murder – innumerable returns of what at its core must remain unrecognizable.

This is why, with regard to the desymbolizing experience of the camps, the survivor's symptoms should, according to Laub & Auerhahn (1989), be understood in analysis as "metalanguages concerning internalized object relations or concerning an absent object" (p. 396). This absent object, which for the authors is a "state of objectlessness", is held to be at the root of the fact that the survivor experiences himself as absolutely alone and absolutely other; moreover, according to them this clarifies an essential feature of all forms of trauma. Faced with an experience inaccessible to psychoanalytic interpretation – which more typically has to do with polysemous phenomena conducive to imaginative play and choice (Laub, 2015a) – bringing unarticulated meanings back into play, in an interpersonal language, is the only way of re-establishing the empathic tie to an object, a tie that has been so radically lacking in a dehumanized environment.

As we read these texts, we realize that the relationship between the conception of après-coup, as discussed earlier, and the function assigned here to empathy could not be closer. The healing function of narration results from this relationship. It is a caring function which is valid for the survivor himself because it allows him to reconstruct an autobiographical, coherent and complete story of his experience, without being subjected to the irruption of primary processes. But it is equally valid for the surviving child because "transmission" – this word constantly comes up in the writings of all the authors – lies in the gap between the scene that was seen but that is not representable by the mother and the scene imagined by the child, which does not trigger a sense of "horror" linked to the external spectacle but an internal sense of "terror" linked to what he experiences mentally. Between horror and terror, there is the difference between the outside and the inside. But there is also the gap that governs the situation of trauma in the theory. While trauma is what cannot be understood by the survivor, even though it preoccupies him so completely that it prevents him from establishing any empathic relationship with his child, the return in the child of the parent's experience leads the child to "dream" the parental experience, which may be seen as an "attempt to assimilate a meaning that was transmitted but not comprehended" (Auerhahn & Prelinger, 1983, p. 37). In other words, the observation and treatment of the children of survivors reveals the formation of a totally permeable membrane between the child and the mother preventing the child from separating from this parent. In reality, the theoretical versions are variable here. For sometimes the complete permeability of the membrane puts the child in direct contact with the black hole, considered as a defective transmission; and sometimes the membrane is totally impermeable, which explains both the encystment and the covering of the present by the past. This "transposition" confines the child to the place of the missing: hence the pathology of impossible mourning carried over from generation to generation. In all cases, not only does the child constantly demand total empathy which is denied to him by the narcissistically defective parent, but he is himself placed in the position of an empathic listener who seeks to interpret what would otherwise remain in the darkness of a fully fragmented memory.

If indeed trauma in the usual analytical sense has a meaning, it can only have that meaning in the context of the second generation. For the parent who lived in the camps, the experience was indeed so devastating that one looks in vain for isolatable and identifiable events allowing one to suppose that a second phase might be engrammed in the first, in such a way that the first restructures all subsequent events and makes possible the retrospective historicization of the experience. On the other hand, for the child, the repetition of the experience in the relationship with the mother restores the very possibility of interpretation. The survivor's child, through his role as a witness and empathic listener, suffers from a *vicarious* trauma which is a repetition of the parent's experience, but "with a difference in the direction of interpretability"; for repetition, as "interpersonal repetition", can be seen as an attempt to "integrate experience". Thus the child and the mother form a common front in face of the very heart of the traumatic experience of the camps, according to Nanette Auerhahn and Dori Laub (see Laub, 2015b, 2015c). The loss of all interpersonal "mutuality", as well as the lack of any presence and an environment capable of giving a human and reliable response, condemn the victims to an irremediable search for lost empathy and their children to the search for answers and protection from their mother that is unobtainable.

The unfolding of the two stages of the trauma over two generations is actually never as clearly stated as I am doing here, any more than the ambiguity of the term "empathy" is elucidated, for the psychic process to which it refers remains ultimately opaque, except for the fact that it constitutes a "bridge" between oneself and the other, and between the present and the past.

The constitution of this bridge becomes a purposive idea when, faced with the disorganization of the empathic process, the adaptation of the analytical setting to the treatment of survivors must be reconsidered; for the loss of the other, internal and external, has distorted any reference to "compassion". So much so that, although it has seemed to certain authors that the subsequent psychic distortions were to be attributed to the process of defence constituted by identification with the aggressor, Nanette Auerhahn and Dori Laub feel it is necessary to ask themselves whether this alleged identification is not the equivalent of an attempt to substitute the empathic other in oneself. Such an internal creation would result in the catastrophic capture of the image of the *"self"* by the aggressor, who has become the sole object of a deserted world. As a result, the reconstitution of the empathic link will lead analyst and patient to re-establish an "empathic memory". Only such an interpersonal bond, made of the same material as the mother-child relationship, could be expected to make up for the survivor's fragmented memory. And only a coherent account of the traumatic event could be supposed to bridge the junction with the lost pre-traumatic past.

One may wonder why there is such an emphasis on the mother in these texts. Certainly, the psychoanalytic model of the foundation of the object relationship in early childhood makes the maternal reference necessary. It is for the same reason that the fracture of the protective shield in traumatic experience is linked to the rupture of all the early schemas of the organization of our relations with each other, since this organization is predictable, synthesizing and pre-symbolizing. But on closer examination – that is to say, in a note (Laub & Auerhahn, 1989, p. 388) – we discover that the *absence of the father* in the destruction of the linguistic reference to otherness conceals a more complex hypothesis. We see in particular that, if the parental figures are essentially related to the maternal presence, it is because in the universe of Nazi barbarism, the paternal order failed in its protective function. Under the blow of destruction, the father lost his place as representative and guardian of the law, leaving the maternal image with the role of an omnipotent presence with the power of life and death. The father, a figure of weakness, henceforth unable to awaken hope, had ceased to be a living psychological force and had become the memorial of a world that had disappeared.

This is how the child, an empathic listener, becomes the mother's empathic listener, because it is from her, from that other – and how can we not mention the theoretical pun used here on (m)other, the "good other" (Laub & Auerhahn, 1984, p. 334, 1987, p. 387) – that the reconstitution of a story ensuring the permanence of identity is expected. Because the story allows for mastery, and mastery, after all, must be flawless. That "authentic memories" are identifiable by their coherence and that their coherence is attributed to the proper functioning of the associative network says enough about the strange fate that befalls the fragment, and the even stranger fate that befalls the memory of the survivors which is expected to be full.

What remains of the erasure of the murder, "constructed by the products of its forgetting" – to use the title of an article by Marie Moscovici (1989)? Nothing or almost nothing. The virtues of narrativity have done their work, in a to and fro between contextualization and interpersonalization, the continuity of the narration being strictly modelled on the permanence of the object. And what is left of guilt? Almost nothing again, if we consider that it is the other means, pathological in this case, of maintaining internal permanence, even if it has to be paid for at the high price of internalizing the persecutor in place of the superego; this theme comes up more than once, and in particular under the pen of Bergmann (1985). Of course, one does not remember, but one carries the camps inside oneself, just as they are. And this is not a matter of the compulsion to repeat but of psychic abrasion.

"Psychoanalysts of the Shoah" are unable to take into account the fact that sadism, in spite of everything, seems to play its part quietly, that sexualization deeply penetrates forgetting and not-forgetting, and that, without being named, masochistic positions seem to reorganize the scenario of an intolerable submission. This is because two elements escape them. On the one hand, the trauma model involves much more than a "shock", a shock, moreover, that is "emotional"; and secondly, the search for mastery, which is not a feature of narration but of the compulsion to repeat, should involve the scripting of a violent and repressed sexual scene, in which desire ultimately finds its place. However, neither of them is admissible by these authors because both would imply paying attention to the modalities of countercathexis brought into play in the process of the trauma itself.

In *Beyond the Pleasure Principle*, Freud states that trauma is not the direct result of being flooded with large amounts of stimuli, that it is not simply a phenomenon of invasion but also a matter of the "anti-cathexis" on a grand scale that is set up, for whose benefit all the other psychical systems are impoverished. In other words, the remaining psychic functions that are paralyzed have their mode of expression in psychic life – if only in the form of the mechanisms of binding (or attempts at binding) and their correlate, the compulsion to repeat. However, specialists in the "trauma" of the Shoah can only misconstrue or ignore these expressions; to take them into consideration would require them to review the whys and wherefores of the introduction of the death drive into drive life, and of its alloys with the libidinal arrangements which supported the survivor in his survival, even if he was greatly bereaved. But it is as if the libido itself, in the face of the atrocity, had lost its qualities, as if it were indecent to make the libidinal impulse coexist with the atrocious facts of history. It is an eminently moral affair, of course, but one that ultimately forces us to wonder how the survivors survived.

And it is not the treatment of guilt in this process that will help to get this psychoanalytic line of thinking out of the rut, because the victim cannot be guilty. Silence cannot therefore be conceived as the product of guilt, except for having survived. There is barely any mention of the fact that the inner voice of self-accusation resonates in the ear of the one who has returned, that it reminds him in so many different ways how each of his gestures as a survivor, each of his choices to subsist, made him a murderer, how he owed every extra day to a crumb of intelligence and to a fragment of territory which the other person who disappeared that day, lacked. And the sexualization of punishment is mentioned even less. The defence mechanisms invoked, such as denial, splitting and disorganized/

disorganizing fragmentation leave the question of murder squarely in the murderers' camp, while the psychically simpler and less onerous version is undoubtedly the unthinkable nature of the void, the only real survivor being the one who was virtually constituted by the Muslim who would not have succumbed to "psychogenic death".[1] This is how the modification of the analytical setting is constantly justified in such treatments. Quietly or expressed out loud, the clinical argument for disorganization tends to legitimize the sidelining of everything in the analytical setting that could lead to the revival in the transference of destructive savagery.

The need to put on the clothes of the cruel superego, the obligation not to soften anything in a transference that only asks to be caught again in the nets of compassion and admiration would in fact force the analyst to re-establish his sense of terror in a process of reflection where it would not be the lack of representation but its murderous overload that would come to the fore. A double-sided murderous overload: in analysis, where hostility has the colour of a crime; in civilization, where hostility to culture makes its way in the wake of every civilizing movement.

But if murder is qualified in terms of the materiality of events, and if all that remains of trauma is the pre-analytical version of the impact of real and indisputable facts, then it is the whole of the psychoanalytic structure that is abraded. The argument put forward is one of clinical operativity; it allows for adjustments of the setting, but it will also allow for relativism. But to what sort of renunciation or capitulation of thought does the shortcut made between the fact and its effect testify? What warning signal should we discern in the falling back of cultural clinical analysis towards the back line of individual clinical analysis? What sort of surrender is reflected by the mere fact of subsuming the Shoah under the term trauma? Are we to understand that the hatred expressed by Nazi barbarism towards psychoanalysis would have found here the method of its success, if only in the form of the subsequent revocation of drive complexity? Without it, however, we would not be able to grasp the motives which led a host of humans to rob themselves of their conscience and their autonomy by robbing their fellows of all human form.

Note

1 It is also remarkable that the category of survivors changes over the course of the studies: from the survivors to their children, from the fighters of the Warsaw ghetto to the escapees who took refuge in the Polish and Lithuanian forests, it regroups quite indiscriminately those who resisted annihilation in the camp itself and those who survived in hiding, for example, in the south of France.

References

Auerhahn, N., Laub, D. (1984). Post-traumatic memory as pathway and obstacle to recovery. *The International Review of Psycho-Analysis*, 11: 327–334.

Auerhahn, N., Prelinger, E. (1983). Repetition in the concentration camp survivor and her child. *The International Review of Psycho-Analysis*, 10: 31–46.

Bergmann, M. (1985). Reflections on the psychological and social function of remembering the Holocaust. *Psychoanalytic Inquiry*, 5: 9–20.

Cohen, J. (1980). Structural consequences of psychic trauma. *International Journal of Psychoanalysis*, 69: 421–432.

Cohen, J. (1985). Trauma and repression. *Psychoanalytic Inquiry*, 5(1): 163–189.

Cohen, J., Kinston, W. (1984). Repression theory: A new look at the cornerstone. *International Journal of Psychoanalysis*, 65: 411–422.

Fairbairn, W.R. (1952). *Psychoanalytic Studies of the Personality*. London: Routledge & Kegan Paul.

Jucovy, M. (1985). Telling the Holocaust story: A link between the generations. *Psychoanalytic Inquiry*, 5: 31–49.

Kardiner, A. (1941). *The Traumatic Neuroses of War* (Revised Edition: *War Stress and Neurotic Illness*). New York: Hoeber, 1947. *War Stress and Neurotic Illness*, by Abram Kardiner, with the collaboration of Herbert Spiegel, Second Edition of The Traumatic Neuroses of War. New York: Paul B. Hoeber, Inc., 1947.

Kohut, H. (1971). *The Analysis of the Self*. New York: International Universities Press.

Laub, D. (2015a). À l'écoute du témoignage de ma mère. *Le Coq-Héron*, 220(1): 13–28.

Laub, D. (2015b). Rétablir le "Tu" intérieur dans le témoignage du trauma. *Le Coq-Héron*, 220(1): 112–124.

Laub, D. (2015c). Arrêt traumatique du récit et de la symbolisation: un dérivé de la pulsion de mort? *Le Coq-Héron*, 220(1): 67–82.

Laub, D., Auerhahn, N. (1989). Failed empathy – A central theme in the survivor's Holocaust experience. *Psychoanalytic Psychology*, 6: 377–400.

Moscovici, M. (1989). Un meurtre construit par les produits de son oubli. In: *Il est arrivé quelque chose: approches de l'évènement psychique*. Paris: Ramsay, pp. 387–416.

Winnicott, D.W. (1960). Ego distortion in terms of true and false self. In: *The Maturational Processes and the Facilitating Environment*. New York: International Universities Press, 1965, pp. 140–152.

10 The liquidation of tragedy

How does the individual who, before being included in a group, had his own continuity, his own consciousness and his own field of activity, accept disappropriation? The loss of individual characteristics and the enigma of such renunciation may be seen as initiating the questions posed in *Group Psychology and the Analysis of the Ego* (Freud, 1921). That the equation between the leader and the hypnotist and the all-powerful father figure makes it possible to understand the process whereby large numbers of individuals, who have all put one and the same object in the place of their ego-ideal, are led to identify with one another, does not tell us what happens to each person's uniqueness within the social group. Of course, the model is that of the state of love, and this is never more than a "normal psychosis" (Grubrich-Simitis, 1993, p. 153).[1] In both cases, the loss of reality invalidates the capacity for criticism emanating from personal consciousness and makes one forget inclusion in the world. This is then no more than the universe formed by the closure of the group around its leader, individual feelings and personal intellectual acts proving too weak to claim any autonomy. If the hypnotist, by creating a group of two, can awaken in each one this obscure part of the archaic heritage, we can see how the group is able to lead any individual along the path of regression: the leader in turn obtains the surrender of each individual's personal will, since his power and dangerousness make even looking at him prohibited. When together, men "behave as if they were similar in shape", and when the conscious personality wanes, the restriction of individual narcissism is paid for in return by the tremendous extension of narcissism bestowed by membership of the multitude and its power.

This Freudian model was developed, in fact, at a watershed moment. On the one hand, it drew on the Darwinian source of the primal horde – that which underpins *Totem and Taboo*; on the other, it corresponded to the first transposition of the theory of narcissism into the elaboration of cultural formations. At the junction point between the two, the family, the germ-cell of civilization, allows for relations between the group and the individual (Freud, 1930, p. 114, 1921, p. 123): on the one hand, the first social group of any person is the environment constituted by

DOI: 10.4324/9781003301660-11

these "others" (1921, p. 69) who are parents and siblings; on the other, the group may be a revival of the primal horde because group psychology is the oldest human psychology. Between the two, progress is conceived by the yardstick of the primitive family imprint sealed in the form of the modern family. Of course, the family state is profoundly modified because there are now several fathers, who were once brothers, and who have renounced the position of single leader, and because the limitation of their powers results from both the fraternal pact and their multiplicity. The transmission belt remains: "from the very first, individual psychology is at the same time social psychology" (ibid.), which makes it possible to grasp the phenomena at work in primitive groups thanks to the psychic life of individuals today, and conversely, to elucidate the phenomena observed in individual analyses thanks to the hypotheses put forwards concerning groups.

But this picture, which Freud himself calls "the myth of the primal family" (ibid., p. 140), implies another component which, on its own, makes it possible to marry genesis and persistence, origin and continuity. I see this additional component in the implicit reference to Aristotle, to be very precise, in the opening to his *Politics*: if it is "obvious that the city is a natural reality", it is because any city (*polis*) is a community (*koinônia*) and man is by nature destined to live in such a *koinônia*, endowed as he is with speech. However, this is not limited, like any human or animal voice (*phônè*), to expressing pain and pleasure. As *logos*, it has above all the power to say things that are useful and harmful, just and unjust (*Aristotle's Politics*, Book 1: 1253a 1–15, in Barnes, 2016). It is necessary to highlight this implicit source if we want to understand the impact of Nazi barbarism on the ideas that civilized humanity has forged of itself and, with regard to what interests us, on the theories that psychoanalysis initially developed about culture. For the place of language is central here, whether it is a matter of the heroic story at the basis of the social pact, the picture of the assembly of brothers – a picture that the troop loyal to its Führer dismantled – the notion of equity in speech or in the treatment of each person by the group, or, finally, the function of guilt as borrowed by Freud from Greek tragedy. In a word, treating the Shoah as a trauma, that is, as an event, invalidates this essential element of the dislocation engendered by Nazism: the liquidation of tragedy. To clarify this point, we must therefore return to the Greeks.

Jean-Pierre Vernant (1962) sees one of the turning points in Greek thought in the function of the *logos* linked to justice, when the notions of *isonomia* – the equal sharing of power – the role of public debate, and the birth of law all appeared at the same time. This emergence was the fruit of a slow process of secularization, but one of its main foundations was the interaction between the spheres of mathematical thought and social reflection. The assembly was a circle held together by the balance of its geometry, whose central space, the "middle" [Greek: *meson*] remained open because it was not occupied by an exclusive holder of power: each in turn could move towards this *"meson"* in order to take a seat and speak. While Vernant sees this as the device that led to the invention of democracy, he also shows how the conception of equity and right speech resides in the historic way of dealing with conflicts within the aristocratic elites: from the time of Hesiod, the demand for equality was conceived in a bond of similarity in which rivalry took shape (*passim*, here p. 42).

Freud made this demand for fair treatment one of the springboards of his demonstration concerning the morphology of groups. If one of the engines of the cohesion of organized groups, army or church, is the granting of equal love by the great figure around whom they are organized, conversely, and in line with Simmel, he identified the source of war neuroses as lying simultaneously in the inhuman and unjust treatment of those who fought in the Great War. The feeling of solidarity and duty, which is what underlies the strength of community spirit, Freud adds, presupposes equality: we deny ourselves a great deal so that others in turn do the same. No one should distinguish themselves from others, all should do and have the same things: such manifestations undoubtedly result from jealousy, social feeling ultimately being based on the transformation of an initially hostile feeling into a positive attachment which, basically, is merely an identification.

Singularity and similarity, unity through love for the same leader and unity through love for the same father: Freud here links the combined interplay of attachment and hostility in groups with the relationships that are established in a child's bedroom. For it is in the "natural group formation" (Freud, 1921, p. 125) of the family that the reversal of jealousy into solidarity and the metabolization of narcissistic positions takes place, when these cease to be used as a reason for hating others. Certainly, the older child welcomes the younger as an intruder. At first, he wants to push him aside, strip him of his rights. But, in the presence of the equal love that parents show towards all their children, and due to the impossibility of maintaining a hostile attitude in the long run, an identification finally takes place between the children, and with it, a first feeling of community. This is how identification transmutes intolerance towards the rival into the cement of an alliance. Within a circle, the children share the love of the parents. Within a circle, they stop opposing each other and discover this mode of agreement which implies recognition in the other of something like oneself which allows hostility to be suspended. Within a circle, the identificatory modifications, required by the renunciation of the sexual goals of infantile love, order the intertwining of being and having, where each individual finds the grounds for their first affective community. The web of individual narcissism – its Oedipal vicissitudes, the place devolved to the "model" of the father – and the chain of collective narcissism thus form the material for collective libidinal organization, for the family of childhood is not organized any differently from the vast primitive human family from which we all come. Children are brothers, that is to say sons, the relationship to the primitive father being both at the origin of the first social pact between equals and the source of the immense nostalgia which cannot find any other outcome than in the mythical story of the birth of the community.

Yet this family circle, with its strange power of transforming jealousy into a feeling of solidarity – this applies to children and also, in the same way, to members of the social community – does not erase the hypnotic effects of the love-object, of its authority, of its power resulting from the immense protective power that is attributed to it, which the leader, by taking the place of the ego ideal, embodies.

Admittedly, as Freud notes, the capacity to reactivate these archaic situations varies from one individual to another – which the hypnotist recognizes when confronted with a rebellious subject – because not everyone has the same ability to exchange one's ego ideal for the group ideal embodied in the leader: either the distinction between the ego and the ego ideal is not completed, and the ego still possesses its very first narcissistic completeness, in which case the leader is then purely and simply clothed with the omnipotence of the ideal ego; or the ego ideal does not find its full and complete embodiment in the leader, and the subjects are then carried along "suggestively", that is to say, through identification.

Is this really a minimal "correction", as Freud suggests? (1921, p. 129). Nothing is less certain, if we judge by what becomes of this difference in Freud's subsequent reflections. It seems to me that it is the source of the praise for neurosis that Freud offers in the final summary of *Group Psychology and the Analysis of the Ego*. And, above all, it is the source of the very possibility of the mythical story.

The astonishing apologia for neurosis – astonishing because I do not think he makes this assertion so strongly elsewhere in his writings – arises when he comes to the ultimate study of the respective roles of the direct sexual drives and the aim-inhibited sexual drives in the various psychic formations that he examines. The comparative project is in itself strange. And yet it forces itself upon him, concluding the long examination of the ways in which man consents to his alienation. From this perspective, direct sexual drives are worth their weight in gold, for they are the guarantors of an individuality that persists even for the individual dissolved in the group. It is thanks to them that neurosis escapes the series of states – being in love/hypnosis/group formation – a series essentially founded on narcissistic drive functioning, the inability of which to obtain full satisfaction – which preserves it from any lowering of energy – supports the durability of the links necessary for the sustainability of the community. It is not only in the neurotic that there is a constant mixture of the two vicissitudes of the sexual drive. In addition, after renunciation and identification with the first love objects, the portion of the drives aggregated with the ego remains constantly in conflict with the portion of the drives that is repressed in the course of the biphasism of human sexuality.

Had Freud read Orwell's *1984* in advance? In any case, the conflict he describes – an infinitely fertile conflict between the portion of the drives that is repressed and the portion aggregated through identification with the ego – bars the way to any homogenization around a single internalized object. The compensation for individual narcissistic impairment due to narcissistic dilation in the group meets its obstacle there: at the point where the freedom that only internal conflict can grant is opposed to the "prodigy" (Freud, 1921, p. 129) of the disappearance of the individual who has exchanged his ideals for those embodied in the Führer. In *1984*, Winston's love for Julia sustains this conflict for a long time, until, helped by the torment of the rats, Winston wants the appalling punishment to be inflicted on her, his beloved. Neuroses, Freud writes, "embrace all possible relations between the ego and the object" (ibid., p. 143) whether the object is retained, abandoned, or erected inside the ego. They therefore guarantee that intrapsychic strife is always maintained on two sides: the repressed drive impulses constantly strive to attain satisfaction and are opposed to the ego, and the relation between the ego and the ego ideal inherits the conflict between the ego and its primary objects. Such a dispute cannot be resolved by massification alone.

It was from this dispute, it seems to me, that the heroic story developed. The epic poet could only step forward into the assembly of brothers because, for each of these sons, the relationship with the father turned out to be the source of deep intrapsychic tension. As individuals and as a plurality of individuals united in a totemic community around the murderous deed and its atonement, they certainly had the ideal of the honoured and feared father in common. But they also carried within themselves the same dissatisfaction (ibid., p. 135). This was what drove them towards new developments. It was also what led them to re-occupy the place of singular fathers, heads of individualized and limited families. Finally, it was what made one of them stand up out of nostalgia and recount the exploits of the first hero. This was a mythical lie that sought to explain why an individual had committed the crime that only the horde as a whole would have been able to carry out. This was an epic invention that transformed reality and brought the possibility of combining the individual and the collective spheres to completion. In fact, the poet was himself the hero. But although he seemed to offer himself as a new ego ideal, it was on the condition that his act of relating the hero's deeds was considered as setting the remembrance of the father and the reminiscence of the sons free from the real deed of murder. In this sense, if the poet transported the murderous deed to the level of imagination, it was not to embody the ideal in his own person. It was in some respects to disembody it. Such a disembodiment was not as yet a desacralization, of course. However, we must recognize in the operation described by Freud the movement by which the lyric poet draws the circle of listeners without occupying its centre except by exploring nostalgia and fiction.

He was a narrator, therefore, who recounted the crime, spoke of inaugural guilt, and laid the foundations of the community. It was the mythical genesis of the political "We". A historical genesis if one considers that the heroic lie contains in a distorted way a nucleus of historical truth; but a genesis, nonetheless. In *Les Origines de la pensée grecque*, Jean-Pierre Vernant (1962) emphasizes the crucial evolution of the term *archè* – a word that can be translated as "power" as well "beginning" – in the journey which goes from myth to the threshold of rational thought. With the reflections of the Milesians (Thales, Anaximander and Anaximenes), with their attempt to define the order of the world in terms of its internal forces and the law of numbers, with the new correspondence between geometric thought of the circle and political thought of a balanced and reciprocal space, the *archè* ceased to designate the origin only in the sense of the hierarchical position within a system of theogonic sovereignty. With the defeat of a divine agent holding power, the secularization of the *arché* involved the registration of genesis and causes in time. This was an "historic" moment of change which took part in the movement allowing man to think of the community in terms of an abstraction, where the divinities gradually became principles ordering the autonomous domain of nature and its physics as well as those of social ethics and their measure. This movement, at the source of knowledge emancipated from the divine, benefited from the whole evolution of moral thought in Greece, and was completed in the spectacle of consciousness divided in the "place" that is tragedy, when Greek man questioned myths through the eyes of the citizen (see Vernant, 1972, 1986).

When, in *Totem and Taboo*, Freud (1912–1913) emphasizes the link between the heroic myth and "tragic guilt" (p. 156), he also indicates the essential role of the chorus in the performance of the tragedy, a chorus whose commentary opens up the enigma of human singularity, the rage of the confrontation between the inflexibility of desire and guilt, the internal torment that is a prelude to deliberation. In other words, by taking over the heroic deed, tragedy in turn breaks down the figure of the mythical hero – the commentary of the chorus, a chorus of assembled citizens, being the very instrument of disintegration. By taking into account individual responsibility, freed from the blind repetition of divine punishment for an original crime, the scene where the tragedy unfolds fundamentally modifies not only the relationship to inner discourse, but the relationship to the power of the truth of fiction. While it is never fate that is tragic but only consciousness of it, imagination tells the story of the soul struggling with exile, and it does so by tearing man not from the reality of world and *koinônia*, but from the actual performance of deeds. This is how, under tension, the We, the I and the You, the "outside oneself" and the "inside oneself", the other and the person, the individual and the collective, the unique and the impersonal, can coexist.

With the mythical lie and the "tragedy of the primitive father", Freud, in *Civilization and its Discontents* (1930, pp. 131–133) and then in *Moses and Monotheism* (1939, pp. 117–118), followed the thread of consciousness of guilt, from its source in the primary ambivalence of feelings – repentance inevitably arising from the portion of love that it encompasses – to its development with the enlargement of the community beyond its first family form, the role of the Great Man to whom "in group psychology the role of the superego falls" (p. 117) and, finally, the historical, "genetic", "evolutionary" continuity of the commandments.

It is precisely this thread that is broken by Nazism, liquidating the tragedy of the primitive father. "I predict a paradoxical surprise in Germany", Freud wrote to Marie Bonaparte.

> They began with Bolshevism as their deadly enemy, and they will end with something indistinguishable from it – except perhaps that Bolshevism after all adopted revolutionary ideals, whereas those of Hitlerism are purely medieval and reactionary. This world seems to me . . . doomed to perdition.
>
> (letter from Freud to Marie Bonaparte dated
> 10 June 1933 in Jones, 1957, p. 182)

This is politically frightening because "in the case of the German people a relapse into an almost prehistoric barbarism can occur as well without being attached to any progressive ideas" (Freud, 1939, p. 54). In other words, as Semprún (2013) has pointed out, it is a *Weltanschauung* that presents itself "without palliatives or ideological pretexts", "quite naked".

The idea that the masses have at their foundations the vector for an ever possible regression towards barbarism has not been contradicted by history. Ideals too, ever since ideologies have brought with them their share of industrialized murders. And identifications, the breeding ground for identity-making, have also seen their trajectory curving in the sky laden with totalizations. In isolation, man can be cultivated; in groups, he has the violence, ferocity and enthusiasm of primitive individuals, that is to say, their irresponsibility. Thomas Mann said this in 1935 in his essay "Europe Beware!" (Mann, 1942, p. 73) citing *The Revolt of the Masses* by José Ortega y Gasset (1961): speaking of the intrusion of new masses who use civilization as a force of nature, and the immense wave of "eccentric barbarism", he pointed out that such brutal fairground customs were the work of primitive groups. But this surge was not the result of the Great War. The latter only accelerated the movement of a decline, of a contempt for the values of morality, art, ideas – a contempt that obtained the intimate consent of the masses, who were only too happy to be able to swap the laborious course of education for the simplifying principle of domination and suggestion. Thus, according to Mann, Europeans were caught in the yoke of hypnosis, unable to regain awareness of themselves. "The mass of the people take things easily" wrote Freud (1933, p. 142). And all the more easily if they are spared the pains of confronting reality and truth.

How can we fail to note in this situation an echo of Freud's note in *Group Psychology and the Analysis of the Ego* concerning the "mystical" character of the hypnotic phenomenon? (1921, pp. 115, 77–78)) How can we not note it if we consider that it is at the source of consent to illusion and preference for the unreal? It is from this mysterious "We" that the group derives the feeling of its omnipotence, and that the individual who is part of it gains the certainty that the impossible no longer exists. We can recognize here the confiscation of reality-testing by the *Führer*, when the masses have given way to him as the critical authority, and the measure of the miracle achieved by this psychic montage. But to me it seems above all remarkable that it is around this same notion of "everything is possible", around this same abolition of the group's relation to reality, that Hannah Arendt (1958) describes the onion-like structure of the totalitarian system (pp. 413 and 430). The "shapelessness" (p. 395) of the totalitarian state, the multiplication and duplication of all services, the abrogation of a hierarchical system of responsibilities, however disastrous, and the resulting confusion of authority not only contributes to the disintegration of individuals; the method also determines the formation of a "phantom world" (p. 445) and nonetheless materialized world, a whole that is both realized and fictitious. This paradox, according to Arendt, results from several factors, including that humanity is organized as if it were formed only of individuals "reduced to a never-changing identity of reactions" – a sort of human species resembling the animal species, whose only "freedom" would consist in "preserving the species" (p. 573).[2] As for the leader, he relies on the wish of all humans to take their desires for reality, that is to say to be satisfied with unverifiable stories, rumours strictly fomented by subjective mirages, stories that are "indisputable" in the true sense of the word. The fictitious world is thus provided with all the sensory data of reality, but it lacks the consistency and responsibility without which reality remains only a mass of incomprehensible data. Finally, the successive envelopes overlap, ranging from the leader and the elite to individuals atomized by terror, including sympathizers, who validate the credibility of fiction without lying, since lies are reality itself.

In this situation, we can see that the notion of "myth", even if the Nazi theorist Alfred Rosenberg (1982/1930) makes full use of it in *The Myth of the 20th Century*, is stricken with inanity. The Nazi myth does not refer to mythology but to "limitless absolutes" which Philippe Lacoue-Labarthe and Jean-Luc Nancy (1991) have shown are the source of a an utterance of the life force itself. The aim of the myth of the race is to achieve the universality of the type in "the naked power of its own affirmation" and to obtain the "mystical" adhesion of the people – by the word "mystical", Rosenberg means beyond a simple belief, total participation in the type. As I have already mentioned, all the great German Aryans of the past centuries took to fighting once the philosophical term of *Weltanschauung* had been misused. But nothing remains of mythology, of the Greek narrative of myths, even though the mimesis of Hellenic solar power and of its "archetype" is at the heart of the fabric of identity of the National Socialist masses.

As for the function of the epic story, it has vanished. The assembly of the brothers that it presupposes is not even conceivable in the ghostlike universe created by Nazi self-realization. There is no place for the hero who narrates, no place for his gestures since the gathering of the community takes place only on the territory of the naturalness of blood and of race, and this territory is not a circle: it is the *Lebensraum*, where one speaks in the idiom of survival.

For those who would like to oppose, for those who would, despite everything, like to claim autonomy for their thought, their destiny and their words, the path here is too narrow for the fiction which would be its depository, like a defile that is too narrow for the power of poetic speech to slip through. It is a real bottleneck for anyone who tries to elevate the murderous deed to the level of imagining the act, for the reality of mass murder inhabits the world as both its foundation and as a fictitious vapour. This is how the question of knowing how to account for the actual unreality comes up over and over again in the testimonies of those who returned from the camps. The impossibility of dealing with this reality which had lost all connection with the imaginary sphere – and consequently with reality itself – is always spoken of in the impossible reconstruction by the narrative of the exact opposite of what is dreamable, to which the abysmal degree of unreality must nonetheless be restored. Whether it is spoken of in the terms of a universe whose violence stems primarily from its unintelligible character or in those of a language diverted from its normal meaning and degraded into jargon – the reasons for the inability of language to speak are revealed in many ways – each time there is this knot that the civilizing narrative once again wants to untie, a knot that seeks to link mass extermination to some origin of murder and destruction, and attempts in turn to thwart its repetition. But the knot, this time, works like a noose.

Yet this is the challenge of Kertész's work which, in principle, seeks to weaken the narration of the experience by disrupting its method. "There is nothing impossible that we do not live through naturally", he writes in *Fatelessness* (2004, p. 262). Such therefore is the other focus of this "naturally", of this *natürlich* which punctuates his texts: to confound seems obvious and especially to deny the account of the experience of the treacherous slope of the epic drama, even though it was one of disaster, which would be the denial par excellence of what there is to say (Kertész, 1992, p. 29).

It is in this sense that we must understand Kertész's affirmation, repeated over and over again, that he owed his survival after the camps to the fact of having known the coherence of continuity, of having never placed his hope in any catharsis that a free life would allow, of having had to write in an "extended present of Auschwitz". Unlike Levi, Améry, Bettelheim, Celan and many others who committed suicide, he was neither haunted by hope nor affected by the wave of disappointment experienced by those who returned, and who encountered head on the impossibility of restoring, more than horror, its indecipherable logic (see Kertész, 2013, p. 11, 159). By speaking of totalitarianism with another totalitarianism, he has now been able to speak for all. For the freedom he found in the dark time that immediately followed the dark times owed nothing to hope or confidence. It was oppression itself that created it, "denying it day after day and day by day making its existence more evident" (2009, p. 219, 1992, p. 33). Are we to understand that Kertész found in Stalinist totalitarianism the route that allowed him to reconstitute imaginatively the circle of ruination by forging a new circle of resistance? And further that, in his eyes, this was the condition for successfully transforming the experience of the camps into a human experience and for bringing the discovery of this new form of universality, "the absence of fate" into culture? But to do that, it was still necessary to invent a language.

"I like to write in Hungarian because it makes me feel better about the impossibility of writing" (Kertész, 2009, p. 233, see also 1992, p. 56). Is that enough? Certainly not, because language, even when it is impossible, must nevertheless bear witness to the loss of a common language. It must indicate in its usage the impracticable plural of "They" and their consensuality. The worst obstacle is, moreover, this inflation, this globalization of the Holocaust, this circle so widened that language itself has definitively sealed it off, by transforming the memory into a ritual, by assigning it to a ossified, immovable place (Kertész, 2009, p. 216, 253, see also 2013/2006, pp. 67–68, 143–144). The survivor, this new type of man in European history who accepts its linguistic conventions – who resigns himself, in doing so, to this whole set of words: victim, persecuted, ordeal, pain, atrocities, unthinkable, unrepresentable, etc. – is isolated by the very linguistic forms of the Holocaust discourse, by their modelling. He gradually realizes that all these words have made the Holocaust a sacred generic term that does not even touch the reality of extermination, and "he gives up". And yet, adds Kertész, if the survivor of the Shoah is content with exile, to emerge victorious from the expatriation of oneself as a writer only means that one is a crook or a liar. In the community of life of a "prisoner on leave", which is that of Stalinist terror, language remains borrowed. How can one take hold of this language of others so that it speaks the truth, while not denying the fact that its power, here, now as before, remains that of the mystical We of any totalitarian state; that here, now as before, there is no more I or You; that, between "the state control of thought" and "the organization of enthusiasm"[3] man is functional and immorality collective?

If Kertész prefers to use the name Auschwitz rather than the Holocaust to describe the universe of the Nazi concentration camps and mental upheaval that followed, if this is the name of a fact and of its essence, it is then necessary to "invent", to "create" Auschwitz in such a way that everything is born "hermetically" and that "moving forward in history, a feeling of perdition invades the reader" (Kertész, 2009, p. 44, 51, 2013, pp. 4, 8–9, 68–69). To find concrete details, the memory of the Auschwitz football field, that of the eiderdowns in the *Revier* [infirmary] in Buchenwald, to think of children playing in the absurdity of the crematorium, to imagine that the sick were fed with milk and honey in order to gradually remove their guts. But above all, words are needed that speak of deprivation, the very ones that Celan (2005) invents in "Conversation in the Mountains", not to signify the reconciliation of words with the world, but to understand how through Auschwitz, that terrible property of the Jew, the latter has lost his tongue. Nothing "which belongs to him in truth, nothing which is not lent, borrowed", it is with a "language in use here" – "a language, not for you or for me – because I ask you for whom is it meant, the earth, not for you, I say, is it meant, and not for me, – a language, well, without I and without You, nothing but He, nothing but It, you understand, and She, nothing but that" (p. 151) – it is with it, this language that has let you down, that you simply have to write and "sketch out a reality" (see Kertész, 2009, pp. 213–215; Celan, 2005, 1986).[4]

"At a certain temperature, metaphorically speaking, words lose their substance, their content, their meaning; they simply deliquesce, so that in this vaporous state, deeds alone, naked deeds, show a certain tendency for solidity; it is deeds alone that we can take in our hands, so to speak, and examine like a mute lump of mineral, like a crystal" (Kertész, 2017, p. 43). A language that acts. The deed, and the liquidation of the deed by the act, to state its singularity. To tame the raw material because nothing is hiding. To tell the story not of what is unrepresentable but what cannot be distorted. In short, to tell the story of B., born in Auschwitz, who committed suicide. But how should one tell it: "objectively? dramatically? or as in a transcript style, so to speak?" And yet, "[l]ook at the subject that I am providing you with": a child is born in Auschwitz thanks to the mutual help of good people. All the ingredients for the tragedy seem to be there. Only fate is missing. *Liquidation* is in fact the story of the liquidation of heroism and tragedy (p. 18), because the exception, "the result of an industrial accident in the machinery of death" (p. 33) destroyed them (Kertész, 2005b, pp. 26–32). Each survivor only testifies to a particular operating defect, and each of these industrial accidents has a name, the proper name of what escaped the machinery. There is therefore no point in creating pathos from the event. There is no point either in placing hope in the *Witz*, although it persists: "Do you know what this here", [pointing to his chest] "this letter 'U', signifies?" – "*Ungar*, Hungarian". – "No, *Unschuldig*" ["innocent"] (Kertész, 2004, p. 142). It is even more pointless to resort to some sort of Jewish identity: you do not speak Yiddish; "if you ask the 'Finns' where they come from, they reply *'fin Minkács'* . . . or *'fin*

Sadarada' . . . looking at you as if you were thin air" (p. 139).[5] However surprising it is that these business experts hold on to such an irrational thing that ultimately ends up being much more damaging than profitable, it is even more astonishing to feel that something is out of tune with the general idea: to be a Jew among the Jews in the camp.

It was the very principle of identity that was shattered, and not under torture. It was not that of criminals who were sent to the camp for a specific activity, nor was it that of the politicians who were there for actions or opinions to which they had subjectively claimed authorship and who had, as in Buchenwald or Dachau, for a long time patiently taken hold of the reins of the camp. But it was that of the quintessence of the detainees: the group of innocents. It was through them that the civil rights of the entire population were abolished, the legal person assassinated and the moral person beheaded. The corruption of all human solidarity went hand in hand with the invalidation of both consent and opposition, with the aim of ensuring the disintegration of the uniqueness of the person. If ideology is very literally what its name indicates, the logic of an idea, its first function as *Weltanschauung* is above all to emancipate itself from reality for a truer reality thanks to the binding force of its logic: writes Hannah Arendt (1958). "You can't say A without saying B and C and so on, down to the end of the murderous alphabet" (p. 472). An alphabet that is destined to ruin "the singularity granted through will and fate", by exhausting the resources of isolation until the ego abandons itself, when common sense, the experience of a shared tangible fact, the legitimacy of a form of conviction are dissolved.

Kertész's language seeks to make ideological logic fall into its own trap, by dismantling it, by replying "that's obvious". To do this, it describes the good will that exists in the camp, the strange expectation that things and rhythms will settle into place, that the ordinary days of captivity will obey a form of rational prediction, even if that of the worst, that the distractions will be a facade and explanations forthcoming. "The secret of survival is collaboration", (Kertész, 2013, p. 66) the mental collaboration through which one tries to rediscover the appearances of logic. And it is this, the "novelistic" turning point of explanations, that Kertész tries to find by creating his own character as fiction. Kertész, Keserü, Köves, and finally K. make up the file. So many names that he can no longer identify with himself, "vanishing nicely and comfortably between fiction and the facts that are called reality" (ibid., p. 74), succeeding in being there, "naturally", where he was not: there, where the hands made gestures "quite simply" as long as hunger and wasting did not make him understand the limits of absence from his body; there, where, "peacefully, placidly, incuriously, patiently", in the puddle where he had been placed, he felt no cold or pain, and it was more "[his] intellect than [his] skin which signalled that some stinging precipitation, half snow, half rain, was spattering [his] face" (p. 186); there, where he daydreamed, without any unnecessary movement or fatigue. He simply did not recognize that voice, though once so familiar, his own, when he stubbornly wanted to have "one last chance" assuming there was a way, "naturally" (p. 184). Barely calling out, getting carried away on the handcart, berating himself for not being far-sighted enough since he didn't know *"how they did it"* in Buchenwald, just hoping it wouldn't be too painful. Nothing absurd that one could not experience naturally: "despite all deliberation, sense, insight, and sober reason, I could not fail to recognize within myself the furtive and yet – ashamed as it might be, so to say, of its irrationality – increasingly insistent voice of some muffled craving of sorts: I would like to live a little bit longer in this beautiful concentration camp" (2004/1975, p. 189, emphasis added).

Here again, we must read Kertész in the light of Arendt. The private, singular sphere of each individual inevitably stands in tension with the public sphere founded on the law of equality of all – the "difference" of all existence interfering like an intruder in the political construction of the principle of universal justice. Nevertheless, only this construction makes it possible to build a common world, with the same opportunity for everyone to speak and act. It is in this common world, established on the legality of a civic status, that is to say on the law, that, despite the hatred of which he may be the object, the individual in his singularity finds the basis of his existence at the same time as protection. In the interwar period, stateless people discovered that no government authority, no nation-state was ready to offer them guarantees, and that no place was ready to assimilate their community. Excluded from citizenship and from the "family of nations", they were excluded from the "right to have rights", that is to say they were excluded de facto from all of humanity and simply identified by their unique qualities. This is how those who knew the camps understood that "the abstract nakedness of being human and nothing but human" is the greatest danger" (Arendt, 2017, p. 297). Those "without rights", deprived of legal and civic shelter, learned that they were becoming "a human being in general", in other words, that they were reduced "to their absolutely unique individuality which, deprived expression within and action upon a common world loses all significance" (p. 302) (see also Enaudeau, 2011).

Thus the naked man is a man to whom only his own name remains. And the latter is a rigid designator, an invariable mark of a reference independent of the sentences into which it fits, strongly determined as to its location in the networks of names, but weakly determined as to its meaning: an object of history? An object of perception? A component of a logical space? An ingredient in a story? How does it reach reality? (Lyotard, 1983, pp. 47–68, 88–91).

So it is necessary to multiply proper names, Kertész, Keserü, Köves, around the untransformable proper name that is Auschwitz. In the centre, we find the liquidation of the epic saga, that is to say the prohibition of the "beautiful death", of the praise for its courage and its meaning, of its function in the formation of the city, of its power to create a We united around heroes.[6] But at the centre, above all, there is the observation that the "middle" has ceased to be the meson of the circle of assembled citizens. It has become the site of a unique game, "*Lager* poker", which a few opponents gathered clandestinely on New Year's Eve play: "A simple game, simple rules. The players sit around the table and each person says *where they have been*. Only the place-name, nothing else. That was the basis for determining the value of the chips" (Kertész, 2005/2003, p. 51, emphasis added). The value of the tokens is determined on this basis. To be the winner in the game of proper names is to win what? It doesn't matter since the point "value" system is based on exchangeability of the non-exchangeable. B., the other of Keserü, the other of Kertész, the man of what could have been a beautiful tragic birth if fate had not failed, knows in advance that he has the poker in his pocket: the "unbeatable" name, Auschwitz. He leaves for fear of cheating. He leaves this petrified world.

It is necessary to invent proper names on the periphery of the name that cannot be invented, and then invent time. That which, as in fairy tales, sees to it that here seven days are seven years, the time to record "day after day, how much of one has wasted away" (Kertész, 2004, p. 165) these twenty minutes spent on the railroad where everything happens very quickly and imperceptibly, twenty minutes of human beings arriving, women with beautiful smiling faces, young people with intelligent eyes "all of them well-intentioned and eager to cooperate", "twenty minutes of idleness and helplessness . . . "was repeated the same way for days, weeks, months and years on end". The use of time allows us to understand "how it became possible to turn human nature against one's own life" (Kertész, 2003). It is therefore in temporality that the links of the narrative can be rooted. Not the historical temporality of the event. Not that of terror and resistance. But the time absolutely specific to that event, a time related to its materiality, hard as a stone, hard as the naked deeds which punctuate it.

This temporality is nothing more than that of the stubbornness in the camp. A stubbornness of invention, a stubbornness of thought, means practiced by everyone to escape from themselves and regain their share of an "accepted and inalienable possession" (Kertész, 2004, p. 155), a stubbornness that no longer imagines time but "fill it" (Kertész, 2004, p. 250). Because the train is moving, it is still rolling, and its onward course requires the collaboration of the intelligence of things and what they are going to be next. But this "next" is not a future. It only aroused amazement when the two-digit number appeared on the arm of the doctor from Buchenwald, a "dignitary" in his immaculate white coat, with its impeccable folds. Inmates had been living there for four, six, twelve years. So all this time had to be occupied somehow – by counting backwards minute after minute.

"Can we imagine a concentration camp", asked the journalist met by Köves on his return to Budapest, "as anything but a hell? The young survivor replied that he could only imagine a camp since he was somewhat acquainted with what that was, but not a hell (ibid., p. 248). "All the same, say you could?" the journalist pressed. And Köves tried to imagine the camp as a place where it is impossible to become bored even though, under certain conditions, one was of course bored. "How do you account for that?" – "Time". Time helps, it helps everything: to arrive in an agreeable, neat and clean station, where "everything becomes clear only gradually, sequentially, step by step" (p. 249). By the time one has passed a given step, the next one is already there. Time is used to meet the new requirements of each new stage, and it does this in the multiplication of the minutes that have passed by, sometimes over a period of up to twelve years. "It's impossible to imagine it", replied the journalist. And Köves tells himself that must be why they prefer to talk about hell instead (p. 250).

"Of course, naturally". There is the time of returning home. And with it, the collection of stereotypes: punishing the guilty, mobilizing public opinion, the affair of the whole world, dissipating indifference and apathy, bearing witness to the painful ordeal, to its truth, that was not easy for anyone. Times were hard for everyone, when everyone tried to survive, over the course of turning-points and changes. But the story of every "twist, turn and episode" is a dizzying one. It does not come about in "the regular rhythmic passage of seconds, minutes, hours, days, weeks and months" (p. 255). No, the yellow star "came about", the ghetto came about", liberation "came about", a swirl of events that were already blurred, while all eyes were on the future. The returnee is encouraged to imagine the future. The past comes in the form of an incantation, where burden and atrocities punctuate what should now be forgotten so that a new life may begin. But what is a new life if it is impossible to be reborn, if what has happened has happened, if everyone during that time "took steps". Those who were in Budapest, he in the camp: a time in common, but reduced to its "normal course", this perhaps is what remains to be shared in the *koinônia*, provided that its members are willing to stop talking about hell and about horrors. Because these empty words do not tell how the queue on the ramp was constantly moving, how the selection progressed in a dazzling way with everyone taking steps, bigger or smaller ones (p. 257) Time is human because "it didn't just come about", because we were the ones who took it step by step. Of course, looking back, everything seems finished, that is to say finite and unalterable. We can then consider that all this "came about" and, in doing so, give credit to the passage of time. But past and future are "flawed" perspectives that miss the essential point: the length of the twenty minutes was such that each minute had started, endured, and then ended before the next one started. But "every one of those minutes might have brought something new. In reality, it didn't" (p. 258).

If it is with hindsight that one recognizes what appears to be fate, the slow walk, in a timescale fragmented by its own minutes, destroyed this fate. For example, if "Jewish" meant nothing at first, it was the steps themselves that gave it meaning. But what meaning? The fate experienced was a "given fate" and not that of each individual, even if he experienced it to the end. It was a fate from which fault had been obscured, abrogated by the selection of the innocent, clearing them in the eyes of history of all crime as from all responsibility. It deprived them, in doing so, of any inclusion in the unfolding of the story. All the survivors insisted on the accidental nature of their survival. All said they were nothing more than a sign of a mechanical malfunction, a mistake. The question of fate therefore arises only when one must "continue to live", in the irresponsibility of this accident. The impossibility of being only an innocent, of having nothing to do with it, of having "only been honest in [one's] given fate" is then revealed. Not only is the random nature of the return commensurate with the inanity of any discourse dramatizing murder and guilt, but hatred, which we may try to substitute for the "bombastic" language of horror and suffering, will not express any better the irreversible loss of both singularity and the common world – because this hatred is no longer that of the gods, nor that of men; it has its place here, its role. The liquidation of the tragedy in which it participates speaks of the inability to convert it into a thought about oneself fulfilling one's own destiny. Its "usefulness" merely testifies to the consensus shared by men who have become functional.

Besides, what is fate? If it exists, then it is allotted to you, and freedom does not exist. And if there is freedom, then there is no such thing as fate since we ourselves are fate. Yet to say of the mass murder that it struck the innocent is to permanently strip the survivor. Neither victor nor vanquished, neither cause nor result, he was relegated to a dead end where, having failed, he nevertheless did not commit any crime. So he can only "adapt". Conformity, adherence to the consensual "We" built on the ruins of the mystical "We", will certainly grant an honourable life, "in harmony with reality" (1992, p. 17). Yet if reality is nothing other than ourselves, and if the facts are nothing but the absurdities of life, the conformist himself will inevitably become a fact, an absurdity. That, in *Fiasco* (Kertész, 2011a, the only reference to Goethe's autobiography is the diary of the executioner Berg, reveals the height of the sarcasm – I will come back to this (2011b, p. 286ff). Let us simply say that the destruction of tradition is here at its peak: it is suddenly put in the service of the liberation of the weight of any singularity, since the "crystal clear act" that results in the massacre does not even arise from the character of the person, of his inclinations, of his nature, but only from the situation imposed on him. Experience in sense of *Erlebnis* now resists narration, even if the deciphering of the history of the murderer, that is to say the genesis of the murder, perhaps lends itself to it – that is what the "*detective story*" still proclaims.

"What can art do since the type of man it has always represented (the tragic man) no longer exists?" (1992, p. 11). It can speak about this new era which has broken with autobiography, which has rejected the "place" of the tragic spectacle, which carries within itself the squandering of the circle of brothers. This account makes no concessions to nostalgia, does not rely on any repentance, does not invoke any "shadow" of the deed. It only wants the atonality of discord where the consensual illusion reigns so freely. It only wants "to reach the depths of characters and concepts with the means of the surface" (ibid., p. 25). For it is in the surface that gaps return that are capable of making the absolute tremble without limit, without remainder, and that the psyche rediscovers the first mesh of detachment. For Kertész, the gaps are those of writing itself: the "no" of *Kaddish for an Unborn Child*; the "no" opposed to the German dream of a fiction supporting the reconciliation between the singularity of a fate and the common fabric of a culture; the "no" rejecting the redemptive virtues of love, even if it were that of writing. Loves, lovers can do nothing against the exhaustion of time and the "comical situation" of the survivor, when everyone sees only solutions instead of lives.

However, in *Liquidation*, the sexual thing, among the rare differences still available, seems to be the only one capable of reintroducing division and rift. With this, in the midst of irreversible losses including that of disappointment itself, while the liquidation of the characters is the means of signifying the bankruptcy of heroism, we see the infiltration of the living part, that of disorderly, insane moments, without continuation, of the meeting of two human beings. Had Kertész also read Orwell? Such a method, in any case, resistant to auto-fiction and its suspicious narcissistic inclination, sets in motion the waltz/hesitation between two forms of annihilation, which are two forms of return to zero, and it sets it in motion in the atonal version of time, its minimalism, so that Auschwitz manages to become part of the culture.

In this sense, the multiplication of proper names is a "surface means" which shatters the hero's unique name. And time is the same surface means, which otherwise dismisses the form of totalization to which any narrative can become hostage.

> The absence of fate is all that is determined from the outside. . . . In contrast to this absence, I call fate a possibility of tragedy, of downfall, of failure in action. It is the classical fate, in which we recognize ourselves, as well as one's faults, one's greatness and one's peculiarities. We recognize the Gods, to maintain the theme of Greek tragedy. With the absence of fate, all of this no longer exists. It is also the end of tragedy.
>
> (1999, p. 90)

But what detour can one take to consider both the formation of the community and its possible destruction, to grasp the interweaving of restored narcissism and the corruption of the heroic narrative, the utterance of which nevertheless seems essential to the pact ensuring the constitution of the socius?

Notes

1 Kertész (1992, p. 77) quotes Freud's phrase in *Totem and Taboo* to the effect that states of love are the normal prototypes of psychoses.
2 Hannah Arendt refers in a footnote to Hitler's *Tischgespräche* [Table Talk], the fragment of which is as follows: "I [strive] for a condition in which each individual knows that he lives and dies for the preservation of his species. It is our duty to encourage this conception that the man who distinguishes himself in the service of the species is worthy of the highest honours."
3 Expression used by É. Halévy in "L'ère des tyrannies", a paper presented and debated at the *Société française de Philosophie* on 28 November 1936. Halévy hesitates between the term dictatorship and that of tyranny, the term "totalitarian" not yet being created to designate this new political phenomenon.
4 Kertész notes that "the *Kaddish* is built involuntarily and without 'premeditation' on *Todesfüge*".
5 *Fin* in Yiddish is equivalent to German *von* [from]).
6 I am referring here to the work of N. Loraux, and more particularly to the (1993) book *L'Invention d'Athènes. Histoire de l'oraison funèbre dans la "cité classique"*.

References

Arendt, H. (2017/1951). *The Origins of Totalitarianism*. London: Penguin.
Barnes, J. (ed.). (2016). *Aristotle's Politics, Writings from the Complete Works*. Princeton, NJ: Princeton University Press.
Celan, P. (1986/1958). *Speech* on the occasion of receiving the literature prize of the Free Hanseatic City of *Bremen*. In: *Paul Celan: Collected Prose*, trans. Rosmarie Waldrop. London: Carcanet Pres, Ltd, pp. 33–37.
Celan, P. (2005/1959). Conversation in the mountains. In: *Paul Celan: Selections*. Berkeley: Uniiversity of California Press, pp. 149–153.
Enaudeau, C. (2011). Réfugiés et apatrides: des droits en moins, des hommes en trop. In: *Témoigner. Entre histoire et mémoire*. Bruxelles, n°110, September 2011, pp. 100–111.
Freud, S. (1921). *Group Psychology and the Analysis of the Ego*. S.E. 18. London: Hogarth, pp. 65–144.
Freud, S. (1930). *Civilization and Its Discontents*. S.E. 21. London: Hogarth, pp. 57–146.
Freud, S. (1933). *New Introductory Lectures on Psycho-analysis*. S.E. 22. London: Hogarth, pp. 1–182.
Freud, S. (1939). *Moses and Monotheism*. S.E. 23. London: Hogarth, pp. 7–137.
Grubrich-Simitis, I. (1993). Verliebtsein ist die Normalpsychose. In: *Zurück zur Freud texten, Stume Dokumente sprechen machen*, Ilse Grubrich-Simitis (ed.). Frankfurt: Fischerverlag.
Jones, E. (1957). *The Life and Work of Sigmund Freud*, Vol. 3. London: Hogarth.
Kertész, I. (1992). *Journal de galère* [Galley-Slave's Journal]. Arles: Actes Sud.
Kertész, I. (1999). Le vingtième siècle est une machine à liquider permanente. Interview with G. Moser. In: *Parler des camps, penser les génocides*, C. Coquio (ed.). Paris: Albin Michel, pp. 87–92.
Kertész, I. (2004/1975). *Fatelessness*, trans.T. Wilkinson. London: Vintage International.
Kertész, I. (2005/2003). *Liquidation*. London: Vintage.

Kertész, I. (2009). *L'Holocauste Comme Culture*. Arles: Actes Sud.

Kertész, I. (2013/2006). *Dossier K.*, trans. T. Wilkinson. Brooklyn: Melville House.

Kertész, I. (2017/1990). *Kaddish for an Unborn Child*. London: Random House.

Kertész, I. Moi, le bourreau . . . In: *Le Refus*. Arles: Actes Sud, pp. 289–306.

Lacoue-Labarthe, P., Nancy, J.-L. (1991). *Le mythe nazi*. Paris: Aube.

Loraux, N. (1993). *L'Invention d'Athènes. Histoire de l'oraison funèbre dans la "cité classique"*. Paris: Payot, new edition.

Lyotard, J.-F. (1983). *Le Différend*. Paris: Minuit.

Mann, Th. (1935). Europe beware! In: *The Order of the Day: Political Essays and Speeches of Two Decades*, tran. Helen Lowe-Porter. New York: Books for Libraries Press, 1969, pp. 69–82.

Ortega y Gasset, J. (1961/1929). *The Revolt of the Masses*. London: Routledge.

Rosenberg, A. (2017/1930). *The Myth of the Twentieth Century*. London: Black Kite Publishing.

Semprún, J. (2013). *Morales de résistance: Husserl, Bloch, Orwell*. Paris: Climats.

Vernant, J.-P. (1962). *Les Origines de la pensée grecque*. Paris: Presses Universitaires de France.

Vernant, J.-P. (1972). Le moment historique de la tragédie en Grèce. In: *Mythe et tragédie en Grèce ancienne*, J.P. Vernant and P. Vidal-Naquet (ed.). Paris: Maspero, pp. 13–17.

Vernant, J.-P. (1986). Le sujet tragique: historicité et transhistoricité. In: *Mythe et tragédie en Grèce ancienne Vol. II*, J.-P. Vernant and P. Vidal-Naquet (eds.). Paris, Maspero, pp. 79–89.

11 The temptation of kitsch

Trauma, après-coup, historical novel: how are we to represent things? How, on the crest line between reality and the power of forgetting and reminiscence, are we to think about what will never be pure testimony nor even the application of relativism to history. The problem is all the more crucial in that, as Saul Friedländer (1992a)[1] insists, Nazism did not so much destroy language as cause an unprecedented mismatch between words and historical experience. If *Probing the Limits of Representation* remains a reference volume, it is because the role of fiction is tackled head-on. First of all, this is because of the debate that opposes Hayden White's historical relativism – according to which the "plot" of the historical canvas always supposes the admixture of fiction and its rhetoric – and Carlo Ginzburg's historical objectivity or Browning's detailed study of the facts. But also because it reopens the "historians' quarrel" which had been raging since 1985, that is to say since the publication of the articles and books by Ernst Nolte and Martin Broszat, tempering Nazi crimes (see Nolte, 1987; Broszat, 1981; and also Friedländer's (1987) criticism) by different theoretical means.

But more specifically, it is Dominick LaCapra's (1992) paper that I would like to focus on here. Because while his contribution is centred on the "historians' quarrel",[2] it is unique in that he insists throughout his work on the notion of *transference* at work in all historical reflection on the Shoah. Transference is involved in the different points of view. But above all such transference is implied by the historical narrative itself, which necessarily conveys a form of repetition. Just like Eric Santner (1992) in his paper, "History beyond the pleasure principle: Some thoughts on the representation of trauma" – a paper that deals with the "fetishistic narrative" which he opposes to the work of mourning according to Freud[3] – LaCapra poses the problem of the role of "psychic mastery" in the work of the historian. In his view, the "routine" opposition between scientific history and historical fictionalism, far from being relevant, serves as a defence mechanism, just like the pure and simple alternative between the grandiose identical reproduction of trauma and the redemptive virtues of narration.

DOI: 10.4324/9781003301660-12

He thus takes into account the function of the "transference on to the object of study" which affects every historian. "The tendency in psychoanalysis to emphasize the importance of transference in the relationship between analyst and analysand has often had the unfortunate consequence of distracting attention from the role it plays in other places" writes LaCapra (2002, p. 42), who quotes Freud's (1925) *An Autobiographical Study*:

> It must not be supposed, however, that transference is created by analysis and does not occur apart from it. Transference is merely uncovered and isolated in analysis. It is a universal phenomenon of the human mind . . . and in fact dominates the whole of each person's relations to his human environment.
>
> (p. 42)

To LaCapra, historiography is no exception to this generalization. It is at this price that historians can construct the past, and especially that relating to the Shoah: between continuity and discontinuity, between repetition and change, historical temporality will necessarily be subject to *Nachträglichkeit* [*après-coup*]. Further, whether the author likes it or not, this transferential movement participates in the return of the repressed in the present. "German nationalistic historians", the defenders of Heidegger or the director of *Schindler's List* fail to recognize, that is to say repress, the transferential links that they have with their objects. Conversely, these links are necessarily present in the different points of view, depending on whether one is a survivor, the relative of a survivor, a former Nazi, a young Jew or a young German, more distant from the immediate terror. Marked neither by empathy nor by pure critical distance, the transferential links uniting the historian and his object, the "narrative", are made up of loss and absence, mobilizing the experience of lack at the individual level – including the traumatic lack of castration. Only the assumption of loss can open up the possibility of dealing with the Shoah while renouncing a totalizing rationality. If LaCapra (1997) defends Claude Lanzmann's film with such conviction, it is precisely because he sees in it the determining role of reiterations, silences, tonal modulations, in the slow implementation of repetition and its "hallucinatory reincarnation in the details of the present". LaCapra is therefore protesting against "sentimental humanism", such as that which sought to mobilize, for example, the sculpture of George Segal in Lincoln Park in San Francisco. According to him, it is only a "simulacrum of dead bodies" casually littering the ground, since the scene is ultimately aimed at appeasing the beholder. The kind of pleasure thus communicated through the harmonization and sentimentalization of what is most shocking is in fact *kitsch*.

LaCapra is not alone in raising the issue in these terms. When Friedländer opposes both Steiner, who requires only silence in the face of the unspeakable, and the aestheticizing productions among which he places those of Visconti, Michel Tournier and Anselm Kiefer, it is the same "aesthetic thrill" that he is targeting. "Aroused by the contrast between the harmony of *kitsch* and the constant evocation of the themes of death and destruction", this thrill feeds on "a desire, aroused both by the eroticization of power, force and domination and, simultaneously, by the representation of Nazism as a place of all such outbursts, of all such transgressions" (Friedländer, 1982, p. 16). Thanks to the juxtaposition of these two contrary elements – the call for the most immediate emotional communion and the solitary terror – the *kitsch* of death tries to exorcise extermination by means of the elation of a sensitivity that insinuatingly brings relief. This is what Ruth Klüger (2005, see postface, pp. 324, 326) calls "the aura of *kitsch*", which allows one to fantasize far removed from reality and in a way that is so satisfying for oneself.

Certainly, the reflection on the function of literature in the testimony of survivors – of which Catherine Coquio (2015) drew up an exhaustive picture in *La Littérature en suspens* – goes far beyond the boundaries of psychoanalysis. Nonetheless, one of the points of contact between the analytical and literary spheres is the role of empathy that these narratives do or do not arouse. More precisely, she questions the very position of the "stage" with regard to whether or not it allows emotion to be mobilized, and whether it can or cannot become the territory of a collective reappropriation of the event. Thus, when Shoshana Felman (2001) attributed the Eichmann trial with a force of "emotional explosion", at a time when in Israel silence reigned over the final solution, it was to defend the idea that this emotional wave allowed a "conceptual revolution" to be accomplished in the victims. Thanks to this legal act, they were able to appropriate their history, establish their identity and find their legitimacy as a community. If with the Eichmann trial the law was able to restore the meaning of the word "humanity", it was because the trial took place on a "monumental stage" – which she said, gave it "monumental significance". From this point of view, the legal event enacted a legal conception that exceeded the ideological and conscious intentions of its organizers. It turned it into a "narrative event" – she refers to Rorty here – which reorganized the relationship between the individual sphere and the private sphere. Because, according to Felman, "a victim, by definition, is not only someone who is oppressed, but also someone who has no language of their own, someone who has had their language, in which he could have articulated his victimization, stolen". The revolutionary character of the trial lay in the fact that it was a "transformative act" which gave the Shoah the value of a story endowed with semantic and collective authority.

Felman therefore challenges the position taken by Arendt, for whom justice requires discipline, asceticism and historiographic radicalism. According to her, the trial involves on the contrary a spectacular staging of emotions intended to "give birth historically to the history of the victims". As a moment of linkage between the Nuremberg legal narrative and future law, it elevated a singular legal event to the level of a "sacred or canonical narrative". This newly born sacred tale was and could only be a saga, a "collective fable of mourning". Both a legal parable and a legal reference, it created "the privileged text of a popular tale of justice".

While giving Felman the credit for her very precise reading of Arendt in order to better distinguish himself from the latter, we are irresistibly led to think of those other theatre pieces that David Rousset put on as early as 1948. "A play. With only one actor. Imagination plays no role here. . . . In the scene of grand mastery, you will hear him order the murder. But you will not see the murder come to pass. . . . What matters to him is the killing machine and how it works. . . . It's just that he got the idea of a slight refinement". *Le pitre ne rit pas* [The clown does not laugh] brings together official documents and a number of letters of denunciation, archived from 1943 (Rousset, 1948, pp. 8–11, 30–31). "The boards have been put up in Berlin"; the crowd is there, a real crowd; but "you will quickly find that under this magnificent variety of natural interests [the Father, the Woman, the Professor, the Madam], it is always the same face, the face of our unique actor". "You will see how he makes love, how he steals, how he kills". But while humanity in the world may laugh at itself – and that is its health – the clown does not laugh, "he believes". He said, "I will build my house in the purity of blood, for the sins of the father fall on his children for seven generations and more". "The play begins. It is far more important than anything we have to say. It lives". There follow ordinances from the General Commissariat for Jewish Affairs, letters addressed to Darquier de Pellepoix, always written in the familiar and good-natured style of well-ordered management between co-tenants, official decrees and details of their application. They are just small documents, woven into the fabric of this play which counters the monumentalism of Hitler thundering from the rostrum. Just countless little things, and in particular, no sign of the emotional outburst – the very outburst that had made the crowd gathered on the *Reichsparteitagsgelände* in Nuremberg really vibrate – which is what Rousset has in the sights of his virulent satire. And there is nothing of the "pathic configuration" either, whose power of attraction allows mimetic and compassionate identification so well.

Concerning this "illusion of the direct which is based on an immersive logic", Philippe Mesnard (2007) emphasizes that it provides no guarantee of understanding the facts, any more than tears are of lived experience (see also Mesnard, 2009). This is why he contrasted the pathos that pulls one into the "bottomless" vertigo of suffering emotion with, on the one hand, "symbolic configuration" and, on the other hand, "critical configuration". With the first, he shows how, by transposing lived experience into a symbolic system as Elie Wiesel and Primo Levi each do in their own way, it is a matter of approaching reality without any hope of accounting for it, while forming a picture of it such that a form of intelligibility is accessible thanks to distance. As for "critical configuration", Philippe Mesnard shows that, if the witness attests to an experience that he has survived, the testimony does not play on the "as if" dimension or on striking images, but on the contrary sees to it that the critical capacity of the recipient is not lost. The very usage of language then reflects the mourning of a form of omnipotence, of a fusion between oneself and the world. His ethical requirement – "to accept loss so as not to lose reality, for it is realism that loses reality" – rests on the recognition of the limits of the narrative and the limits of the imagination. Both Imre Kertész's reflection and Claude Lanzmann's film, *Shoah*, are thus based, according to him, on the rejection of any unified vision. Against exhaustiveness, against the mimetic appeal to the other who will "understand", the enunciative devices are visible, making room for the lacuna, amnesia, the confusion of temporalities.

On the other hand, with emotional inflation, *kitsch* is never far away, playing on the mainsprings of aestheticization. In contrast, taking negativity into account – silence, caesura, hatred, repression, internal conflicts – involves the creation of new formal modalities that will deal with memory differently. This is the position taken by Kertész who, on the one hand, attacks the sentimental din of *kitsch* and, on the other, maintains that "the concentration camp is conceivable exclusively as a literary text, not as a reality (even – and maybe especially – when one has experienced it)" (Kertész, 1992, p. 222). But there is no easy path between "the refusal of the gigantic and of the apocalyptic" (Perec, 1963, p. 94), between compassionate kitsch and the need that "words should [nonetheless] have an effect, in the sense of '*Wirkung*', that they should enter the flesh" (Kertész, 2005). "The novel that one is writing must 'please' in the sense that the reader must want to turn the page", Kertész told Florence Noiville. "It is a trap into which he is lured so that he is receptive" (Kertész, ibid.). This path is not easy because everything that could be akin to the unfathomable world of myth, harmony, the Bavarian mountains and the "twilight of the gods" – these are Friedländer's words – anything that echoes the romantic heritage which Nazism seized – and this time it is Hermann Broch (2001) who wonders about the concomitance of the appearance of kitsch in art and the rise of romanticism in the bourgeois world – makes us forget that Hitler "was an absolute supporter of *kitsch*": "He lived bloody *kitsch* and he loved the *kitsch* of street theatre. They both found them "beautiful" (pp. 34–35; see also Broch, 2005). A lover of "eager beauty" like Nero, he cared nothing for ethics; only the aesthetics of political achievement mattered.

It is a question of the degradation of values, but, above all, a search for emotional outpourings and their effects: it is from this perspective that we must understand the praise that Broch (1966) gives the work of Schönberg in his "Remarques à propos de *La mort de Virgile*" [Remarks on *Virgil's Death*"], as well as the dedication he made to him in his "Réflexions relatives au problème de la connaissance en musique" [Thoughts on the problem of knowledge in music] (Broch, 2005). In Broch's eyes, the "new music" carries within it the motive forces of the criticism of kitsch and the intimate ecstatic pleasure that comes with sentimental flashiness.

This is a remarkable point, in my eyes, if one considers that, "for [his] own use", Kertész specifically called the language that he tried to invent to speak of the collapse of the cultural "convention" inflicted by Auschwitz, an "atonal language".

> At the time of *Fatelessness*, I was haunted by atonal music: Berg, Schoenberg. . . . In the same way, I wanted to create an atonal language. Atonality is the cancellation of consensus. No more D major or E flat minor. The tone is abolished, like the values of society. The basso continuo is also destroyed, which means that the ground (not the note, but the ground on which you walk) is no longer fixed and that this base of references which gave a foundation for action disappears.
>
> (Kertész, 2005)

The reference to Adorno and to the *Philosophy of New Music*[4] is explicit; he considered that, faced with the commodified aestheticization of works of art, music, with its capacity to refuse harmony and ornament, with its power to explore deeply the discordances with sentimentality, and to break conciliatory sequences by suspending sound, was a line of resistance.

It was a matter, then, of writing an atonal novel, then, which would thwart affectivity and the staging of the drama, which would reject the artifice of feigned passions. In fact, the reference to Adorno was present as early as July 1970: "What concerns me is this: having read Adorno, I can see again clearly that my novel uses the technique of twelve-tone composition, that is, serial and therefore integrated. This eliminates the free characters and the possibilities of twists and turns in the narrative. The characters become thematic motifs that appear in the structure of a whole that is external to the novel; the structure levels each of the themes, erases all apparent depth, the 'developments' and variations of the themes being in the exclusive service of the guiding principle of the composition: the absence of fate" (Kertész, 1992, p. 27).

It was a matter of writing an atonal novel, but what is the tonality of a novel? "A defined moral basso continuo, a fundamental note that resonates throughout the text. Does such a fundamental note exist? If so, it is dried up. So it was a question of writing a novel in which there was no static morality, only the original forms of lived experience, experience in the proper and mysterious sense of the term" (ibid., p. 67). A mystery which, however, sacrifices nothing to the elation of the unification of a life, which knows how to free itself not only from hope but from despair, like Beckett, the one who "speaks from the other side" (ibid., p. 199).

Because "life and writing are two completely different levels" and because "the Holocaust is not describable", it was a question of "finding a language that would be an expressive language – expressive, in the sense that it contains what cannot be described". "So the narrator in *Fatelessness*, who is a child, may effectively appear to readers to be a boy. For me, it's nothing other than language", says Kertész (Hähnel & Mesnard, 2003). And the same is true for the narrator of *Kaddish*, "for him, too, it is about language". In the choice offered to the writer – either to describe the individual in the mass situation, or else to describe individuality in so far as it is suppressed by the event of massification – writing must account for the process of the deprivation of individuality, this dispossession called "fatelessness".

That is the reason why there is no place for heroization. If Kertész frequently refers to Beckett and Adorno, it is because he finds material in the "negative dialectic" for his attempt to give shape to cultural negativity (Kertész, 1999b).[5] You have to "construct the novel so that it contains its own failure, contains the betrayed cause" (Kertész, 1992, p. 68). To pretend that creation is a naively natural manifestation of talent is an attack on the human condition. Conversely, the feeling that "the author began by being destroyed by the truth he discovered before being resuscitated by it" (p. 134) determines the credit given to the work. This has nothing to do, therefore, with the canons of the Holocaust, sentimentalism, its system of taboos, its ritual language, its "products of the Holocaust for the consumption of the Holocaust". It has nothing to do with the patheticization of "exceptional" fates, such as those of Jerzy Kosinski or Binjamin Wilkomirski who, caught up in the ruins of horror, made themselves the artisan impostors of memory, arguing that they were "there" to validate both the salvational function of testimony and its historical value. Now this is an ethical matter, an ethics entrusted to language itself, which involves the status of values. "Meanwhile, we dwell in the midst of Spielberg's saurian kitsch and with the absurd chatter emerging from the fruitless discussions over the Berlin Holocaust monument" (Kertész & McKay, p. 269).

The sort of consolation which results from it, namely, the story of the sufferings, the self-glorification of the victims, their video recordings and "the gentle waves of belated solidarity" suggest that Man with a capital M – and with him the notion of humanity – would have got out of Auschwitz safe and sound. In so doing, they legitimize the separation between the possibility of Extermination and our lives today. They strive to push its consequences beyond human experience, and pathos is the weapon of exclusion.

If one looks at things more closely, one tells oneself that the immediacy of emotion, in accordance with empathy and consensual discourse, played a major role in what so deeply disconcerted psychoanalysis. The repression of the indignity that emotional sharing and its thrill inflicted on history and overlooking the contribution to infamy made by the discourse on identity appear surprisingly in empathic attitudes. Certainly, they claim to be a reversal of such crimes into their opposite. Nevertheless, this remedial solution, which avoids taking a critical look at emotions and their ambiguous function, appears to be a probable consequence of what Nazism did to psychoanalysis. However, if, in Kertész's eyes, any representation that does not implicitly contain the ethical consequences of Auschwitz is kitsch, we must of course understand that these consequences do not relate to reparation but rather to the anatomy of liquidation.

Liquidation is the title of Bee's play, which speaks all at once of the liquidation of the author, of the liquidation of the Hungarian dictatorship, the liquidation of the Auschwitz camp and the liquidation of tragedy. Why the latter? Because there are no more tragic men, but above all, as Bee argued, because of the material itself, this objective reality that is so difficult to tame and which will necessarily "become a story". So, must we tell Bee's story? A child came into the world at Auschwitz. "The kapos put down their sticks, their whips and, feeling very moved, they lifted up the crying baby". Of course, told like this, it's kitsch. But it can be told differently. "Impossible, what is kitsch is kitsch". Yet it did happen. Sure, but "it wasn't true. It was an exception. An anecdote. A grain of sand fell into the machinery for crushing the corpses". In the midst of "the daily magic of evil", in a world where "effects did not always derive from causes, nor did causes always seem adequately grounded points of departure" (Kertész, 2005, pp. 36–37), to tell the story, it is to tell it to oneself by answering the *"whys"* with *"becauses"*. This is why we were on the train jolting towards Auschwitz, this is why the doctor who made the selection at Birkenau did not push us to the left, this is why benevolent hands lifted us out of a heap of corpses, and so on. The story, starting from the final point, necessarily becomes a march towards the goal. It achieves the outcome of the story, the survival of a poor guy. "Every particular story is kitsch, because it escapes the rule". Thus, kitsch makes it possible to escape a mutilated life by restoring wholeness and its orderly arrangement, while the narration should be "characterized by a certain lack, the lack of 'fullness of life' . . ., a lack which corresponds moreover perfectly to this period of mutilation". This means "that instead of 'representing', the work becomes what it represents" (Kertész, 1992, p. 28).

This route is close, in some respects, to that taken by Beckett. A route which, in *Liquidation*, involves two reversals. First, kitsch turns against itself and asserts itself as a negation of kitsch thanks to the embedding of the piece kept safe in the forever missing novel. And second, reality turns against itself in a negation of the hero, the product of a theatrical fiction in search of the insoluble enigma of final destruction. The absent novel thus gradually becomes a "disappeared" novel and ends up as a "burnt" novel. In the centre is an impossible synthesis and the writing which can only be incomplete. And on the fringes, reality, crushing in its non-existence, that only the very structure of the novel causes to exist. Did not Bee say that "if one examines the contemporary arts more closely, one discovers that only one branch of art has been developed to perfection, and that is the art of murder"? (Kertész, 2005, p. 112–113)

"You told an Auschwitz-tinged love story, Judit", Adam says in *Liquidation*. Judit, who has walked through this open-air museum that is now Birkenau, replies: "I was there, I saw. Auschwitz does not exist" (Kertész, 2005, pp 121–123). Everything she knew well from the photos was there, but "everything seemed incredible, like a copy of the original". But what original?

Notes

1 This volume brings together the contributions of an important colloquium held in 1990 at the University of California.
2 Friedländer (1992b) takes up the theme of transference and après-coup in an article written very shortly after, citing LaCapra: "Trauma, transference and 'working through' in 'writing the history of the Shoah'". In his book *Reflections of Nazism*, Friedländer (1982) told Stéphane Bou that he had done an analysis.
3 Santner takes the game of *Fort/Da* as well as anticipatory anxiety as his starting-point for thinking about the modalities of the reconstitution of a protective shield at the collective level.
4 See Adorno's analysis of Schönberg's *Erwartung* [Expectation] (op. 17) in Chapter II of *Philosophy of New Music*, "Atonality" (Adorno, 2006).
5 According to Clara Royer (2017), it was on this date that Kertész became aware of Adorno's texts, thanks to a publication in Hungarian. Nevertheless, Kertész's references to Adorno are complicated since, in his essay "Ombre profonde", he wrote: "We all know of Adorno's famous statement: 'to write poetry after Auschwitz is barbaric.' I would qualify this, still in general terms, by saying that after Auschwitz, you can only write poetry about Auschwitz" (Kertész, 1998b, p. 54). But in 2006, he said of this same statement that it was "a moral stink bomb that needlessly pollutes air that is already rank enough as things are" (Kertész, 2013, p. 105).

References

Adorno, Th. (2006/1949). *Philosophy of New Music*, ed. and trans. R. Hullot-Kentor. MN: University of Minnesota Press.

Broch, H. (1966/1955). Remarques à propos de La mort de Virgile. In: *Création littéraire et connaissance*. Paris: Gallimard.

Broch, H. (2001). *Quelques remarques à propos du kitsch*. Paris: Allia.

Broch, H. (2005). Réflexions relatives au problème de la connaissance en musique. In: *Logique d'un monde en ruine*. Paris: Éditions de l'éclat.

Broszat, M. (1981). *The Hitler State. The Foundation and Development of the Internal Structure of the Third Reich*, trans. J. Hiden. London: Routledge.

Coquio, C. (2015). *La Littérature en suspens. Ecritures de la Shoah: le témoignage et les œuvres*. Paris: L'Arachnéen.

Felman, S. (2001). Théâtres de justice: Hannah Arendt à Jérusalem. Le procès Eichmann et la redéfinition du sens de la loi dans le sillage de l'holocauste. *Les Temps Modernes*, 615–616(4): 23–74.

Freud, S. (1925). *An Autobiographical Study*. S.E. 20. London: Hogarth, pp. 7–74.

Friedländer, S. (1982). *Reflections of Nazism: An Essay on Kitsch and Death*. Indiana University Press.

Friedländer, S. (1987). Réflexions sur l'historisation du national socialisme. *Vingtième Siècle, Revue d'histoire*, 1(16): 43–54.

Friedländer, S. (ed.). (1992a). *Introduction to Probing the Limits of Representation: Nazism and the Final Solution*. Cambridge, MA: Harvard University Press.

Friedländer, S. (1992b). Trauma, transference and 'working through' in 'writing the history of the Shoah'. *History and Memory*, 4(1): 39–59.

Hähnel, C., Mesnard, Ph. (2003). Imre Kertesz: écrivain et prix Nobel. [interview with I. Kertész], *Mouvements*, 25(1): 115–122.

Kertész, I. (1999a). Ombre Profonde, ed. Kertész, 2009, pp. 53–61.

Kertész, I. (1999b). Interview with Gerhard Moser, "Le vingtième siècle est une machine à liquider permanente" In: *Parler des camps, penser les génocides*, C. Coquio (ed.). Paris: Albin Michel.

Kertész, I. (2005). Briser de l'intérieur les limites de la langue. Interview with Florence Noiville. *Le Monde des livres*, 9 juin.

Kertész, I. (2017). *L'histoire de mes morts*. Paris: Actes Sud.

Kertész, I., Mackay (2001). Who own Auschwitz? *The Yale Journal of Criticism*, 14(1): 267–272.

Klüger, R. (2005). La mémoire dévoyée. Postface. In: *Refus de témoigner: Une jeunesse*. Paris: Vivianne Hamy [R. Klüger (1994) Missbrauch der Erinnerung: KZ-Kitsch. *Gelesene Wirklichkeit: Fakten und Fiktionen in der Literatur*. Göttingen: Wallstein Verlag, pp. 52–67].

LaCapra, D. (1992). Representing the Holocaust: Reflections on the historians' debate. In: *Probing the Limits of Representation: Nazism and the Final Solution*, S. Friedländer (ed.). Cambridge, MA: Harvard University Press, pp. 108–127.

LaCapra, D. (1997). Lanzmann's 'Shoah': 'Here there is no why'. *Critical Inquiry*, 23(2): 231–269.

LaCapra, D. (2002). Liaisons et déliaisons. *Espaces Temps, Michel de Certeau, histoire/psychanalyse. Mises à l'épreuve*, 80–81: 38–54.

Mesnard, P. (2009). *Entretien avec Alexandre Prstojevic et Luba Jurgenson, Consultable on Line* (www.vox-poetica.org/entretiens/intMesnard.html).

Mesnard, P. (2007). *Témoignage en résistance*. Paris: Stock.

Nolte, E. (1987). *La guerre civile européenne (1917–1945): National-socialisme et bolshevisme*. Paris: Édition des Syrtes, 2000.

Pérec, G. (1963). Robert Antelme ou la vérité de la littérature. In: *L.G. Une aventure des années soixante*. Paris: Le Seuil, pp. 87–114.

Rousset, D. (1948). *Le pitre ne rit pas*. Paris: Le Grand Pavois.

Santner, E. (1992). History beyond the pleasure principle: Some thoughts on the representation of trauma, S. Friedländer (ed.) (1992a), pp. 143–154.

12 What about hatred?[1]

Kertész never gives up the fight against "professional humanists" (2011a, p. 37). Those who persist in explaining away Auschwitz or the Gulag by invoking economic reasons or social structures or those who pretend to ignore the fact that "the withering away of the world has a deeper origin, much deeper than anything history could reach through reason or science" (2008, pp. 57–58), when "there are only half-dead left who burn the dead, and storekeepers who sort objects" (1999a, p. 84). But also those who, like the journalist met by the young deportee who had returned to Budapest, loudly deplore the "pits of the Nazi hell" that was Buchenwald. "You must have seen a lot, young fellow, a lot of terrible things!" Silence from Köves. "The main thing is that it's over, in the past", continues the journalist, who asks the young man what he is feeling now. "Hatred", Köves replies. The journalist understands this feeling: in his opinion, "under the circumstances", hatred also has its place, its role "and even its uses"; and besides he assumes that they both agree, he knows who Köves hates. To which the young man replies: "Everyone" (2004, p. 247). In *Dossier K*, Kertész makes clear that this answer was one of "the most misunderstood or perhaps better, misinterpreted sentences in *Fatelessness*". Is this the time to explain it? No, Kertész continues, "It's a good thing for a novel to have certain words that live on in readers like a blazing secret" (2013/2006, p. 84).

But how does the term "hatred" relate to blazing secrets here? Is it because it fascinates the journalist to the point of making him lose his patience? "Why do you keep on saying 'naturally' about things that are not at all natural?" Because "in a concentration camp, they *were* natural", Köves replies. Is the blazing secret linked to this "natural" character? Consider the paradoxes of the experience. Think of the very end of *Fatelessness*: "There even there, next to the chimneys, in the intervals between the torments, there was something that resembled happiness. Everyone asks only about the hardships, and the 'atrocities', whereas for me perhaps it is that experience that will remain the most memorable. Yes, the next time I am asked, I ought to speak about that, the happiness of the concentration camps" (2004, p. 262).

DOI: 10.4324/9781003301660-13

What the "natural" aspect of horror rejects is the insane cohabitation with happiness – the contradiction that professional humanists cannot grasp, just as they overlook the fact that experience is modified through writing. But what does it mean to distil unspeakable reality into signs, and to dilute the "impenetrable secret" into generalities? "If I am incapable of looking at it with a stranger's eyes, why am I unable to read *my own* novel with *my own* eyes?", asks the narrator of Fiasco (2011a, pp. 71–72). And, as the sentences had organized themselves as he wanted them to, why didn't he recall "what had happened *before* those sentences, the raw event itself? How could it be that those sentences for me contained merely *imaginary* events, an imaginary cattle truck, an imaginary Auschwitz, and an imaginary fourteen-and-a-half-year-old boy – even though I myself had at one time himself been that fourteen-and-a-half-year-old boy?" (ibid., p. 72). Anyway, what had happened to what is called *Erlebnis*?

In his Stockholm speech, Kertész reiterated how it took the operation of resurrection, ensured by the Stalinist dictatorship, for the details of the past to resurface, like Proust's madeleine soaked in tea (the comparison was made by Kertész himself). A heavy price to pay, surely, for the virtues of the aftermath or the insanity of memory. "For a time, I awoke each morning on the barrack forecourt at Auschwitz. It took a while for me to realize that this perception was evoked by a constant olfactory stimulus. A few days before, I had bought a new leather strap for my wristwatch. At night I always put the watch on a low shelf directly by the bedside. Most likely that characteristic smell, reminiscent of chlorine and a distant smell of corpses, had lingered on the strap from the tanning and other processes. which reminded me of chlorine and the distant stench of corpses. Later on I even used the strap as a sort of sal volatile: when my memories flagged, lay low inertly in the crannies of my brain, I used it to entice them from their hiding places" (ibid., p. 74).

Was this the insanity of memory or a sudden implosion? The narrator is walking through a stifling Budapest. The sky is white, irritation is at its height, and there is an inexplicable outburst of rage from a dog. A bus rolls in: "Screw you!" Köves thinks. "Either pull out or just run over me" (ibid., p. 42). After the screeching of tyres, the driver and pedestrians vent "their impersonal venoms". He still has absolute trust in the excellent driver: the narrator knows full well that "bus drivers are loath to kill under certain circumstances. Driving over a limp body – that is the privilege of tanks. Murder is something else, and mass murder something different again". (ibid., p. 43). This was how an earlier idea of his came back to mind: "A plan for a dissertation, on a not too ambitious scale, concerning the possibilities for an aesthetic mediation of violence" (ibid.).

But there you are: if killing is one thing, and massacre is another, writing is yet another. But "the problem with facts, however important they may otherwise be, is that there are too many of them and they rapidly wear fantasy down". "We are ever more alienated as we gawk at them", because cumulative images of murder become as lethally tedious and exhausting as the attendant work itself. "There can be no doubt about", he adds, "that is what put paid to tragic representation!" (ibid., pp. 45–46). What's more, as soon as Köves starts to write, he stops remembering. It is not that the memories disappear, but simply that, arranged as a product composed of abstract signs, they change. How can creation and the "obsessive monotony" of the experiences of the camp be held together, when this is what the imagination constantly struggles against? How can one recreate the assassination, in three weeks instead of the required six, of a group of Dutch Jews deported to Mauthausen? "These 340 deaths on the rocks might rightly find a place among the symbols of the human imagination", writes Kertész – but on one condition: only if they had not occurred" (p. 47).

The rupture lies there, in the clash between sublimation and literary experience. There is neither overview nor symbolization: not only are the gods and the devil, those who guaranteed us the tragic virtues of fate, dead; but Goethe is buried. And the absence of fate is not an individual loss; it is a mass condition. Kertész's words to Moser in "The Twentieth Century is a Permanent Liquidating Machine" (see Kertész 1999b, pp. 89–90) say it again: in Goethean times, inspiration came from admiration; today the "negative hero" of *Fatelessness*, crushed by fixed time, only allows this cultural negativity to take form and come to an end. Elsewhere, Kertész remarked that *Fatelessness* is "an inverted *Bildungsroman*".[2]

In short, the opposite of Semprún's (2005) approach in *The Long Voyage* where, according to Kertész, the portrait of Ilse Koch as Lucrezia Borgia of Buchenwald – pale complexion, fair eyes, daydreaming about a deportee's parchment-like skin used as lampshades, a Beethoven concerto – in short, blood, lust and the demon "can be fitted with no trouble at all into the ready-made toolbox of my historical imagination" (p. 48). What are we to make of the insurmountable disproportion between actions and speaking? Semprún, who Kertész met after receiving his Nobel prize, did not seem to be alarmed about this disproportion. According to Kertész, he was a fragile, sensitive, gentle man who, in Buchenwald, was part of the underground Communist camp organization, without which children like him would never have survived. But he was a politician who described the Resistance, the martyrs, the heroes and who, in doing so, was drawing on an ideal, using a pre-Auschwitz language, a language that makes narration easier (2011a, pp. 47–48).[3] Incomparable experiences, and also an incomparable perception of the world, concludes Kertész. An incommensurability that the very modalities writing must attempt to express. But how? Because, on the one hand, "[it] is to be feared that formulations that have been steeped in the solvent of literature never again their density and lifelikeness" (Kertész, 2009b, p. 40) but, on the other, "[o]ne should strive for formulations that totally encapsulate the experience of life (that is to say, the disaster); formulations that assist one to die and yet still bequeath something to posterity" (ibid.). Hence the antinomy in which Kertész seeks to position himself as a writer, affirming testimony on the one hand while, on the other, considering the other solution which would be "a life passed in muteness without being formulated as a formulation" (ibid.)

Is this the secret of the hatred that was to give rise after Auschwitz to a radical misunderstanding? And which, moreover, led Agamben to create a "imaginary concentration camp" where the "Muslim", the paradigm of a man who has lost all humanity, appears as the zero degree of testimony, that is to say his *Urbild*, his prototype. Here we should take up in detail the study carried out by Philippe Mesnard (Mesnard & Kahan, 1991) in *Giorgio Agamben à l'épreuve d'Auschwitz* (see particularly pp. 50–57). Mesnard shows how, despite countless testimonies, Agamben neglects the multiple strata of power in the camps, entangled in the multitude of languages and the multiple heterogeneity of temporalities, all woven into the labyrinth of prohibitions, rules, laws, however unfounded they were. And how, despite the very complex accounts left by the members of the *Sonderkommandos*, he reduces this period to "a story limited to a silent film of an emaciated body, itself recycled into a figure of rhetoric" (p. 51). The terror, the horror, the unrepresentable, dramatized in the figure of the Muslim, are from this point of view the products of "a rationale in which the real is reified in its own representation" (p. 55). It is the ultimate stage in the scope of hatred, certainly; but a *patheticized* stage in this unique form of radical desubjectivation.

Under the effect of "this concentration camp reduction", the mediatized victim invades public space and leaves untenable paradoxes behind, for the benefit of a mythical story. Anne-Lise Stern (2007) is more radical in her criticism: "[T]o claim to be from Auschwitz, thus to advertise it, and the 'Muslim' at the same time, does not work" (p. 257).[4] It does not work because "those who hit the bottom", "the 'Muslims', the swallowed up, the integral witnesses" did not come back to testify.

Avoiding pathos, then, and its betrayals, while at the same time showing how "exemplary death" was ruined along with the mirages of humanism was what made (Kertész, 2011b) take another path. A path opened up by the question: how has the haunting liquidation of humans by themselves destroyed hatred? Let us hear it: hatred according to the language before Auschwitz.

However, on this other path, without his ever being mentioned, one has the strong feeling that Kertész has, so to speak, met Günther Anders. Because for the latter too, hatred, which has now become superfluous, is to be stored in the antiques department. All that remains of it is utility. A utility that belongs to the field of illusion, and this political illusion is only a manoeuvre so that the masses "do not feel only like butchers" (Anders, 2007, pp 46–48). "I give them hatred every time it is required", said President Traufe, the fictitious interlocutor of "Appetite comes with eating".

They get it from me *for free at home*. Just like water, gas, electricity and TV. And this hatred which is channeled to them, they then *consume* it, and exactly in the way I want: because they throw themselves full of hatred into the politically opportune struggle. . . . Wouldn't cold, emotionless assassination contradict all our ideas of Western values?

The illusion of affect is therefore necessary, because it still maintains what the good old days guaranteed us, when ferocity was embodied in evil individuals and fighting them made it possible to think that we were fighting against evil (Anders, 1999, p. 185). At that time, writes Anders (2007), hatred was "the *primary* (pre-theoretical) *form* of negation" (p. 51) involving, simultaneously, pleasure in destroying the other and self-constitution by negating the other. Whatever the violence, it had its marks of nobility, which were still open to the imagination. Today, the overtaking of humanity by the products of its technical skills in the industrial age (whether it was the Nazi camps, Hiroshima or the Vietnam War) has invalidated this psychic function of hatred. The abysmal discrepancy between what modern man makes and what he is able to imagine, that is to say to form a picture of, precludes him from any possibility of identifying with his creations. Because actions are hidden from perception and escape memorization, this discrepancy prevents him from having any inner conception of the consequences of what he has made. In a time when heroes no longer fight but "just annihilate" (ibid., p. 33), *"hatred is definitely superfluous"* (pp. 91–92) destructive events being reduced to the carrying out of missions. It is therefore blindness to the *telos* of the action, to its ends, that brings destruction.

If there seems to be a meeting-point between Kertész and Anders, it is because what Kertész calls "the functional man" is precisely this human being robbed of his relationship to purposes, that is to say to the determination of destiny. Whereas, ever since the time of the Greeks, hatred had given destiny its verticality, the founding axis of tragedy as well as of politics, with Auschwitz, man lives his own reality "without living the existential experience of his life" (Kertész, 1992, p. 9). "His life is usually a tragic mistake or transgression, but without tragic consequences; or it is a tragic consequence devoid of tragic causes" (ibid., p. 12). Do you want, Anders asks, your people to fight or eradicate an element A unknown to them, not perceived by them, equally impossible to perceive and to hate? Well, breed in them the hatred of an element B they think they know – hatred that inflames or poisons them enough so that they kill A" (Anders, 2007, p. 72). But make no mistake: the act here is one of "total indifference" and affect is dissociated from the performance of the act. Quite simply, because it is necessary, as a decoy, for the enemy to remain a hateful other, he will be made so by substitution.

Is Anders' point really new? How far does it differ from what Freud envisaged in terms of the technical perfection of destruction, in his exchange with Einstein, and to which he returned in *Moses and Monotheism*, emphasizing the surprising nature of a remarkable period in which period "progress has allied itself with barbarism" (Freud, 1939, p. 54)? What was his purpose in thus underlining the irremediable separation of scientific progress and progress in the life of the mind?

Because this observation goes far beyond the interchangeability of the objects of hate. This was the subject of an anecdote recounted by Freud several times, including in *The Ego and the Id*, to describe the displacements effected by the primary processes. If three tailors from a village are hanged because the only blacksmith has committed a capital offence, it is because the path of instinctual discharge is indifferent to the specific nature of the hated object; what matters is that the hateful stasis does not last. But this interchangeability takes place, in fact, in a theoretical universe where love and hate are conceived as interdependent on the terrain of the conflict between pleasure and displeasure. If "the ego hates, abhors . . . all objects which are a source of unpleasurable feeling for it" (Freud, 1915, p. 138), writes Freud, if, in doing so, hate, which is "older than love", originates in the rejection of an external world that is a source of stimuli, it is still the case that the contact between the disturbing object and the narcissistic ego takes place on a common instinctual drive base. The reversal of an instinct into its opposite, the turning round upon the subject's own self, and the reversal of content indicate how much the mobility of instinctual movements, repression included, were still predominant in this first topographical conception.

With the second topography, the matter becomes much more complicated, because it is no longer a single instinctual drive source but two distinct sources that are pushing towards discharge. From the moment Freud introduced the antagonism between the death drive and the life drive, he was faced with the question of how the switchover between love and hate occurs – "a direct transformation of hate into love [being] incompatible with the qualitative distinction between the two classes of instincts" (Freud, 1923, p. 44). He thus came to conceive of an undifferentiated energy that was capable of attaching itself to one or the other of the two instinctual drive impulses, giving prevalence now to the erotic pole and now to the destructive pole. But Freud located the source of this energy in the reserve of desexualized narcissistic libido which is formed in the course of renouncing primary objects. In other words, Freud placed at the centre of this seesaw (which is no longer a transformation) an energy supply resulting from the narcissistic process of identification by which the abandoned infantile object is introjected into the ego. The role of hate therefore acquires greater complexity on two counts; for this narcissistic process, operating through processes of internalization, is also what leads to the setting up of the superego at the centre of the infantile ego. Thus the superego inherits the link to the Oedipal configuration along two axes: on the one hand, it is the guarantor of repression in the name of ideals; and, on the other hand, it is armed with the hate that was once directed at this important childhood configuration.

But – and this is a further source of the complication – at the junction between these two modalities, the superego also drains the portion of unbound energy coming from the death drive. It was the evolution of this portion of internal destructiveness, not projected outside in the form of aggression, which led Freud to describe the second topography as a "heresy": according to this theory, he wrote to Einstein, moral conscience, a product of the diversion inwards of aggression, also has its origin in the death drive itself. (Freud, 1933, pp. 209–211). As André Beetschen (2003) writes, the intersection between the narcissistic economy of the superego and the death drive in fact places at the centre of the ego "an invasive hostility which, different from hatred or murder and their purposes, sets up within the ego what is unknown and formless, what has not or not yet been represented, the echo of the primitive (pp. 1474–1475).

It is in this tension that hate loses the sharp outline that it had in the first topography. Until then, the affect of hate had been a way of maintaining links to the object. Henceforth it could rage without the hated object being identified as an external object. This is how destructiveness, operating within the closed perimeter of narcissism, can cause the superego to attack the ego melancholically, an ego which is identified with the object of hate. In addition, the superego, which has its origin in the id, knows very well how expensive drive renunciation is, and how small are the compensations offered in return. This creates a formidable cleft stick: on the one hand, the superego commands the renunciation of infantile goals, hatred included, in favour of sublimatory and cultural goals; but on the other this renunciation itself fuels an inevitable hostility against culture. Thus the inclination to aggression is reinforced by that which should curb it.

For Freud, it was this situation that was at the origin of the ravages of war. The wish to eliminate the rival, the enemy, the stranger, fuelled by hatred, is not enough to explain the blindness of devastation. It is also necessary to take into account the two factors which ensure the cohesion of the socius: on the one hand violence, which can also work in the direction of respect for the law; and, on the other, identifications which form the basis of the community. In other words, to explain the astonishing enthusiasm that accompanies war, it is clear that one must take into account the "the lust for hatred and destruction" (a term initially used by Einstein) (Freud, 1933, p. 201). But to this must be added the reinforcement provided by the interplay of identifications and ideals. Apparently mobilized by the quest for perfection, it is also activated and aroused by the effect of the narcissistic petition.

The superego feeds in part on the destructive source that inhabits each human being, insofar as the latter finds in the leader material to reactivate the infantile wish of a narcissistic omnipotence (which immersion in the multitude promises), and so we can see how ideals, demanding perfection, draw on the portion of the death drive that has not been deflected outwards and can find themselves enslaved to destructiveness:[5] "Even where [the death instinct] emerges without any sexual purpose", wrote Freud in *Civilization and its Discontents*, "in the blindest fury of destructiveness, we cannot fail to recognize that the satisfaction of the instinct is accompanied by an extraordinarily high degree of narcissistic enjoyment, owing to its presenting the ego with a fulfilment of the latter's old wishes for omnipotence (1930, p. 121). Besides the fact that this alliance between narcissism and the death drive, associated with the perfection of the instruments of destruction, could lead to the destruction of the antagonists, it is clear, writes Freud (1933), that "in its present-day form, war is no longer an opportunity for achieving the old ideals of heroism" (p. 213).

What hero is Freud talking about here? Is it the one who, advancing into the circle of brothers, manages to speak of the murder of the father, the inaugural transgression, and establishes himself, by his very story, as a new ego ideal? A mythical invention, an epic invention, which allows the fraternal circle to transmute hatred as much as nostalgia, leading them towards the assumption of the prohibition of murder. Since *Totem and Taboo*, the heroic narrative has participated in the structure of the conflict which presides over the elaboration of common laws. It unfolds the tragic horizon of the clash between the inflexibility of desire and guilt, contributing to the establishment of tutelary figures that gradually dematerialize.

However, it is precisely the re-materialization of these figures in the form of the leader that overlooks the price of hatred and transgression. It repudiates loneliness and tragic torment. At the same time as the hated object loses its contours as an object, the individual, who has become part of a group, "no longer needs to be saved because he is no longer responsible for himself". These are Kertész's (2009a, p. 102) words, which converge surprisingly with those of Freud in *Group Psychology and the Analysis of the Ego* (1921, pp. 76–77). With the difference that, for Kertész, it follows a duty of art, "the artist's choice can only be radical".

It is only under the conditions of leaving nothing to the illusions of hatred, abandoning nothing to tragic mimesis, releasing language from the rags of heroism and conceding nothing to the autobiographical narrative (remember that *Fatelessness* is "an inverted *Bildungsroman*") that we will try to "approach the unapproachable" (2009a, p. 14). The unapproachable, that is to say the "naturally", the "it goes without saying", that the words before Auschwitz inevitably lack. Kafka, Orwell, too, saw "the ancient tongue melt in their hands, as if they had set it on fire, only to show the ashes, in which new and hitherto unknown images appeared".[6]

However, among these ashes, no doubt, there are those of *Poetry and Truth*. The reference to Goethe is explicit in *Fiasco* when Kertész introduces the diary of the torturer Berg. Köves chats with the man who says he had "talents" – talents for everything, that is to say anything, especially for writing (2011a, p. 215). Writing *I, the executioner*: the book of a life, "the true story of my life", an interesting and instructive life, "a life exemplarily solved", "because", says Berg, "we need to know how to appreciate our fate" (p. 297). Admittedly, "the beginner is confronted with wonderful examples, more enlightened, indeed entrancing examples from the Enlightenment era" (p. 299). He does not claim to outstrip them but at any rate "to take courage from their finely-nuanced accuracy, their heroic honesty, their gratifying endeavour to strive constantly to draw a lesson" (ibid.) You can "shake your heads disapprovingly at the mention of these lofty models" when this man who is going to appear in court with the deaths of thirty thousand people on his conscience [is] able to transcend [his] fate"! "But at least pause before the phenomenon with the admiration it deserves" (p. 300). Because this executioner feels the urgent need to furnish "a more complete picture of [himself] to flesh out the false reality, [his] acts in other words" (p. 301), even though these were in opposition to his ideas. This opposition, in truth, did not affect his original conviction. And don't laugh at the literary reference! He too has gone through certain depths of life and conceives of it with sufficient "human grit and happy creative power" for it to be relevant to the general" (pp. 302–303). Of course, you prefer to regard Berg as a being totally foreign to your nature. But are you so sure that your nature is akin to that of this "an aristocrat of sensitive soul who was blessed with a gift for expression and a vivid imagination . . . who was made great by his talent and innocuousness" (p. 302).

This is how Kertész goes against the grain, and almost word for word, of the program of *Poetry and Truth*. Because it is indeed an autobiography whose aim is to transmit the experience of freedom in a way that is "not by means of my aggressively real but my magical appearance" (Kertész, 2011a, p. 304). That this freedom is "perverse", that the *Erlebnis* is one of fear, does not change anything. In this "outrageously individual" journey, it is necessary to recognize a truth of the world, since Berg did not live out this fate against you, against us, but in our place. It is a matter of particular sensitivity, which can also be elevated to the rank of universal, if we understand that external compulsion only played a small part in the first criminal act, that it only offered itself as a favourable reality and subsequently became an inner compulsion.

Sarcasm is at its height here – a real bite into the flesh when internal servitude to hatred and fear is said to return to "its original form" (p. 305). Kertész here directly alludes to Goethe's morphogenetic theory, the matrix of the conception of *Bildung*. It is a theory not only of human fulfilment but of the experience of life itself, when this, from the state of empirical experience, of *Erfahrung*, becomes lived experience, symbolizing *Erlebnis*. For Goethe, life is the task par excellence, one that requires each of us to turn their personal constellation into a trajectory oriented by the aesthetic invention of its meaning. Under the sign of the Pindaric injunction: "Become what you are", it orders the metamorphosis of life in the unfolding of the creative form, which is driven by the original form received as an inheritance (on this point, see Cohn, 1999). "Nature" is therefore here,

that which provides a model – that of the morphology of plants – a prototype which is as it were the precondition of symbolic formation. At the
start of *Fiasco*, the opening lines of *Poetry and Truth* were quoted without
reference: "it was on the 28th of August, 1749, at the stroke of twelve noon,
that I came into the world in Frankfurt on the Main. The constellation was
auspicious" (Kertész, 2011a, p. 89). "An auspicious moment" in a "cosmic
order" which makes the great creator "a mythical hero" coming down to
earth.

But now the order has changed direction and the hero has become
negative. While the difference between crime and guilt remains the only
important thing, it is a very unfortunate demand to expect henceforth the
sentence to be "transfigured" and "raised to an intellectual plane" by my
consciousness of guilt, says Berg. One cannot expect a liberating effect,
when the fate of the executioner has been shaped by common consent,
thanks to the silent capacity of a "consensual we". So there remains this
autobiography, in the form of "sweet vengeance on the world". Sweet
revenge, that is to say, perhaps, the ultimate metamorphosis of hatred that
has its last word there. "For a long time, man was superfluous, but free . . .
Now though, man is just superfluous, and he can only redeem his superfluousness by service", says Berg (p. 311).

But then what is the source of this first act, committed under pressure
of an external compulsion, without the external force being present at
the time? Nevertheless, it determines its interior trajectory. In truth, says
Berg, that is a "decisive, I might almost say, crystal-clear passage in the
construction" (p. 314) The construction of the psychic life of a man not
invaded by, but deserted by hatred.

Notes

1 This chapter was first published under the title "Le héros négatif" in J. André
  (ed) Les territoires de la haine, Paris, PUF, pp. 49–68. It is reprinted with the
  permission of the Presses Universitaires de France.
2 Interview with the newspaper *Libération*, dated 11 October 2002.
3 Reference to Semprún (2005/1963, pp. 175–176), as well as the statement made to
  the newspaper *Liberation* on 9 June 2011.
4 Anne-Lise Stern herself refers to Levi (1989, p. 97).
5 Highly suspicious motives, writes Freud, which in their time served as an
  excuse for the cruelties of the Inquisition, but which today [let us remember that
  it is 1933, the date of the great famine organized in Ukraine and the first purges]
  underlie the Bolshevik wish for an ideal society without hatred.
6 I. Kertész (2003), Speech delivered on receiving the Nobel Prize for Literature,
  under the title "Eureka!" Also in Kertész (2009b, pp. 253–265).

References

Anders, G. (1999). Désuétude de la méchanceté. *Conférence*, 9(Autumn), 167–187.
Anders, G. (2007). *La Haine à l'état d'antiquité*. Paris: Payot & Rivages.

Beetschen, A. (2003). L'accomplissement et l'atteinte. *Revue française de psychanalyse*, 67(5): 1455–1527.

Cohn, D. (1999). *La lyre d'Orphée. Goethe et l'esthétique*. Paris: Flammarion.

Freud, S. (1915). *Instincts and Their Vicissitudes*. *S.E.* 14. London: Hogarth, pp. 117–140.

Freud, S. (1933 [1932]). *Why War? (Einstein and Freud)*. *S.E.* 22. London: Hogarth, pp. 199–215.

Freud, S. (1939). *Moses and Monotheism*. *S.E.* 23. London: Hogarth, pp. 7–137.

Kertész, I. (1992). *Journal de galère* [Galley-Slave's Journal]. Arles: Actes Sud.

Kertész, I. (1999a). *Un autre*. Arles: Actes Sud [(2004). *Someone Else: A Chronicle of the Change*, trans. T. Wilkinson. *Common Knowledge*, 10(2): 314–346].

Kertész, I. (1999b). Le vingtième siècle est une machine à liquider permanente. Interview with G. Moser. In: *Parler des camps, penser les génocides*, C. Coquio (ed.). Paris: Albin Michel, pp. 87–92.

Kertész, I. (2003). 'Eureka'! Nobel Prize Lecture, 2002. *World Literature Today, Norman*, 77(1), April-June, 2003(4). Also in Kertész, 2009b, pp. 253–265.

Kertész, I. (2004/1975). *Fatelessness*, trans. T. Wilkinson. London: Vintage International.

Kertész, I. (2008). *Sauvegarde. Journal 2001–2003*. Arles: Actes Sud.

Kertész, I. (2009). *L'Holocauste Comme Culture*. Arles: Actes Sud.

Kertész, I. (2009/1991). *The Union Jack*, trans. Tim Wilkinson. Melville House.

Kertész, I. (2011/1988). *Fiasco*, trans. Tim Wilkinson. Brooklyn: Melville House Publishing.

Lévi, P. (1989). *Les Naufragés et les rescapés*. Paris: Gallimard.

Mesnard, Ph., Kahan, C. (1991). *Giorgio Agamben à l'épreuve d'Auschwitz*. Paris: Kimé.

Semprún, J. (2005/1963). *The Long Voyage*, trans. Richard Seaver. New York: Harry N. Abrams.

Stern, A.-L. (2007). *Le Savoir-déporté*. Paris: Le Seuil.

Conclusion
The foundations of words

In his preface to the diary of Rudolf Höss, the commander of Auschwitz, Primo Levi, wrote: "the author is not a bloodthirsty sadist or a fanatic full of hatred, but an empty man, a tranquil and diligent idiot, who endeavoured to carry out as carefully as possible the bestial initiatives entrusted to him" (Levi, 2015). Could this man have been deserted by hatred, like Berg, or Eichmann, on the day of his trial? And what sort of indifference animated Hitler when – the Russians were at the gates of Berlin – he seemed so unconcerned with the fate of his people, only concerned that his body would not be treated as carrion by his enemies?

Canetti (1976) raises this question when he compares the imperturbability of the Fuhrer's delusions to the coherent nature of President Schreber's; not just to assert the man's paranoid character, but to indicate that like Schreber, Hitler was fundamentally convinced that he was the sole survivor of a global catastrophe – that of the previous war. In his case, survival generated a psychic mechanism in which pleasure in building and enjoyment of destruction coexisted, without either being subordinated to the other. This is evidenced by the architectural projects entrusted to Speer: these were not merely prodigious symbols of a thousand-year-old kingdom; nor did they merely express the consubstantiality of the extension of the empire with the extension of his person. If buildings were designed to attract and contain the masses, it was because Hitler knew how easily they tend to disintegrate. They too must therefore have their place in time immemorial, while their durability depends on the assurance that crowds will remain excitable beyond the present generations. The function of these buildings – colossal squares, religious buildings, places of procession – is therefore to guarantee, thanks to the repetition of gatherings, their continuous growth.

However, beyond excitable living people, these buildings express, in the desire for an eternity that is manifest in them, the wish for survival in death commensurate with the "crowd of the dead" on which Hitler relied. It was to this grandiose mass that he owed his strength when the Weimar Republic was drowned in the erring ways of a democracy it did

DOI: 10.4324/9781003301660-14

not discipline. The crowd of Hitler's dead, those whose names would be engraved on the gigantic triumphal arch planned by Speer, was his "own mass", writes Canetti. This crowd was the source: a crowd of souls who must constantly re-metamorphose into new and expanding masses. This metamorphosis was suddenly reversed when the ruin of the German cities replaced the destruction of the great enemy cities – Canetti evokes "the mass of fire" envisaged by Hitler to destroy London and Paris. It was useless now to protect the people, what remained of the people; no need to think about their survival; no need to think about the mass of murdered victims: this mass also demands its own growth. The enjoyment of survival culminates in collapse. All the more so as Speer, having relied on the Hitlerian maxim "no people lives longer than the documents of its culture", offered models in which we could see the buildings as they might be, thousands of years later, like majestic ancient ruins. This was the luminous logic of the "Theory of the value of the ruins of a building", according to Speer himself; a self-exterminating logic that is specifically Hitlerite, according to Frederik Detue (2013). The fusion of individuals, the lack of distinction between the living and the dead, produced by monumental space, are not merely the instrument of attacks against social ties associating autonomous subjects. Rather, with the abolition of space between men, they create a compactness specific to the uniqueness of the "We" and its celebration (Abensour, 2014). It is this We which, in the eyes of Freud and then of Kertész, is easily transformable into a "mystical We".

As Michel Gribinski (2009) writes, "the scene of analysis can be, for example, in a literary fiction – an immense region where we work to increase our awareness of our reality, to describe its enigma" (pp. 15–16), provided that the analyst asks the writer to do this, rather than offering him an interpretation. I have asked many questions of Kertész, in particular concerning the intertwined role of construction and destruction in what he calls the Nazi "counterculture". How did he navigate the ridge line which both separates absolutely and yet links together the civilizing power of the murder of the father according to Freud and the disintegrating power of the murder called Auschwitz? I have asked this writer, who has looked directly at a humanity hollowed out from within by a dizzying perplexity concerning the very efficacy of guilt, how he framed, or reframed, the question of the inaugural act, and in what his fragile hope of a possible elaboration still lay. In the universalization of consequences?[1]

The question was raised at the very beginning of his work, in 1959, since *I, the Executioner* was a first novel, which remained unfinished and was then integrated into *Fiasco*.[2] The criminal act committed by Berg – "which subsequently proved to be an irrevocable choice, just because it had happened and because it *could have happened*" (2011a, p. 305), but which proceeded "as if nothing had happened, or rather as if everything which happened had happened by accident" (p. 300), without his full attention or his commitment, and even, basically, without his consent – this first murder was only carried out because he had been forced to admit that he could not "refuse the duty that had been assigned to [him], the order and the mission which had been marked out for [him] by a higher place" (p. 301). Yet this first murder, a simple "fact", far from denying Berg any membership of humanity in general, has, whatever it costs us, universal value. Of course, it was individually that the opportunity arose. However, what appears to be an external compulsion did not, in fact, occur in any way. "Because the external compulsion was merely secondary, nothing more than the projection of a genuine will which comes true if the reality favours it" (p. 305).

In addition, this fact initially took the form of a feeling: not hatred, but fear. The fear aroused in people by the mere appearance of these men in jackboots, with belts and pistols, excited the irresistible pleasure which Berg himself nourished with ever-growing passion, "trembling from the desire that others should also experience it; that it should enslave others, eat deep into their souls and stir up in them a licentious freedom" (p. 303). And it is this same fear that he wishes "not by means of [his] aggressively real but magical appearance, that is the representations of [himself] through words and language" (p. 304), by "writing literature", to transplant into us "as a moral lesson". But what morality? If the external compulsion merely allowed the internal compulsion to "return to its original form", the dictum "become what you are" immediately assigns to the acquisition of the inheritance the accomplishment of an *Urform* [primal form] which dismantles the very foundations of the *Aufklärung*. Now this form, far from being the fate of Berg alone, is common to all of us, who await with stifled excitement the continuation of the effects of favourable reality, to horrify us all the more, to horrify us with ourselves and with this "will" expressed in spite of our consciences.

In this prosopopoeia of the executioner, Kertész is perfectly clear. The fact, the source of its realization, is to be sought in the common effort, even if, due to the real individuality of his career, Berg saves our conscience and gives it back to us, at the same time as our childish faith in our ideals. But this faith, reinforced by the world's propensity "to interpret my career as a failure, as a failure primarily in a practical moral sense, and to force that notion on me with self-important fuss" (p. 307), is in vain, as is the hope maintained of a liberating effect of judgment. "The demands of life", says Berg, "will soon exceed the bounds of man's moral capacity" (p. 311), that is to say their sensitivity to crime, or more precisely their sensitivity to the accusation of being at fault – when this itself is the crime. Of course, without guilt, man is superfluous. But in fact, it is thanks to his superfluousness that man can be saved from dereliction. As for the first act, this "decisive, I might almost say, crystal-clear passage in the construction" (p. 314), it is as necessary as the original parricide, except that it has lost its essential components: hatred, distress and repentance. There remains therefore the epic narrative to which Berg resorts, now stripped of all the features which determined the purposes of the social pact. Far from founding it, the force of attraction of the mob, the intoxication of abandonment to this mass marching in unison, and the illusion of finding warmth and security in it bolster humanity's ability to amputate part of itself. "Destructiveness" – is it enough to say that? Perhaps, on condition that this does not also become a pontificating word, and that analysts do not turn into professional humanists.

When Adorno (1973) writes that "the *totum*[3] is the totem" (p. 377), and that only the aesthetics of the fragment, of the dislocation can counteract the slope of identity, he joins Kertész in developing his "inverted" *Bildungsroman*, the first stone placed to disarticulate a language immobilized in its single meanings, incapable of ambiguity. We cannot ascribe to chance the fact that Berg's manner of speaking, under Kertész's pen, is so cryptic that his interlocutor constantly has to "hang on" to the words. While the coincidence of the act carrying out mass murder and the words to prescribe it have invalidated the secret scene of the crime as well as the obscure characteristics of the criminal, and while words have somehow become tied to things, Berg's enigmatic way of speaking attempts to restore the double basis of language. We can then see the extent to which the very language of ideals has been petrified. "[T]he world places greater weight on the immutability of its notions of morality than on admitting the truth" (p. 300) says Berg, while Kertész draws closer to the crime of being guilty.

For Adorno, such immutability played a major role in the squandering of enlightened promises. By abandoning the immeasurability of singular conflicts, it has worked for the sole benefit of universal rationality, the murderous madness of the totalizing will. By fighting against what Freud called the *Ananké* of nature and its violence, it has never ceased to dominate the "unknown" which threatens it. And in order to take possession of it, it has treated "objectively" any object that presents itself, including man, an equally uncontrollable source of *Ananké*. As close as Adorno may sometimes be to Freud, unlike Freud, he therefore situates the activity of destruction in the frenzied search for knowledge that is subject to empirical science and its concreteness. For the moment comes when the latter "stands in the same relationship to things as the dictator to human beings. He knows them to the extent that he can manipulate them" (Horkheimer & Adorno, 2002, p. 6). Having become "absolutely an object", man has lost his capacity to resist the common measure. The consequence is the stereotyped production of cultural goods, the killing of eccentricity by the entertainment industry, and the reification of man enslaved to pseudo-ideals. Hence the function entrusted to art, which is capable of responding in the singular, marked by its boldness in resisting the exchangeability and interchangeability of goods and people in the community, and able to fight against the mass effect generated by the action of reason itself.

Adorno speaks of "reason"; and he sometimes also speaks of "the ego". Thus, in one of his very last texts, "Resignation", he writes: "No transparent relationship obtains between the interests of the ego and the collective it surrenders itself to. The ego must abolish itself so that it may be blessed with the grace of being chosen by the collective. Tacitly a bit of Kantian categorical imperative has erected itself: you must subscribe" (Adorno, 1998, p. 292). To subscribe, to submit to instrumental reason: the deceptive consolation offered by collective action – the sense of a new type of security – comes at the cost of the sacrifice of autonomous thought. But the worst thing for Adorno is that no higher, less regressive form seems to be available at this time. "But according to Freud", Adorno writes, "whoever regresses has not reached his instinctual aim. Objectively regression is renunciation, even when it thinks itself the opposite and innocently propagates the pleasure principle" (ibid.).

What is this ingenuity of the pleasure principle when the regressed form, seizing the avenues offered by the possible substitution of objects, "subscribes" to what the ego, governed by the collective, commands? To what Freud (1912) discovered in "The universal tendency to debasement in the sphere of love"? Namely, "the possibility that something in the very nature of the sexual instinct itself is unfavourable to the realization of complete satisfaction" due to the diphasic onset of object-choice and to the interposition of the barrier of incest, and thus due to the fact that the found object will never coincide with the original lost object (pp. 188–189). Or is Adorno alluding to the weight in the regression of the partial sadistic components that demand satisfaction? For Freud, this in no way leads to ingenuity. The difference between the pleasure of satisfaction demanded and that which is obtained is on the contrary what pushes us forward, while the limitations imposed by civilization, the price of suffering paid for renunciation, become the source of great cultural works, accomplished by sublimation.

But for Adorno, sublimation lost its marks of nobility at the moment when sex became a "variant of sport". As for Freud, from the masochistic regression evoked in "A child is being beaten" (1919) to the doubt which, in *Civilization and its Discontents* (1930), undermines the value of compensations ("civilization behaves towards sexuality as a people or a stratum of its population does which has subjected another one to its exploitation" (p. 104), his attention is more than ever turned towards the conditions of psychic subjection. In the centre, it is no longer drive activity alone – that which threw Oedipus into the arms of Jocasta with the tragic outcome we are familiar with – but the vicissitudes of distress and narcissism that are also in the spotlight. Because why does civilization demand other sacrifices than that of free sexual satisfaction? Why does it simultaneously demand the sacrifice of a portion of this narcissism which is nonetheless at the basis of the identifications ensuring the cohesion of the community?

I would like to take a detour here by linking what, following Kertész and Adorno, we could call "the ingenuity of the executioner" and the question that Michel Gribinski raised in 2009 concerning *Faire parler le destin* (Kahn, 2005): the current indecision, linked to the collapse of the tragic scene which I had described – and which I continue to describe – is so radical that it is "a matter of urgency to find a *poros*, a means of passage, however meaningless it may be, leading to a decision and subsequent laws, so that at the collective level, regression becomes accessible to reason" (Gribinski, 2009, p. 67). The regression envisioned by Gribinski is the one he discovers and, remarkably, leads us to discover, in the study of the *Lebensborn* experiment and the documents relating to the undertaking of this eugenics program, conceived and directed by Himmler. With regard to these places (originally homes and nurseries to enable unmarried "purebred" women to give birth anonymously and abandon their children to the SS; and then centres welcoming women, who were always "racially pure", so that they could be impregnated by the SS and their children could be trained as the descendants of the Aryan elite; and finally camps where Aryan children kidnapped in conquered countries in order to be Germanized were gathered together, those "unfit" for the program being deported or murdered), Michel Gribinski reveals the planning of the management and the rationalization of the industry they concealed. Both the numbers and the methods indicate, he says, that they went "beyond the principle of hatred which governs mere destruction" (ibid., pp. 74–75).

Of course, he says, we could probably make do with the irrationality of passionate hatred to explain it. But the undertaking seems more opaque to him psychically. It is linked precisely to a sort of "rationality of life" – for example Himmler's real concern for these women and their regime, a real attention to their well-being as expressed in his letters – which coexisted, without the two orientations coming into contact with each other, with "the planning of a genocide targeting, fundamentally, the human species". Not only hatred, then, but "something like self-destruction" (ibid. pp. 78–85). Gribinski concurs here with what Canetti says about Hitler. There, edification and destruction coexisted; here, the coexistence concerns race building and destruction of the species. And Gribinski does not attempt, any more than Canetti does, to dissolve the question, for want of resolving it, with the term "splitting". The enigma – that of a "rational, a-conflictual surface, playing the role of border between crude unmediated fantasies of origins, and a constant regime of acting out" – requires us to wonder about this "dead calm" in which a singular form of love reigns: "the banality of love", he suggests, a love without conflict, without ambivalence, without passion, as described by Berg in Kertész's book. But a love built in such a way that it is ultimately not only the soul of Western civilization (as I had argued) but its very body, its real body, its descendants, that Christendom, having become autophagous, wants to annihilate: this is what the *Lebensborn* experiment shows.

The point of contact between Adorno and Gribinski is situated around what both view as "dehumanization" in the form of the "de-individuation" that reason manages to exercise, carried to its extreme in the practice of treating human beings objectively. The future of consciousness is in the foreground here, when the individual becomes prey to the destructuring organism of the mass. The breaking point lies around what is entrusted to regression. For Gribinski, it is not a matter of renunciation – which would imply a conflict, even if covered over by the pseudo-ingenuity of "retro-graded" instinctual satisfactions. On the contrary, it is a question of a state in which the initial stage of infantile sexuality has not been "absorbed" during the post-pubertal torments of the second stage of sexuality. The lack of communication between the two psychic positions thus prevents the first stage, that which Freud said was "imperishable", from putting the paths opened up during the infantile past in the service of sexuality in the present – which would conflictualize the latter. On the contrary, from the separation of the two trajectories emerges a non-resorbed child in man, a small, immobile giant. No après-coup, no reorganizations, no distor-tion, no displacement, no madness. Nor is there any room for regression in this universe where the intensity of the rationality of symptoms and of their actuality is on an equal footing. Or else, if there is regression, it takes the form of the horde of children portrayed by Golding in *Lord of the Flies*: a neoformation, which is in no way the replica of the primal horde, because the totemic clan is without a father, and the totem without taboo. Drawing on the analysis proposed by Nathalie Zaltzman (2007), who sees in this "the conquering progression of a collective cultural regression" (p. 14), Gribinski (2009) adds concerning the absence of any prohibition: "It's as if *hatred were devoid of the affect of hatred*" (p. 97).

Nathalie Zaltzman, for her part, insists on the connection between individual narcissism and collective narcissism at the foundation of the human community. However, quite apart from of a moral assessment of the result, it is the same process of collective identification around figures of identification – cultural heroes whose rebellion makes it possible to break with the inertia of society – which seems to her to be at work: it does not matter whether it is placed in the service of the work of culture, that is to say of the enrichment of the awareness that man gains over that which surpasses him, or whether it functions in the service of the most destructive regression. Especially as, in the latter case, it is not to the "pre-history" of the human community that the regressive movement leads back, but rather to the formation of a "post-history" as Golding presents it. In these cases where common membership of the human race is denied, where consciousness is no longer able to diagnose evil, where instinctual violence takes precedence over humanization, the narcissistic libido clearly fails as a prop for collective identifying constructions. This is why Nathalie Zaltzman (2009) argues that regression affects not the drive organization itself, but rather the authority of the ego. It is this very point that Freud overlooked when he made the work of culture dependent on the taming of the drives. The cultural superego, she writes, "in its negative treatment of hatred and destructiveness through the injunction of love" ultimately only makes the illusory contribution of its wishful thinking (p. 157).

But, apart from Freud being sceptical about the theoretical value of carrying the notion of the superego over from the individual to the collective, is his position so unambiguous? As the systems of psychic compensation offered by the social community in return for what each individual sacrifices to it libidinally and narcissistically appeared to him more and more problematic, he took the measure of the "enthusiastic prejudice" (Freud, 1930, p. 144) which had guided the *Aufklärer* that he was. Moreover, he underlines the "great economic disadvantage in the erection of a superego" at the individual level – namely that "instinctual renunciation now no longer has a completely liberating effect" (Freud, 1930, pp. 127–128). In fact, as long as the threat of losing parental protection and tenderness governs the restriction of pleasures and self-love, we can understand how, from the outset, anxiety determines inhibition. And how, in doing so – when moral conscience takes over from this anxiety – the fear of losing the love of the superego can, with the same anxiety, lead to avoiding any form of transgression. The chains that check the imperialism of love and hate are the very chains of love and hate. But it is not clear why awareness of guilt is all the more severe insofar as man is virtuous. Why does an abstinent and docile ego, having complied with renunciation, not obtain the confidence of the superego?

At first glance, however, the mechanism allowing civilization to overcome the aggressive ardour of each individual by placing it under the control of an internal watchtower, like a garrison occupying a conquered city, seemed ingenious. It is a mechanism rooted in self-observation which, due to the division of consciousness, secretes an autonomous agency which arms it for its "judging activity" (Freud, 1930, pp. 59–60). Yet it seems that this very armament is the source of the difficulty. It is in fact made up, in part, of the object-libido which, with the renunciation of Oedipal cathexes, is desexualized and aggregates with the ego as narcissistic libido. From this point of view, the superego is in itself the result of compensation. Or rather it could be, if the superego were not also in a position to take over the part of unbound energy coming from the death drive. This is how the activity of the superego, grafted onto the "need for punishment", leads in individual clinical situations to all the variations of destructiveness intertwined with distress. This is especially so since, besides the act, there is the thought of the act, and, when it comes to bad intentions, the superego, because of its origin, knows about as much as the id. Finally, frustration quantitatively increases the energy available to the superego, as a result of which renunciation reinforces hostility against civilization and its limitations. But that still does not tell us why the ingenious mechanism fails in its task.

This is what we must take into account with the third source of the superego's armament. A current which is not immediately subjected to anxiety about loss, but which on the contrary is nourished by that part of the object relationship which continues clandestinely, at the very heart of identification: namely the violence that, as a child, we would have liked to direct against the parental figure. So the ferocity of the internal authority is also nourished by the fury against what was originally external authority and its sovereignty (Freud, 1933, pp. 123–124, 129–130). Is it not at this crossroads that hatred and idealization conclude a pact that allows the imposing tyranny of the Ideal to team up with the deleterious action of the superego? The claim to a narcissistic fullness that one imagines to have been that of the father thus becomes the axis of the regression of the superego function itself. Of course, when the community expands from its first familial form to the socius as a whole, this conflict and the attempts to resolve it take on the various and constantly renewed forms of common institutions. However, if the individual finds material to embody this imposing ideal in the leader, the promise of perfection will lead to a murderous orgy.

We thus discover a time bomb, so to speak, placed at the very heart of the agency of the superego. Freud, in fact, does not only say how the superego, which is at once the residue of the first object choices and the instrument of the categorical imperative, utters two absolutely contradictory commandments: one in the service of identification stemming from the abandonment of the infantile object, the other in the service of resistance against Oedipal cathexes; one which prescribes: "you *ought to be* like the father", the other which prohibits: "you *may not be* like the father" (1923, p. 34). He does not only describe the identificatory evolution of the grandiose capacities attributed to the father; he also describes in a veiled form the precarious evolution of the collective process when the hope of narcissistic enjoyment ensured by their inordinate satisfaction emerges from the shadows. *Civilization and its Discontents* here inherits hypotheses left pending in Group *Psychology and the Analysis of the Ego*, in particular those mentioned in the description of major collective festivals. In these moments of excess permitted by the law where prohibitions and prohibitions are lifted, in these psychic situations where the split between the ego ideal and the ego is temporarily effaced, Freud understands how the abrogation of superego limitations is itself a "magnificent festival for the ego" (1921, p. 131). A manic ego, intoxicated not only by the illusion of its full freedom, but even more by a perfect self-sufficiency, a state it believed to have been lost forever.

It is thus through narcissism that the individual's subjugation to the injunctions of religion is linked, in Freud's eyes, to the compactness of the masses. It may be that the belief in providence is supported by both the figure of a greatly magnified father and the savagery of "pious crusaders" – the promise of eternal life at the cost of the prohibition of thinking; or it may be that each person's willingness to alienate his freedom is illuminated by the gain obtained by immersion in the mass, the assurance of a future golden age masking the underlying hatred – as in case of Bolshevism; or perhaps hatred, racially assumed and practiced, loses its tangible consistency as soon as the incarnation of the fate of the community in the Führer does away with reality-testing.

Canetti (1976) rightly noted the effectiveness of Hitler's crowd control thanks to the idealized host of heroes fallen in combat. But he is infinitely perceptive when he emphasizes that the strength that the Führer derived from it was due to the certainty he had acquired that there was no longer any gap between his disproportionate project and reality. Canetti says in so many words that Hitler had discovered, so to speak, the weak point of reality: the part where it is most fluid, where most, fearing the crowds, shrink back in fear. Fear when faced with the crowds, fear of not being part of them, fear when faced with the crowd of dead: it is this fear that feeds in Berg the irresistible desire "that others should also experience it, that it should enslave others, eat deep into their souls and stir up in them a licentious freedom" (Kertész, 2011a, p. 303).

That fear plays a part in the armament of the superego relates back to its original constitution: the sense of guilt is only a "topographical variety of anxiety" (Freud, 1930, p. 135), and it is from this source that the agency of the superego draws its hegemonic power, with the aim of restricting hatred between fellow citizens. Nonetheless, its supremacy can itself turn into an expansion of hatred. As civilization has no other means of maintaining the social community in a "closely-knit group" than to constantly reinforce this sense of guilt, one day, writes Freud,[3] an increase in the sense of guilt will perhaps "reach such heights that the individual finds hard to tolerate" (ibid., p. 133). Isn't this exactly what Berg describes when he writes: "You have to free yourself of the colossal tension: all of a sudden you cave in and abandon any resistance", relinquishing yourself to the external authority, even if it was the instigator of the most violent and immoral actions? It is in any case in these terms that Kertész describes in *Fiasco* "the crystal-clear passage in the construction" (2011a, p. 314).

Looking at it more closely, we can see that the massified We, an artisan of relief, a crystal clear passage in the construction, resides at the very heart of language. It is that which endorses the lie of the *Lebensborn* experiment and suddenly makes us hear only the "fountain of life" where it is only a question of killings in their rigorous concreteness. This necessarily raises the question of what is at work within language itself, so that it no longer seems to be inhabited by its double meanings and its sexual reminiscences but puts itself in the service of a psychic life subservient to thought "without fiction", rigorously "substantial" – I am using the words of Olivier Jouanjan here. Where is such a use of words rooted, which no longer seems to obey the repression that Freud made the root of the instinctual history of language? The language of Tiresias, that of dreams like that of parapraxes and symptoms, constantly makes use of the amphibological foundations of language, thanks to which the conflictual foundations of psychic life manage to find their manifest forms. If verbal play succeeds in serving disguised satisfaction, it is because, according to Freud, words come from the same primitive root which, on the one hand, continues to express sexual matters and, on the other, is used not to express them. The role of the double meaning, the value of its ambiguous characteristics are here less the representational contents than the libidinal cathexis and the force of affect, intertwined in the contacts of the body, desire and the surrounding world – that is to say the primordial contacts in the appropriation of the language. It is from this point of view that the foundations of language are sexual, even if the censorship subsequently erases them. What Freud calls the *Grundsprache* (basic language), our intimate language of paranoiacs (Freud, 1916–1917, pp. 165–169),[4] our language of projective savages, is none other than this sensory language of desire, repressed by socialized speech, banished by "communication", but secretly deposited.

Thus it is that every word is both the fruit of instinctual drive activity and the product of its repression, and that every word is situated at one and the same time on the terrain of sexualization and that of desexualization. It is for this reason that language is always capable of re-sexualization; and it is for the same reason that, in its current usage, words are stabilized in their function as "moderate acts". This represents an advance in civilization, Freud (1926) stated in *The Question of Lay Analysis* (p. 188). But it is an advance that never erases the intractability of the unconscious that dwells in the foundations of language: language deceives and betrays us, and speaks without our knowing it. Nevertheless, the condition of this advance is that the desexualization of words gives access to a form of compensation. By partially escaping the virulence of the drives, but nevertheless still making themselves the vehicle of psychic fulfilment, words are thus situated economically at a pivotal point. They can be the medium of sadistic cruelty or masochistic enjoyment, but the main thing is that they remain rooted in the psychic solution that constitutes the form of cultural compensation which is the use of speech.

It has to be admitted that this model of a double base of language, with repression of the sexual roots, is supported by a theory of censorship which belongs to the first phase of Freudian elaboration. It ignores the fact that the lever of this operation changes fundamentally with the introduction of narcissism. Once the ego ideal becomes the measure by which the ego evaluates itself and triggers the action of repression, the gauge of failures will inherently contain the ingredient of narcissistic omnipotence. This is tempered, admittedly, and largely contained, having found both in individual and romantic relationships and in cultural creations something with which to ensure self-esteem. However, there is a major gap between the operation of repression determined by civilized moral censorship and that governed by the superego/ideal ego pair. For, in the second case, the prohibition is at the same time anchored to the voice which uttered the prohibition, to the narcissistic claim and to the fear of loss. It is not that the de-sexualization of words ceases; but the process which now catches the words or the embryo of words in a pincer movement between ideals and inhibition is inherently weighed down with the all-powerful infantile figures. What paths will the resexualization of words take when the most attractive discourse or the most brutal harangue recharges them with the power and attractions of the internal tyrant or the internal hero?

When it comes to submitting to them, to seducing or coaxing them in order to share in their power and recover the lost narcissistic fullness, these masters or these despots will always be likely to resurface at the very heart of linguistic usage, taking the path of identifying registrations in the reverse direction. The accents of the voice which resonates within will be embodied, regressively, in the clamour of the voices which resound without. On the day when the grandiose ideal refuses to deal with the torments of ambiguity, words will thus easily become the concrete vehicles of the mystical and threatening "We". It will suffice that the sublime ends are contained in the means of purification, that the act of liquidating is strictly superimposed with its intention, that the autocratic determination of new meanings satisfy the ideal of purity. When myth is reduced to the immediacy of blood, there is no need for interpretation; eugenics has done its work at the very heart of language.

Very strangely, the more the deleterious effects of the veneration of crowds or of the hypnosis exercised by leaders have been confirmed by history, the more psychoanalytic theory has tended to abandon the framework that would allow it to understand the psychic levers involved. The abandonment was carried out in the name of a new freedom that enabled analysts to sidestep the obstacle of authoritarianism. One cannot see, to tell the truth, how the supporters of interpersonal psychoanalysis, after having denounced the consequences of the analyst's so-called "authoritarian" position and the misdeeds of suggestion, can hope to answer for hatred, "dead calm", subjugation and murder, or even murder without murderous intention. How can we expect to bring to light the springs of the unconscious pacts which ensure the captivating power of totalitarianism, if we revoke the libidinal theory on the grounds that it is obsolete, and if we retain only the individual failings and restorative power of narcissism, in the name of its empathic benefits? Such a "politically correct" position in fact dismisses the essential tools for grasping what is combined, in a constant movement back and forth, between the intrapsychic economy of subordination in individual lives and the economy of consent to tyranny, at work in the masses.

In short, it is to forget that "what began in relation to the father, is completed in relation to the group" (Freud, 1930, p. 133). But such an oversight is perhaps precisely the stigma of what Nazism did to psychoanalysis.

Notes

1 "I see only one serious problem that needs to be settled, which is whether the twentieth century experience of concentration camps is a matter of universal or marginal relevance" (Kertész, 2013, p. 107).
2 It was published, together with three other texts by Kertész (2007), under the title *Opfer und Henker* [Victim and Executioner]. The mention of this first essay appears in the background in *Fiasco*, for example, p. 33 and p. 118.
3 Concerning this *"innig verbundene Masse"* which owes nothing to close-knit bonds but everything to their unconscious inextricability, I refer the reader to the very enlightening discussion by F. Coblence (2012).
4 The reading proposed by Jones (1918), as well as the additions to Chapter VI of *The Interpretation of Dreams* in 1914, have often oriented research in the direction of symbols.

References

Abensour, M. (2014). *De la compacité. Architectures et régimes totalitaires, le cas Albert Speer*. Paris: Sens & Tonka.

Adorno, T.W. (1973). *Negative Dialectics*, trans. E. Ashton. New York: Continuum.

Adorno, T.W. (1998). Resignation. In: *Critical Models: Interventions and Catchwords*, trans. H.W. Pickford. New York: Columbia University, pp. 289–293.

Canetti, E. (1976). Hitler, according to speer. In: *The Conscience of Words*, trans. J. Neugroschel. London: Andre Deutsch, pp. 65–72.

Coblence, F. (2012). Ce qui fut commencé avec le père s'achève avec la masse. *Revue française de psychanalyse*, 76(5): 1377–1383.

Detue, F. (2013). Architecture et politique: la 'cathédrale de l'avenir', de l'expressionnisme au nazisme. *Texto! – Textes et cultures*, 18(3). www.revue-texto.net/index.php?id=3298

Freud, S. (1912). *On the Universal Tendency to Debasement in the Sphere of Love*. S.E. 11. London: Hogarth, pp. 177–190.

Freud, S. (1916–1917). *Introductory Lectures on Psychoanalysis*. S.E. 15–16. London: Hogarth.

Freud, S. (1919). *A Child Is Being Beaten*. S.E. 17. London: Hogarth, pp. 177–204.

Freud, S. (1926). *The Question of Lay Analysis*. S.E. 20. London: Hogarth, pp. 183–258.

Freud, S. (1930). *Civilization and Its Discontents*. S.E. 21. London: Hogarth pp. 57–146.

Gribinski, M. (2009). *Les Scènes indésirables*. Paris: Éditions del'Olivier.

Horkheimer, M., Adorno, Th. W. (2002). *The Dialectic of Enlightenment*, trans. E. Jephcott. Stanford, CA: Stanford University Press.

Jones, E. (1918). The theory of symbolism. *British Journal of Psychology*, 9(2): 181–229.

Kahn, L. (2005). *Faire parler le destin*. Paris: Klincksieck.

Kertész, I. (2007). *Opfer und Henker* [Victim and executioner]. Berlin: Transit Buchverlag.

Kertész, I. (2013/2006). *Dossier K.*, trans. T. Wilkinson. Brooklyn: Melville House.

Levi, P. (2015). Monument at Auschwitz. In: *The Complete Works of Primo Levi, Vols 1–3*, A. Goldstein (ed.). New York: Liveright.

Zaltzman, N. (2007). Children are pigs. In: *L'esprit du mal*. Paris: Éd. de l'Olivier, pp. 15–30.

Zaltzman, N. (2009). Le mal: un tabou culturel. *Annuel de l'APF*, 2009(1): 153–172.

Index

For Product Safety Concerns and Information please contact our EU
representative GPSR@taylorandfrancis.com
Taylor & Francis Verlag GmbH, Kaufingerstraße 24, 80331 München, Germany

www.ingramcontent.com/pod-product-compliance
Lightning Source LLC
Chambersburg PA
CBHW070344270326
41926CB00017B/3970